BEHIND CLOSED DOORS
in an English Country Town

PAULINE FISK

First published by Merlin Unwin Books, 2014
Text © Pauline Fisk, 2014
Photos © Pauline Fisk (unless otherwise stated), 2014

Merlin Unwin Books Limited
Palmers' House, 7 Corve Street,
Ludlow, Shropshire, SY8 1DB
www.merlinunwin.co.uk

The right of Pauline Fisk to be identified as the author
of this work has been asserted by her in accordance with the
Copyright, Designs and Patents Act 1988.

A CIP record of this book is available from the British Library.
Manufacturing managed by Jellyfish Print Solutions Ltd.
Printed and bound in Malta by Gutenberg Press Ltd.
ISBN 978-1-906122-69-0

DEDICATION

The writing of *My Tonight From Shrewsbury* was a magical time, not
least because so many people willingly shared their experiences and
expertise and gave so generously of their time. This is my chance to say
thank you. This book is dedicated to you all.

INTRODUCTION

I happen to think I live in a fabulous town, brimming with life by day and even in the darkest night. It's a town worth shouting about. That's why I wrote my blog. For one whole year, as often as time allowed, whatever amused, surprised or entertained me about Shrewsbury I attempted to share. There were buildings I'd always wondered about – I tried to get behind their closed doors. There were people that I wanted to meet; now here was my chance.

Over the following twelve months, my blog grew into what it is now, the record of a year in the life of an English country town. Shrewsbury isn't just about the past, despite its old buildings. Day by day it comes alive because of people making it their own. And that's what I've done with my blog. It's been a personal take. I'm not the local tourist board. I don't represent the town council. I'm not even some great authority on Shrewsbury. I'm just a writer and local resident who was prepared to go on a year-long walk and share what I found.

'I won't always get things right,' I wrote on New Year's Day in my first post. 'There'll be errors here in these pages. Things I misunderstand, mistake or just plain miss. But I'll do my best, and I'll try to travel with an open (and curious) mind. So travel with me, please. My hopes are high.'

And so they are again. *My Tonight From Shrewsbury* was a huge success, garnering an astonishing, worldwide following. Now here it is as a book, and again I'm inviting you to travel with me.

Pauline Fisk,
Shrewsbury
July 2014

JANUARY

1st January: MY TONIGHT FROM SHREWSBURY

I've been writing novels for much of my adult life, but for the next twelve months I'm going to blog on the subject of my home town. There's no grand plan about this. As often as I have time or inspiration I'll sit here at my desk and share whatever the town has been for me that day. Things that have interested me, that have caught my attention, made me

Wyle Cop, Christmas lights

smile, made me angry, joyful, happy or sad; buildings that I love; people who fascinate me; events that have taken place, or extraordinary incidences of natural phenomena – any of these might be included in my attempt to get under the skin of a town that teems with life, and that I happen to love.

I'd like to think that, one year from now, in the pages of this blog, one of England's finest country towns will have been fleshed out and come alive. A daunting ambition, I know, but there's never any harm in aiming high.

One thing I've learned as an author is the importance of letting things take their course. Writing a book is a bit like navigating a river – you never know what's round the next bend. That's the beauty of the journey. And a blog is like a river too.

2nd January: CAGED BEAST THAT IS THE RIVER SEVERN

These aren't the worst floods I've seen here in Shrewsbury. In the autumn of the year 2000, the river broke its banks, filled Smithfield Road and went half up Roushill, filling the basement of the Riverside Shopping

Centre and rendering the entrance to the town inaccessible except by duckboard or boat. That year the town was flooded three times in six weeks. TV cameras and news presenters had scarcely packed up before they were back. And those weren't the worst floods, either. The 1960s might have swung, but they also rained. Funny that – I remember sunshine all the way.

The worst year in living memory though was 1947 when a combination of rainfall, freezing temperatures, snow and thaw caused a catastrophic breaking of the River Severn's banks, closing down Shrewsbury as a commercial centre, cutting it off from the rest of the world. Then the waters around the Abbey church made it up the aisle, reaching a record river level rise of eighteen feet.

But not even *that* was Shrewsbury's worst flood. That title goes to the Great Flood of 1795, an event on a Biblical scale, when quays, warehouses and timber yards were stripped of their contents and completely destroyed, and many of the graves in the Abbey graveyard collapsed inwards, setting their contents free.

Traitor's Gate

And that, of course (you'll be getting the picture by now) was small fry compared to the Great Flood of 1620, or the string of other great floods going back to 1348. Shrewsbury's curse and joy is the River Severn. Built into a horseshoe loop in the river, its inhabitants can't get away from water. Entering or leaving the town involves crossing bridges. Because growth is constrained by the river, Shrewsbury's street plan is much the same today as in medieval times.

Some things have changed, of course, but flooding's most definitely not one of them. This morning, down at Traitor's Gate, a vast expanse of wild brown water raged its way past me, strong enough to carry whole trees under the railway bridge and down towards the weir. Tonight the water is still high, a vast inky expanse surging beneath the arches of the English Bridge. But beyond the bridge, the Abbey stands dry. The houses on Marine Terrace aren't flooded this time. And down at the Welsh Bridge, Frankwell isn't flooded. Unless more rain comes pouring off Plynlimon Mountain, Shrewsbury is safe.

What's the forecast like? I check my phone. *'No severe weather warnings have been issued for the next few days.'* Tonight from Shrewsbury, let's hope they've got it right.

5th January: A CONVERSATION WITH CHRIS QUINN

I was talking the other day to the Radio Pembrokeshire DJ once described by John Peel as 'the real BB Skone', and up came the name Chris Quinn. BB knew all about him from gigs he'd played in Wales and, by coincidence, I was due to meet him today.

Chris has a big smile and always seems to be friends with everyone. Sitting opposite him in the Shrewsbury Coffeehouse, he's continually nodding and smiling as people come through the door. I can't remember the first time I heard Chris in performance, but the last time was a month ago, right here in the Coffeehouse, kicking up a storm with jazz saxophonist Casey Greene.

Chris grew up in Germany, where his dad ran a string of Forces Folk Clubs. 'My first instrument was the concertina,' he says. 'I was five years old. Years before I touched a guitar, I knew my future lay in music.'

Chris remembers going to see one band in particular, up by the speakers, drinking it all in. 'What was happening on the stage felt normal to me,' he says. 'It was just what you did.'

Aged fifteen, Chris learned his first guitar piece and started busking on Pride Hill. Loads of people came up and talked to him, and the money was good. He's no memory of being scared. Playing and performing went hand in hand. A stint at a local Performing Arts Course brought Chris an agent and a series of Butlins gigs. This was followed by a Blues Brothers show touring the South Coast. By the time Chris turned up at the Dun Cow in Abbey Foregate to play with fellow Shrewsbury musician, James Hickman, he was already a seasoned performer.

'That's the night The Badgers were formed,' Chris says. 'It took a few beers and a few more nights before we came up with the name, but by then the gigs were pouring in. We could have played seven gigs a week if we'd wanted.'

Chris and James perform together to this day, and separately too, James most notably with Dan Cassidy, brother of the legendary Eva, and Chris as part of the Robin Nolan Trio, playing Django Reinhardt gypsy jazz. His current tour with Robin Nolan culminates in a Jazz FM gig at the Royal Albert Hall. For a Pride Hill kid-busker, Chris has come a long way.

Chris Quinn

He's writing songs too, ploughing his own furrow with an album due at the end of the year. Sometimes he plays his gypsy jazz guitar, sometimes his Martin D28, bought from Eva Cassidy's father. Chris remembers a long afternoon in the Cassidy family barn playing Eva's own guitar. A privilege indeed.

Chris has played small gigs and large ones too. Playing to a 10,000+ audience, along with Jools Holland, was great for his and James's album sales, he says. But a private party for a family of four on a special birthday in their living-room was just as special. 'It may seem crazy to make a four hour journey just for four people and their dog,' says Chris, 'but there are reasons why some things are worth doing, and it's always about the music.'

Who are Chris's musical heroes, I wonder. Chris says it's hard to know who to mention and who to leave out. John Doyle is up there for Ireland, he says, along with Paul Brady; then there's Dougie McLean and Dick Gaughan for Scotland; Martin Carthy and Martin Simpson for England; and for America there are Tony Rice, Doc Watson, Tim O'Brien (listen to his Dylan album, *Red on Blonde*) and Nanci Griffiths.

Chris enjoys the musician's life, including the travelling, but he loves coming home to Shropshire. This summer, he and partner, Jessicah Kendrick, are having a baby. The bump shows already. The scan's been broadcast on Facebook. When Baby Quinn-Kendrick (Kendrick-Quinn) makes his/her triumphal entry into Shrewsbury, I'll let you know.

ONE BOOK, ONE GARDEN, THREE MARKET HALLS

At the moment, I'm reading *The Gift* by Lewis Hyde, which explores the concept of giving, going back to the earliest of times. He warns against exploiting what he calls 'the essence' and encourages giving back as a means of assuring the fertility of the source.

This was on my mind earlier today in the garden of Castle Gates Library. Even in winter its lawns and variegated foliage create a green haven in the busy heart of town. Its gardener and I got chatting and here definitely, I thought, was somebody whose tender care assured, in Lewis Hyde's words, 'the fertility of the source'.

Later, still with those words ringing in my ears, I visited Shrewsbury's indoor market. Yet again, surrounded by quirky-minded, independent, enterprising and imaginative traders, I had a sense of something being given back. These market stallholders don't sell the way they do in Sainsbury's, but by plying their trades in their own way, their enrichment of town life is inestimable.

Pengwern Books in Shrewsbury Market

We have three hidden market halls in our town. The first is the indoor market, housed on the first floor of a modern building with a 1960s clock tower. Then there's the Old Market Hall in Shrewsbury's main square, which houses possibly the only medieval cinema on stilts to be found in the UK. Then there's the Antiques Centre round the back of the Square – an underground market down a set of stairs, giving little clue to the subterranean delights beneath.

I'm fascinated by the idea of Shrewsbury behind closed doors. How many people, including local residents, have been inside the leaning tower on Town Walls? Or Old St Chad's, or the Unitarian Church on High Street? And how about our town's gothic railway station? Or the Ditherington Flax Mill and Maltings? Who's been into them?

There are private houses, too, that invite you to find out more about them. Shrewsbury's shuts and passages are dotted with interesting-looking front doors with glimpses of lives lived behind them, and so are the Georgian hills and streets behind the Old Music Hall. Hopefully during the year I'll get the chance to look at some of them.

12th January
YIKES! AN ENID BLYTON MOMENT IN A CARPET SHOP

You must have read it. If not in Blyton's Castle/Island/Mountain of Adventure series, in some other children's book. The moment when Jack, Lucy and/or their parrot/dog go into the innocent-looking, friendly local shop run by an innocent-looking, friendly nice man, and catch that first glimpse of adventure in a ruined archway half-hidden from sight.

Well, here I am in Castle Carpets asking for a quote and, behind the stands of carpet samples, something *very interesting* catches my eye. 'What's behind there?' I ask, wondering if it's deliberately been hidden and if so (wearing my child-hero crime-busting hat) *why?* 'It's very old,' says the innocent-looking, friendly nice man, who couldn't possibly ever be involved with anything untoward. 'Yes, but what is it?' I ask.

It turns out it's a window – which given that Castle Carpets is built into the side of a real live genuine castle (the sort featured in Enid Blyton, and lots of other children's books), is very interesting indeed. The carpet man suggests that I might see it better in the sandwich shop next door. 'It looks out on their yard,' he says helpfully.

I go and introduce myself. The sandwich lady says she doesn't have a yard. It's long since been boarded up and plaster-boarded over. She does, however, show me a long, covered passageway running behind the whole parade of shops, parallel to the much higher public walkway used today. This lower passageway is covered in, but once it would have been open to the castle walls.

There are rumours of other passages too, the sandwich lady says, secret passages running between the castle and the library, which once housed old Shrewsbury School. What a tangle the town is once you scrape beneath the surface – or walk into the pages of an Enid Blyton book.

Hidden window in Castle Carpets shop

Back in Castle Carpets, still curious about the window, the nice man, Jake, takes pity on me. If I come back at lunchtime when there'll be someone to help him, he says, he'll remove the sample stands so that I can see what's behind.

On the dot of one I return, armed with cameras in the plural in case one konks out (in Enid Blyton books, the children are always prepared; in fact, if they'd been here they'd have brought a seed-cake too). Jake and helper roll back the stands and out into the light of day emerges one of the most ancient-looking windows I've ever seen. I mean, *really* ancient – medieval mystery ancient; Ellis Peters, that sort of thing. And it's enormous too. Not some little peep-hole. More like a 16th century version of wall-to-ceiling plate glass.

What's the history of this extraordinary window, buried in the back of a carpet shop? Jake doesn't know. 'If history interests you, would you like to see our cellar?' he volunteers.

Pinch me and I'll wake up in a minute. Either that, or I really *am* Lucy and the crooks are about to reveal themselves in the next chapter on the other side of the cellar door. Jake leads me to the back of the shop and pulls the rusty old bolt on the cellar door. 'Go down there,' he says, stepping aside. 'And mind your head.'

Are you excited too? You should be. Are you scared? There's no need to be. There are only carpets behind the door. But they're housed in a series of low arched vaults, looping off into the distance with occasional portals of light from some hidden source. Jake says he and his father, Eddie, had some castle expert in and he reckoned these cellars were much like the castle ones and were probably part of them at some time.

I'd like to know more. This calls for detective work. I leave the shop in a daze, glimpsing yet more wonders in the scallop-shell decorative archway over the door. Following me, I notice, is a mysterious short woman with her hair pinned up in an elegant bun/French roll. Was she following me earlier? I don't know. Outside when she speaks to me, I find myself returning to ordinary life. What can I have been thinking of? She's my daughter's mother-in-law – someone I count as a friend.

Tonight from Shrewsbury I can tell you categorically that there are no spies, crooks or hardened criminals in Shrewsbury. Or, at least, there aren't in Castle Carpets. Of that I am sure.

16th January: DR DANNY BEATH

One of the people I'd hoped to interview over the coming year was the photographer, Danny Beath, whose death was announced today in the Shropshire Star. Until moving house last weekend, Danny was a sort of semi-near neighbour, though not one I knew personally. I knew who he was of course – everybody in Shrewsbury knew who Danny was – but our paths had never crossed and I'd no idea, until the Shropshire Star told me, that he was *Dr* Danny Beath, with a PhD in Tropical Ecology.

I did know, though, that Danny was an outstanding photographer with a great love for the natural world, especially here in Shrewsbury and across Shropshire and the Marches. Last November he became The Sunday Times Magazine's Choice Award Winner in their 'Take a View' competition, and had his image projected over the rooftops of London. This winning photograph – of a misty view across the Welsh Marches – took ten years of planning. 'It was a case of getting the right time at the right place,' he said in a recent Photography Monthly interview. 'Something that came together after a long period of waiting.'

A nine-times Shropshire Photographic Society's Photographer of the Year, the county – and indeed his home town, Shrewsbury – is rightly proud of Dr Danny Beath.

17th January: OPEN STUDIO: THE SUNNY SIDE OF THE STREET, WITH LINDA EDWARDS

I first came across the illustrator Linda Edwards strolling between the stalls in Shrewsbury Market. She was a nice, smiley lady with blondish, quirkily-cut hair, wearing bright colours and wheeling around a basket on wheels. I'd always wanted one of those, so went up and asked where she'd bought it. Then, not long afterwards, she set up the Shropshire Illustrators' and Children's Authors' Café, and ever since then we've been friends.

Today I'm sitting in Linda's kitchen, beneath an array of woven baskets that hark back to her Kenya days. Tea is served in her 'Sunny Side of the Street' mugs, with its frieze of iconic Shrewsbury buildings all drawn by her.

There's an abundance of sunny side in Linda's work. Early in her career, she realised what people wanted was sunny and that's what she's been giving them ever since. In her illustrated Usborne Children's Bible, even the camels are smiling.

Linda Edwards' Sunny Side mug

Linda studied Geography at Cambridge University, but was drawn to painting in her spare time. 'I used to sell on the railings in the King's Road, Chelsea. My work always sold. Even then I seemed to have a feel for what appealed.'

In 1993, a relative newcomer to Shrewsbury with two young children to support, Linda joined forces with Ludlow-based card publishers, Clare Maddicott. It was one of her Clare Maddicott cards that brought her to the attention of Usborne Books. 'From then onwards, it all took off,' Linda says, 'it all' referring to nineteen books for Usborne, cards, stationery and gift-wrap for Clare Maddicott, kitchen textiles, ceramics, enamelware and numerous of Linda's own illustrations and distinctive merchandising, all in the vibrant and uplifting style she's made her own.

Whilst we're talking, Linda leads me through her house and down the garden to her summerhouse. It's a Georgian house in miniature, just large enough for a chaise to sprawl against a crumbling wall, covered in cushions and rugs, with a rusty candelabra hanging over it, an old record-player and tiny red apples stacked in trays completing the scene. In its picturesque setting, against a backdrop of the river, sloping grass and trees, it calls to mind another of Linda's merchandised slogans 'Life is But a Dream – in Shrewsbury'.

It's not hard to see where Linda finds her inspiration. In the centre of her garden is an enormous Himalayan birch with snow-white branches, a few tenuous leaves still clinging on from autumn. Linda planted this tree when she first came to Shrewsbury. It was just a sapling then, but now it's put down roots and so has she. In fact, the Tree of Life is the perfect leitmotif for Linda's working life.

We return to the studio, and trees of life are everywhere – in packs of cards, on tea cloths and framed in endless variations on the walls. Linda apologises for everything being so tidy. Recently she's been clearing up, but she wouldn't like me to think her studio is normally like this.

It's a lovely studio, full of light. I browse amongst Linda's bags, mugs and framed prints, shelves of books and stands of greetings cards. Along with her 'Sunny Side of the Street' mugs are coasters, bags and prints, all featuring her drawings of Shrewsbury's finest facades. So successful has this range been, Linda tells me, that she and her partner, Nigel, are planning to take the Sunny Side format to other towns, including several London Boroughs.

Linda's whole house is full of artwork. Even down in her basement I find the Rusty Bike Gallery where Linda shows her paintings, some inspired by Chinese poetry. Then it's upstairs to the hall where, beneath a Jane Ray painting, I notice a cabinet full of fine porcelain elephants, and another of jewel-like, brightly enamelled miniature teapots.

Linda lifts one out, decorated with the design that first caught Usborne's eye. Together she and Clare Maddicott donated her card designs to the charity Trade Plus Aid, which funds development projects in Africa, Asia and South America. The charity's aim is to alleviate poverty and assist disadvantaged communities to become self-sufficient. To date, enough of Linda's enamelled teapots have been sold to build *two whole schools*.

I am astonished. I challenge anyone to spend an hour with Linda Edwards and not feel uplifted. As I leave, I ask what Shrewsbury means to Linda – what makes it stand out from anywhere else she's lived, and why she's stayed. People in other places have seemed more competitive, Linda says. It may be a sweeping generalization, but people in Shrewsbury seem more willing to share. Take the Shropshire Illustrators' and Children's Authors' Café – people come to show their work, pool their knowledge, offer each other professional advice. There's no point-scoring. The atmosphere is friendly and laid back.

'Shrewsbury can appear a bit sleepy,' Linda says, 'but it's not when you get to know it. And especially not now. The town is buzzing with life. It's full of new people, exciting prospects, shops opening, people coming up with ideas, trying things out, giving them a go.'

Linda is rooting for Shrewsbury – and her work is too. It might be dark outside as I write this, but across town the sun's still shining on Linda Edwards' street.

20th January: LET IT SNOW, LET IT SNOW, LET IT SNOW

Welcome to the *My Tonight From Shrewsbury* Snow Special, and thank you Sammy Cahn and Jules Styne – in Hollywood, on one of the hottest days in the summer of 1945 – for writing a song to remind us that the last word on snow doesn't have to be 'White Christmas'.

> *Oh the weather outside is frightful,*
> *But the fire is so delightful,*
> *And since we've no place to go,*
> *Let It Snow! Let It Snow! Let It Snow!*

Well, I can tell you for a fact that *let it snow* was NOT what I could be heard singing earlier today when I locked myself out of my house. As I trudged the streets, my mind turned to the Great Frost of 1739 when the River Severn froze hard enough for stalls to be set up on it, and carriage trips to go up and down.

One of the highlights of that Frost was the attempt by famous daredevil Robert Cadman to tightrope walk across the frozen Severn to St Mary's Church. This happened on February 2nd, 1739. The river was crowded, and so was the area around St Mary's, where Mrs Cadman shook the collecting tin. The plan was for her husband to tightrope walk up from the Gay Meadow (in its pre-Shrewsbury Town Football Club incarnation) to St Mary's spire. So confident was he of success that he stopped halfway up to fire off pistols and perform tricks. He made it safely to St Mary's, but then requested the rope be slackened for the grand finale when he would simulate flight.

However, Cadman's assistant misheard his instructions. Instead of slackening the rope along which his master would fling himself, attached to a wooden breastplate with a central groove, he tightened it. And that fatal error proved the end of Robert Cadman.

Many people died in the Great Frost of 1739, but Cadman's the only one remembered to this day.

A snowy Castle Gates library garden

'Good night, you madman, poor Bob Cadman,' someone scrawled on the ground where his body fell. And that spot is still commemorated:

> *'Let this small Monument record the name*
> *of Cadman, and to future time proclaim*
> *How by'n attempt to fly from this high spire*
> *across the Sabine stream he did acquire*
> *His fatal end. Twas not for want of skill*
> *Or courage to perform the task he fell,*
> *No, no, a faulty Cord being drawn too tight*
> *Harried his Soul on high to take her flight*
> *Which bid the Body here beneath good Night.'*

25th January
POMONA, ANCIENT APPLE QUEEN OF CASTLE GATES

Two thirty in the morning and Des is up and out, heading for the market in Birmingham. Once he ran a business with a massive turnover and forty-five employees, but now he's on his own, nosing into the darkness on behalf of Shrewsbury's newest greengrocery.

Pomona, goddess of apples, celebrated in poetry by William Morris, and in tapestry by Edward Burne-Jones, can be found on Castle Gates, lit up in her latest incarnation by night, and dressed like a stage-set by day, her windows and adjoining pavements in full harvest-festival mode.

'We always reckoned we had a good shop in us,' Des says, the 'we' in question being himself and partner Debra, who's to be found most days behind Pomona's till, and has the equally important (and not always enviable, I guess) role of hauling Des back when his enthusiasm runs ahead of him.

Des Walker

Des certainly doesn't come across as a man who lets the grass grow under his feet. I'm sitting opposite him in the Shrewsbury Coffeehouse, and his drink is already downed whilst mine still sits in the cup. He describes himself as gung-ho and instinctive, and in his cloth cap, tweed jacket and shopkeeper's apron, that's exactly how he looks – in a greengrocery sort of way.

An unnamed source once described Des to me as like an onion – 'you just keep peeling back the layers'. So here I am, attempting to do that. What brought Des and Debra into fruit and veg, I ask. Des puts it all down to an appreciation of food, both as consumers and members of the eating public. 'I've always loved to grow,' he says. 'I love cooking as well as gardening. In 2001, when Debra and I left London we started Boxfresh along with Mike Hamilton.'

Boxfresh turned into a multi-million pound business, supplying customers from Bristol to Manchester. But it grew too fast, Des says. 'I ended up spending all my time in meetings. It became an office job, and that wasn't what I wanted. I'd lost the hands-on say about quality. I'd lost the direct contact.'

Des and Debra bought an apple farm in Herefordshire, and struck a deal to sell Boxfresh, though sadly partner Mike Hamilton never lived to see it through. He died on May 11th 2011, around the time Des and Debra took the keys to Pomona.

'We'd heard that the Crabapple Community were looking for a new tenant for their shop,' Des says. 'Its potential was obvious. We looked at its mirrored wall and two bay windows and saw immediately how it could be. We'd learned a lot from the Boxfresh years. And I've always had a bit of an eye.'

On the subject of Des's eye, I ask what he's looking for at 4.00am in Birmingham. Quality, he says. He's looking for taste, and for products that might be interesting and different – salsify, for example, or fresh figs in season. And, as much as anything, he's looking for price. Pomona's not some high-class wrap-your-potatoes-in-gold-foil shop. It's a regular greengrocer's, and its prices prove the point, high street rather than high end.

I ask what happens in Des and Debra's lives apart from the shop. They have three daughters, Des says. They live quiet lives. They're not the life-and-soul-of-the-party types – but Des does play in a band. He sings, plays mandolin and bass. Irish music. The band is called Star of the Sea. They play regularly at the Irish Centre in Birmingham, and locally too. There's a gig coming up at the Lion Hotel Ballroom, proceeds to Shrewsbury-based charity, Village Water. 'This is a great town for charities,' Des says.

It's time to go. On the way home I call into Pomona. Debra confirms everything Des has said. I browse around the shop. This is high street as it ought to be, not what it often is. In the window, as I leave, a William Morris poem catches my eye:

I am the ancient apple-queen.
As once I was so am I now.
For evermore a hope unseen,
Betwixt the blossom and the bough.

Ay, where's the river's hidden gold!
And where the windy grave of Troy?
Yet come I as I came of old,
From out of the heart of summer's joy.

27th January: BE THERE OR BE WITHOUT A SQUARE

A building technique with roots in the Middle Ages lies behind a Public Inquiry taking place in Shrewsbury this coming Tuesday. In its day, this technique was a means of increasing a building's size, reducing its tax bill and providing a more efficient way of spanning floor joists without impacting detrimentally on its surroundings. Right here and now, however, in 21st century Shrewsbury, that building technique is in danger of becoming something of a battle-ground.

In case you're wondering, I'm talking about overhangs. Here in Shrewsbury we have some of the finest examples in the UK. Whether it's Henry Tudor House on Wyle Cop, Bear Steps, Grope Lane, The King's Head in Mardol, Ireland's Mansion or Rowley's House, in large part, they define Shrewsbury's character.

Back in the 1960s and early 70s, when developers sought planning consent for new buildings, they attempted to mirror in concrete our Tudor overhangs, anxious to find ways to fit in with the architecture for which the town was famous. Stand, for example, at the St Julian's Church end of the High Street and look towards the Square and you'll see that every building, old and new alike, has an overhang. It's like an echo running down the street. There may be people who don't like our modern buildings, but undeniably there's been an attempt at harmony.

Not for much longer, however, if the owners of one building have their way.

The building in question is Princess House in the Square – a building which owes very little to its surroundings other than its massive overhang. What's being proposed is that the public highway underneath that overhang should be stopped up allowing Princess House to be built out, increasing its size to the detriment of the Square, and depriving the town of part of its public thoroughfare.

Is this what we want? It's certainly not what *I* want. The Square is the heart of our town. It houses thriving markets, an annual World Music Day, even full-scale operas. Everything from morris dancing to brass band concerts take place in the Square, along with open-air exhibitions, New Year celebrations and the switching on of Christmas lights.

The Square also houses some of the town's most iconic buildings.

The axis formed by the Music Hall (due to be opened later this year as the town's new multi-million pound museum), the Old Market Hall and the Robert Clive statue, with a backdrop of fine Tudor buildings and Georgian/Victorian facades (of such quality that they were used in the Hollywood movie of Dickens *Christmas Carol*) proclaim that the Square is the town's premier civic space. Already Princess House has intruded into that space with three storeys of overhang. Now it wants to protrude even more.

Hardly surprising then that the proposed change to the character of the Square isn't universally popular – but there's a potentially even more worrying issue. If Princess House is allowed to stop up the land beneath its overhang, then the owners of every overhang in town might look to their perceived

Town Crier, Martin Wood, in Shrewsbury's Square

rights to extra floor space. And if they were to be successful in claiming precedence, pavements could disappear and buildings change shape all over town. Maybe it sounds melodramatic to say that Shrewsbury's essential character could be in danger of disappearing, but there's no doubt that the delicate balance between old and new would be lost.

This coming Tuesday, a Public Inquiry has been set up by the Secretary of State at the Shirehall from 10.00am onwards. What happens at this Inquiry is important for our town. This is one of those occasions when being there really matters. I'll be there, and I hope you will too.

30th January: THE PUBLIC INQUIRY

'It's 10.00am. This Inquiry is now open,' announced John Wilde, the Secretary of State's Inspector. On either side of him, at long tables sat representatives of Rockspring, the owners of Princess House and representatives of all the major objector groups. The rest of us sat between them in rows.

Everybody was free to have their say, the Inspector said, but could we please bear in mind that this wasn't a Planning Inquiry. For good or ill, permission for the Princess House proposals had been granted. All that was being considered here were issues to do with stopping up the highway.

Up to this point, the atmosphere was convivial. The room was packed, but more people managed to squeeze in. 'It's very cosy isn't it? No one's going to sit on my lap, I hope.' Unless I'm mistaken, it was Inspector Wilde who said that. Everybody laughed.

At least they did until the two points for consideration were spelled out. Firstly, was it absolutely necessary to stop up pavement under Princess House? Secondly, what were the dis-benefits to the Square should this stopping up take place?

The Rockspring side was represented by a young man with a shaved head, a bigger man called Mr Tibble (spotty handkerchief in pocket, lots of floppy white hair,) and a tall, grey man, Mr Renshaw, from Town Planning company Stride Treglown, who'd written the Proof of Evidence report that started the proceedings.

Princess House, a building which sat 'uncomfortably in its context of historic buildings' (groan from the floor), had been bought by Rockspring with a strategy in mind to 'regenerate this building for the benefit of the town' (titter from the floor). Their planning application to stop up the publicly-used pavement under the building's overhang had come about as a result of shop tenants' complaints, and the threat of some of them moving elsewhere. The company had spent six months making their proposals acceptable to everybody from English Heritage to the County Council, and it had been successful in getting planning permission. There were no objections to what they wanted to do.

In addition, their desire to take custody of the pavement beneath the overhang was backed by surveys into the pavement's use. Granted one day their CCTV camera had had its view blocked by delivery trucks, but another day Mr Renshaw had been out in person and counted only a small handful of people walking beneath the overhang in the course of an hour.

After this, Mr Renshaw was available for cross-examining. I wouldn't have liked to be him. Opposite sat Sheila Sager and Alan

Princess House

Shrank, representing town centre residents, and they were looking very mean indeed. The town's councillor for the ward in question, Andrew Bannerman, looked slightly more jovial, but only because his cheeks, I've noticed, have natural high colour. Next to him, white-faced and stern in his dog collar, sat the Civic Society's representative, the Reverend Richard Hayes – a man I know to have a razor mind and to never be lost for words. And flanking this group at either end were the equally determined-looking Town Clerk, Helen Ball, and a representative of Shops in the Loop, the town's retail interest group, John Hall.

Slowly they picked their way through the evidence. Those shopkeepers' complaints – had they been unsolicited? (It turned out that no unsolicited complaints had been made.) Did Rockspring deny offering assurances about outdoor seating arrangements being retained if the proposals went ahead? (Yes they denied it, though later it turned out they had). That survey Mr Renshaw had conducted, with such low numbers for people's use of the overhang – was it true that it had been taken during a snow storm?

After Mr Renshaw's cross-examination, it was the objectors' turn, starting with Town Clerk, Helen Ball who, when facing cross-questioning, ably fielded Mr Renshaw's attempts to tie her in knots. 'I couldn't possibly answer that question,' was her bemused, and not infrequent reply, 'Why are you asking that?' to which Mr Renshaw replied, 'I'm meant to be asking the questions, not you,' to which, in turn, Ms Ball replied, 'Well, ask me something I might know.'

I'm sure that gives you the idea. Somewhere in the midst of objectors' concerns about views being impeded for oncoming traffic, the loss of café culture and the forcing of pedestrians out into the public highway, one of the Rockspring people wondered whether Shrewsbury understood the way the retail sector worked. As a large number of those present were retailers, this was met by indignant groans.

People talked about the Square being Shrewsbury's only large public space. Its civic role was mentioned, as was its role as a neighbourhood amenity. Sterling work had been done by Alan Shrank for the Town Centre residents on acceptable distances between pedestrians and highway. He was dry. I'd even push out the boat and say on a couple of occasions, though his face moved not a muscle, he was droll. Certainly he wasn't to be tripped up. And then up stood Richard Hayes. The Reverend Richard Hayes – Shrewsbury's white knight. If the town had been a damsel in distress, she couldn't have been better defended.

For those of you who haven't had the privilege of meeting Richard Hayes, he's the quintessential English cleric. Slight stoop, almost imperceptible stutter, sweep of white hair, sharp mind and, though quietly spoken, the sort of tongue that is equally sharp. Beginning by knocking on the head the idea that Shrewsbury people – including himself, who'd been a parish priest in the City of London, at the heart of the banking culture – had little understanding of commercial/retail interests, Richard Hayes launched into words of praise for what he called 'our Saxon town'. The Square at the heart of it, he said, was a place of harmony. Did Rockspring realise the damage they were doing, not just to the town, but to themselves? Rockspring wanted to attract customers to their tenants' shops, he said, but they were creating an unwelcoming environment. He used the phrase 'shooting yourselves in the foot'.

'Abandon this ill-considered plan,' said Richard Hayes. 'Refurbish Princess House as you see fit, but leave the shop fronts where they are. If you do that, you will win the goodwill of local people, and financially it will be to your gain.'

The rhetoric was really ramping up by now, ably followed by Councillor Bannerman who challenged Rockspring's assertion that objectors to one seventh of the Square being removed were 'only a little cabal.' 'To quote Churchill,' said Councillor Bannerman, drawing himself up to his considerable height, and looking round the packed room, *Some cabal.'*

I could go on. There's lots I'm leaving out here. Points were scored. There were weaknesses in arguments, and twists and turns of facts. Final statements were made for and against. When Mr Renshaw, for Rockspring, dismissed the town's objections as pure emotion, an emotional roar rose to the rafters of 'What do you expect?'

Inspector Wilde said he'd submit his report to the Secretary of State. After that – he raised his hands. This was government we were talking about. No way of knowing how long their decision would take.

'This Inquiry is now over,' he declared. 'Can we thank you for the good-humoured spirit in which you've conducted it,' said ex-Chair of the Town Centre Residents, Professor Lalage Brown, rising to her feet. Claps all round. Everyone agreed. There had been humour in the day. Allowing for the strength of feeling, on both sides, it could have been so much worse.

FEBRUARY

2nd February: FISKING ABOUT

Have you met Shroppiemon on Twitter? He tweets in the old Shropshire dialect of bygone years, and I attempt to tweet back, though not half as well as he does. Recently our tweeting has been about fisking – an old Worthen word, according to Georgina Jackson's *Shropshire Word-Book*, which means to 'go wandering'.

Shrewsbury's a great town for fisking. Yesterday the sun was shining, I'd had a busy week and reckoned I deserved time off. The river was flooded again, and as my dog fell into it last time it was this high, I

Fish Street

decided it would be safer to take him across town.

One of my favourite dog walks takes me round the back of St Mary's Church, past Drapers' Hall, across Dogpole, past the Loggerheads pub (which, yesterday was packed with ladies in extraordinary hats), on to St Alkmund's Square, whose proud boast is that it houses not just one church, but two.

The first, St Alkmund's, has a dedicated congregation and regular weekly services. The second, St Julian's, is owned by Andrew Wright who until recently lived in its tower. Tall and angular with a bushy grey beard, back in his hippy days Andrew ran a wholefood shop in that church's shadow, on Fish Street. I used to buy my black-eye beans off him. In more recent years, I've enjoyed looking up at his church tower at night, imagining him and wife Lexie in their lonely fastness, keeping those old stones lived in and alive.

On the far side of St Alkmund's Square lies the complex of Tudor buildings known as Bear Steps. Down those steps I continued my fisk, small brown dog pulling on lead, across Fish Street's cobbles, down Grope Lane, about which much could be said but maybe another time, across the High Street and into the Square.

This was being set up for market. But it was another market that I was heading for – Shrewsbury's indoor market housed in its 1960s Market Hall building. Here in the Bird's Nest Café, I drank coffee, ate cake (beetroot and raspberry, yum) and watched children clambering over sofas. Susan of Pengwern Books came by and said hello. Julia Wenlock sat and chatted about making chocolates for a living. Yum to that as well.

After Julia had gone, I fisked around the stalls, bought a Coalport cup and saucer for a mere three quid and lingered by the fish stall, which had some nice organic salmon on the slab. Then it was time for home. On the way I called in at the Farmers' Market in the Square, resisting cupcakes and meringues, but falling for soda bread with walnuts and a roasted hog bap. On the way up Pride Hill I stopped to talk to the fire-juggling man. Then I bumped into my dentist, Gareth Jenkins, whom I'd seen on telly in *Come Dine With Me*. Briefly we chatted about his moment of fame, then I headed on home, fisking over for the day.

(PS. Thanks to the owners of those lovely hats for allowing me to photograph them. I hope you had a good night, girls.)

6th February: I WISH HIM WELL

Last night out dog walking round town, my husband found a lad standing beneath an overhang, sheltering from the pouring rain. We should help him, he said. Plainly the lad was in trouble. We made cheese sandwiches and took them out with a mug of tea. The lad looked very young. He was adopted, he said, and his relationship with his adoptive parents wasn't easy. He kept getting into trouble, some of it involving Social Services and police.

Now his mum had had enough and he'd nowhere else to go. He'd hung around all day with friends, but they'd gone home. No, he didn't need a coat. His aunty had bought him some thermals, so he was fine.

Returning home we started phoning round. Surely there was somebody who could help this lad. Where was the out-of-hours Social Work Team when you needed it? Failing completely to track it down, we had no choice but to phone the police. The lad wasn't violent or making trouble, we explained. He wasn't threatening anybody. He was just standing in the rain, and had nowhere to go.

Shelter from the rain

Back at the overhang, while we waited for the police to arrive, the lad chatted about what he was studying in school and his ambitions to become a chef some day. It was his GCSE year. He was good at maths. He always got 100%. He could easily be in a higher group. He wished he could be moved up.

The police arrived. They spoke to the boy by name and were gentle with him. He shook both our hands. His face is before me now as I write. He could be any boy in any country town across the UK, as much a part of the fabric of life as anybody else. This is his Shrewsbury too, which is why I'm writing about him now.

I hope he gets sorted out. I wish him well.

8th February
KATE GITTINS & SHREWSBURY MARKET

Kate's office is in the corner of the gallery. You knock. Go in. Kate's on the phone. You hesitate. Is this a good moment? Kate looks up over her specs, the perfect picture of a busy woman interrupted. Then she smiles. 'It's *you*,' she says. 'Do you know anything about medieval culverts?'

Kate's the dynamic force behind Shrewsbury Market Hall's current success. She's been manager for nearly seven years, and was shopper and market champion for twenty before that. When the job came up, she reckoned it had her name on it. Now, having been in post for a mere seven years, she reckons she couldn't possibly leave – there's still so much to do.

I imagine Kate managing the Market Hall from her bath chair – which, in case you're wondering, isn't likely for a good few years. Everything to do with the fabric of the building, from its iconic 1960s clock tower to its street level units, is in her care. Even the medieval culverts don't escape her beady eye. Kate has responsibilities in the market too, letting out the units at Gallery level and around the market's outer edge, whilst the market floor stalls are let by Shrewsbury Council.

Kate grew up in a Sussex farming family and studied at Riseholme College of Agriculture before coming to Shropshire to work for the Limousin Cattle Society. She worked for the BBC on *On Your Farm* and *Farming Today*, and ran her own garden design and IT businesses. She brought to her current job considerable experience of marketing and PR.

The market's history is long and distinguished. Until the early sixties it was housed in a fine Victorian building, which was pulled down to make way for the current Market Hall. This opened in 1965, trading in fruit and vegetables, bread and cakes, meat and poultry, much of it locally sourced, as well as flowers, fish, delicatessen, books, china and antiques.

A decade ago, sensing that the market's image needed revamping, a company was commissioned to help attract shoppers from Shrewsbury's increasing number of out-of-town supermarkets. They devised the market's current look, controversially bringing in striped awnings to create divisions between individual stalls. They also started tackling the problem of the market not having a street level face.

Since then, the fortunes of the market have turned about. And in no small measure, that is down to

Kate Gittins

the arrival of Kate as Manager. *Passion* and *vision* are the words that spring to mind when she's talking about the market. She wants to put the market on the tourist trail as a must-see destination. 'What we have here is nothing short of Sunday supplement material,' Kate says. 'In its own way, it's every bit as much a treasure as Rowley's House, Shrewsbury Castle or the Square.'

Kate would love to turn what's become recognised as an *awnings problem* (views across the market hall, particularly at Gallery level, hampered by a sea of green-and-white stripes) into a national competition utilising the height and airiness of the market hall to create art installation-type awnings for a 21st century market. The space and drama of the building's interior, she feels, isn't being used. This would be one fascinating way of putting Shrewsbury Market on the map.

With or without new awnings, however, the market is certainly on the up. New stallholders have come in, bringing a whole new generation of shoppers. Kate's delighted to see arts and crafts flourishing alongside vintage clothes, hairdressing, Pengwern Books and art classes for kids.

Then there are the cafés, which are always full, whether the sofas and twinkling lights of the Bird's Nest Café, the tables of Moroccan café, Mezze, or the bar stools of Ian's seafood bar, where champagne and oysters are on the menu. 'Do you like fresh mackerel?' Kate asks. 'You've got to taste Ian's special way of cooking it. Get him to do it for you. Tell him I told you.'

The phone rings. While Kate's answering it she's also digging through her press cuttings. Here's the town's new marketing strategy – 'Shrewsbury: The Original One-Off'. Here's the prize the market won last year – Best Council-Run Market in the Country. Already Kate has the accolade 'Britain's Best Loved Market' in her sights. But as important as any award is seeing people come in and enjoy the market.

What next, I ask when Kate gets off the phone. Improving the entrances, she says. It's vital for a market housed at first floor level to be able to draw people in. And vital, too, to emphasise Shrewsbury Market as a foodie destination. It's full of interesting characters too. All the stallholders have their stories. I should get out there and hear some of them. They're a colourful bunch.

11th February
A BABY'S-EYE VIEW OF SHREWSBURY – MMM & CO

So, what's life like in Shrewsbury from a baby's point of view? I decided to find out by visiting Mmm & Co. The letters stand for 'Monday Morning Mums', not that they're particularly hung up on names. They're too relaxed for that.

Mmm & Co is a place to chill out, have a laugh or share tales of woe with other mums who know what life's like with babies and young children. For the babies, it's a place to roll about on rugs, eye each other up, grab all the best toys, attempt to toddle upstairs (and be brought down again) snuggle up, feed and generally hang loose whilst the focus isn't just on them. It's on their mums and the need for coffee and chat.

Monday Morning mum and child

Meeting weekly at the Shrewsbury Coffeehouse, this is an adult space. It's not municipal or clinical. It's somewhere for mums to feel at home, entirely within their comfort zone.

That *feeling at home* is crucial. The mums who come – whether with first babies, or pregnant-and-in-waiting – are in a transition between their lives as individuals with responsibility for themselves alone, and becoming parents with all that entails. They're facing a new life, including new ways of thinking. Some steep learning curves are happening, and it's good to have a place to meet and share.

Sitting breastfeeding next to me is pink-haired Simone, with a pretty baby in a daisy-print dress. She lives on the outskirts of Hanwood, but drives in for Mmm & Co every week. She's not the only one either. People plainly feel this is worth travelling for. Some mums know each other from school, but others – like Simone who comes from Switzerland, and met her Shrewsbury partner in Thailand – are newcomers. One person in the group came to the Coffeehouse anyway, saw what was going on and joined in. Another caught sight of a tangle of buggies through the window and came in to find out more.

'There's a natural progression,' says Su Barber, 'Mums tend to come in either when they're pregnant or with new babies. They make friends, have their babies, keep on coming, develop networks and gradually slope off.'

The group's loosely held together by Su and co-founder, Marina, who both work as *doulas*. The word '*doula*' is taken from the Greek, meaning 'woman caregiver', in practice an experienced older woman who offers emotional and practical support during pregnancy, childbirth and its aftermath. Mmm & Co is a natural extension of that support.

Another Sue comes in with baby Frank who's five weeks old and fast asleep. Frank's a sweetie. Everybody coos over him. But he's not such a sweetie at home, his mum says. He's not settling well and this is hard. Sue wants to know what to do, and immediately the advice is there. 'What we used to do...' someone says, and 'I've sometimes found...' says someone else. 'It's easy, isn't it, to get upset...' says someone else, and this is quickly followed by, 'It seemed to help with us to...' and 'Have you thought about...?'

All the while the mums are talking, the babies are either sleeping, snuggling, rolling, staring wide-eyed at the world around them or attempting to crawl or trot. What's Shrewsbury like for babies, I ask. Someone says the cobbles are a pain, but someone else reckons cobbles help jiggle babies off to sleep. I ask about breastfeeding. No problem everyone agrees. And shopping, I ask? Some find a few of the more old fashioned shops hard to get round with buggies, but generally people agree that it's a welcoming town. The sofas are great in the Bird's Nest Café. The new café, Eat Up, has very helpful staff, a lift and lots of toys. There's the Square for sitting in on sunny days, and there's the Quarry Park too. The babies love the ducks in the Dingle. And the swings and slides are always worth dropping by.

At some point, almost imperceptibly, the meeting takes on a more formal air. Smaller groups of chatting mums merge into a more coherent whole. Phinn's had a cough, says Marina, and Laura's Luke has too. Sue's Frank has been grizzly and Willow has been off her food. Sam and

Baby Evie are working on a new bedtime routine, helped by Lyndsey who's Evie's other mum. Everybody has had bedtime issues at one time or another, so they all pitch in with advice. But it's gentle advice. Nobody's getting heavy with anybody else.

Somebody starts singing Twinkle, Twinkle, Little Star. Soon everybody is joining in. It's a lovely quiet moment at the end of the morning. 'See you next week...' 'Are you up for coffee sometime...?' 'Have you seen my nappy bag..?' 'See you. Goodbye...' 'Goodbye, goodbye.' The room has emptied now. The babies have gone and it's my turn too. Tonight from Shrewsbury, goodbye, goodbye.

14th February
DO NOT TRY THIS ONE YOURSELVES AT HOME!!

There are urban explorers across the world in all its major cities, and they're here in Shrewsbury too. I know this because one of them called last night to show me his photographs. The way he sees it, Shrewsbury is a succession of secret worlds, waiting to be discovered. And he's the man to discover them.

By coincidence, I'm currently reading the science fiction crime novel, *The City & the City*, by author China Miéville. Its two separate cities, trained to unseeingly inhabit the same space, chime with my visitor's view of Shrewsbury. 'Most people live inside a box,' he said. 'For them, a drainpipe is for channelling rainwater, not scaling. But if they lived outside the box, they'd see a drainpipe as an opportunity. There'd be no barriers in their brains.'

According to my visitor, the rooftops of the High Street are a practice run and Pride Hill is 'the rat run'. All Shrewsbury's public buildings have been scaled, and not only under the cloak of darkness, as his photographs attest.

Don't think because I'm writing this I'm recommending urban exploring as a sport to take up. This is total craziness – a health & safety nightmare at the very least. It takes living outside the box into some very tricky areas. 'We do have a code,' my visitor insisted. 'No domestic buildings (so your houses are safe). No break-ins (so your shops are safe). No taking anything (so we're all safe). Move in silence. Leave as you find. Take nothing but photos, leave nothing but footprints behind.'

My visitor came across as thoughtful and serious-minded. In his

spare time he wrote, acted in and shot films. He wanted to make something of his life, he said. He was full of curiosity, and a strange sort of courage. Whatever I might think of the wisdom, or legality, of streaming over rooftops and creeping underground, I have to admire the courage, tenacity and spirit of adventure that these enterprises entail. *This is my town as much as anybody else's,* my visitor seemed to say, *but it's mine in my own way.*

Look out tonight for a dark figure with a glint of danger about him. He won't

Photo courtesy Verbish, Market Hall tower in background

be on the rooftops – more likely in the Yorkshire House drinking to Verbantine's (no, *not* Valentine's) Day. Verbantine's

Day is for people who aren't afraid to be alone. 'As individuals we have the power to decide whether our lives are enjoyable,' said my visitor. 'Any love interest is just a bonus. The 14th February shouldn't just be amazing for lovers. It should be amazing for *everybody*.'

17th February: A BOG, A SQUARE AND ONE BIG STINK

Gullet Passage leads from the Square to Mardol Head. In the Middle Ages a stream ran down it to a place of wet horribleness known as Mudholes, which drained into the River Severn. The source of that stream was a bog that stood on the site of present Princess House – subject of controversy at a recent Public Inquiry.

I suspect Professor Lalage Brown knew this when, at that Inquiry, she suggested that Princess House might sink into a watery swamp if allowed to be built out any further. The suggestion was quickly refuted, however. Even back in 1881 when the old Shirehall was built on the current Princess House site, that bog had long since been drained. However, it's an interesting fact that its filthy water was once the town ducking pool (clean water not reckoned necessary when it came to retribution).

So how far back does all this ducking go? The Anglo-Saxon word for the gumble – or ducking – stool was 'scalfing-stole', and it seems it was the common instrument of punishment for 'scolds' – in other words women who had too much to say for themselves – certainly in Shrewsbury. In 1266 an Act of Parliament ordered ducking to be meted out to defaulting bakers and brewers too, which meant that the bakers on Shrewsbury's modern High Street – then called Bakers Row – wouldn't have had far to go.

By the end of the 14th century, the bog on the Princess House site had dried up enough for the instrument of punishment to be removed to St John's Hill. A new stool was purchased in 1669, and the Mayor's Accounts for 1710–11 record the payment of sixpence for 'ye carriage of ye Gumble stoole from St John's Hill to ye lower end of Mardol.' As punishments went, this one persisted almost into what we might think of as the dawn of modern times.

Where did I find all this fascinating information? In 'Shrewsbury Street Names' by John L Hobbs, which I bought in Candle Lane Books. And where did John L Hobbs get *his* information? From Shrewsbury Public Library's Calendar of Deeds, St Chad's Parish Registers and Shrewsbury Abbey's Cartulary (available on Amazon, I do not joke, hardcover, *in Latin*, no reviews, four used copies available, eighty quid each).

Don't all rush at once.

19th February
THE LAST DAYS OF THE DANA: 'ART IS MY THERAPY'

What we're currently witnessing here in Shrewsbury, with the closure of the prison because of Government cuts, is the disappearance of a small town within our larger one, a secret town that most of us have never been inside, but which can be glimpsed in an exhibition at Bear Steps. 'Prisoners' Art from the Last Days of the Dana' it's called.

Twenty-First Century scream, by J.M.

Do take a look at this exhibition if you can. Some of it has been produced in the prison education block, some completed by prisoners in their cells. Some paint a pretty world, some a dark one. Some of it finds things to be joyful about. Some of it is very bleak indeed. My particular favourite, for all sorts of reasons, is 'Basket Case – No Meds', from Marcos Phillips, whose parents were bargees transporting wood, cement and coal through the Midlands. Born on the canals, his are the words I've used in this post's title: *Art is my therapy as well as my medication.*

22nd February: OPEN STUDIO – HELEN FOOT

Just round the corner from the gallery on Bear Steps is Butcher Row. I was there the other day in the studio that weaver, Helen Foot, shares with her photographer brother, Richard. Recently, Helen offered to sell me one of her looms (sadly I couldn't afford it). Now it was off to a new home to make space for a big beast of a loom, all 24 shafts of it being made for Helen in the US.

'I never would have been able to afford a loom like that without help from Shropshire Council's Business Enterprise Grant,' Helen said. 'It's great to know that what I'm doing here has their support.'

The county's fortunate to have a weaver of Helen's calibre. She's a hands-on designer/weaver and Royal College of Art graduate, making commercially marketable cloth right here in the heart of Shrewsbury. Her originally designed and handmade scarves are beautiful. Currently she's working with Kate Millbank, a fashion graduate of Central St Martin's, London, on their first batch of Shropshire tweed.

Helen is one of a generation of young people who left Shrewsbury for university and spent years plying their skills in big cities like London, who have recently returned to breathe new young life into the town. She attended Meole Brace School, Shrewsbury College of Arts and Technology and Winchester School of Art, where she developed her knowledge of textiles, discovered the properties of yarns and tried out endless new techniques. It was exciting to be put forward for national competitions, including Texprint, and rewarding to graduate top of her class. However, leaving university for what Helen described as 'a crappy shop job' brought her down to earth with a bang.

Not for long, however. Not long after graduation Helen secured a placement with the Wallace Sewell Studio, which produces innovative textiles for fashion and furnishing exploiting industrial techniques. Helen also secured freelance weaving work for Salt, an interior textiles company based in London, and later secured a second placement with Wallace Sewell. Indeed, when the position of Studio Manager came up, Wallace Sewell gave her that too.

Helen worked there for one year, but then was encouraged by Emma Sewell to take her portfolio to the Royal College of Art. 'I had nothing to lose,' Helen said. 'If I got in it would be amazing. If I didn't I still had a brilliant job.' And Helen did get in – a two-year Masters degree at the top art school in the country, with alumni including Tracey Emin and David Hockney.

'It was tough,' Helen said. 'This was the Royal College of Arts, and there was always going to be a lot of pressure. The place was full of strong characters, big ambitions and amazing talent.'

Helen started out intending to specialise in Jacquard weaving, but ended up hand weaving. The pressure was on all the time, and so was the competition. She narrowly missed a job with fashion designer, Paul Smith, but secured a placement instead at an organic weaving mill on Mull. Creating a business of her own had been a long-term goal, and her Scottish adventure gave her time to reflect on this ambition. She returned from Mull spurred on to give business a go. With her college years behind her, she started working to put together a fully-functioning weaving studio with a range of textiles that would be instantly recognisable within the design world.

'I want to get into Liberty's,' Helen said. 'I want to be known for my designs.' Some of these Helen imagined weaving herself, but others – blankets, for example – she envisaged outsourcing to mills. The Shropshire tweeds she's been working on with Kate Millbank would be made in a mill rather than by hand. It was important that weaving time didn't eat into design time.

Helen frequently takes in graduates on college placements. 'I gained so much valuable knowledge from my student placements,' she said. 'I hope to provide a similarly inspiring experience for the next generation of graduates.' Her latest student helps with warping (a massive undertaking involving up to sixty heddles per inch), does admin and generally helps keep the business ticking over. 'Nothing too challenging!' Helen said.

Helen moved into her present studio tucked away behind Butcher Row in March 2011. Since then she's been getting known across the country, showing at major national craft fairs, developing relationships with stockists and galleries and developing her profile with help from the Craft Council who selected her for their *Helen Foot* Hothouse scheme for emerging makers in 2011. She's also done some freelance work for Alexander McQueen and is working to attract new buyers.

In addition, Helen teaches. When we met, she'd just finished eight 'Introduction to Weaving' sessions with first years at Chelsea College of Art, and she's now lecturing one day a week at Hereford College of Arts. She also has a winter collection to plan for, and recently film-makers R & A Collaborations shot a video of her weaving in her studio, which was selected for the Victoria & Albert Museum's sell-out 'Power of Making' exhibition.

'I know I sound busy,' Helen said, 'but I love it all. The buzz of teaching. Seeing students growing as designers. My own work too. I enjoy the whole weaving process from start to finish – the design, the planning and then the actual making. And I love working *here*. This is a great life. Every day is different. There's no such thing as run-of-the-mill in a business like mine.'

24th February: WHAT DO CHARLES DARWIN AND SAMUEL TAYLOR COLERIDGE HAVE IN COMMON? SHREWSBURY'S UNITARIAN CHURCH

Seeing as it was Sunday, I decided to go to church, and seeing as the Unitarian Church, with its High Street doors usually closed, was amongst the places I'd never been into, that's where I headed.

These were dissenters, so I expected something fairly austere – bare walls, an aversion to heating, pews designed to be uncomfortable. What I found, however, was oak panelling as shiny as chestnuts, polished brass-work, cushions on pews and windows full of light.

I chose a back pew. I've always been a back seat girl. 'Come in with worship', announced the Minister from the lectern, and the service began. The Minister spoke about times in our lives when the lights had gone out, calling on us to think with gratitude of those who'd helped us through. A short prayer was said to the Spirit of Life and Love, then we were into the first hymn: 'Come Together in Love.'

After this, the Minister told a story which smacked of Bruce Chatwin's 'On the Black Hill', recounting how two old friends fell out over a calf. The story concluded with the phrase 'I have more bridges to build'. This was followed by a prayer about walls being built, and bridges coming down, in turn followed by a poem beginning with the words 'What is a friend?'

Friendship, unmistakably was the theme of this service. We sang another hymn and then prayed again. I tried to write down the prayer:

'Spirit of life and love, to want to love and to be human is to be aware of our separation, often feeling alone, not knowing what to do or say. We want to live in harmony with the world around us. We confess our separation as an act of humility...'

That's as far as I got. Something was said next about the presence of God, and something else about grace. A hymn was sung about living together in truth and peace, followed by a prayer about being perfect channels of love, followed by a long, silent pause, during which I thought about the church's distinguished history.

The Darwin family attended church here. Charles Darwin would have sat on these pews until the age of eight when his mother died. Not only that, but the great poet Samuel Taylor Coleridge preached here as a trainee minister. The building itself went up on the site of Shrewsbury's first Presbyterian church, which opened in 1691, only two years after it became lawful for dissenters to have a dedicated meeting place.

A century or so later the church become Unitarian – a system of belief defined by the denomination as Judeo-Christian, but with no creed; rejecting some of the dogma of the established church, including the deity of Jesus Christ and the orthodoxy of the Trinity; stressing the importance of liberty of conscience; each individual free to form their own beliefs.

The service concluded with the Minister's main address (featuring Scott of the Antarctic and tragic heroism) and a final hymn about something of God being in everyone. Then it was time for tea, biscuits and questions. What did it mean to be a Unitarian, I wanted to know. And given the lack of dogma, why weren't Unitarians and Quakers worshipping together? In his *Guardian* blog a few days ago, Andrew Brown wrote, 'I lack the seriousness to make a real Quaker even without the theological commitments. But I do believe we ought to love our neighbours, even when they are miserable, absurd or embarrassing.' This didn't sound too far away from the Unitarians to me.

The Quakers were less formal in their worship, the Unitarians said, but even though Unitarians adhered to the traditional 'hymn-prayer sandwich', that didn't stop them embracing a wide range of beliefs. One person I talked to described herself as a nature-worshipper. Was

Winnie Gordon, Minister of the Unitarian Church

she a Christian too, I asked. She was a *Unitarian*, she said. She'd been brought up in the Unitarian Church but, no, she wasn't a Christian. Some Unitarians were, she said, and others weren't. But the ones who were would call themselves Unitarians first.

Not everybody in the congregation has grown up in Unitarianism, Winnie Gordon, trainee minister for one, and Alison Patrick, Shropshire Council's Tourism Officer for another. She joined the Unitarians through a contact made at work, but others just walked through the doors and found themselves at home.

Outside afterwards the High Street was buzzing. Starbucks full, and Costa too. People were going in and out of Waterstones or sitting in the Square enjoying an unexpected burst of spring. I closed the church door behind me and headed home, glad to know at last what went on inside.

27th February
COFFEE & CARDINALS (WITH A BIT OF BATMAN THROWN IN)

I head down Pride Hill to Starbucks. Usually it's packed, but today there are some empty seats. The girl on the coffee machine shouts my name when my black Americano is ready. I take it and sit opposite a mother, a toddler and a colouring book.

I love the way that Starbucks changes according to its customers' needs. A gang of sixth-formers have created an island by pulling together tables and chairs. There are laptops all over the tables, and sixth-formers sitting two-deep on the chairs.

I love the big windows too, where you can watch what's going on and remain invisible. A lady with a walking-stick goes by, her long coat almost touching the pavement. I wonder if she knows how elegant she looks. A woman with a small dog creates havoc around some skateboarders. Batman enters the Square. He was on Pride Hill earlier, collecting for charity in exchange for being photographed. Now, for some reason, nobody even looks at him.

I pick up an *Independent* newspaper. Its front page shows a Roman

Catholic cardinal looking grim, a Liberal Democrat Lord looking well fed, and a Chancellor of the Exchequer looking 'Defiant Over Cuts Despite Downgrade'. It's Tuesday 16th February and this is today's news.

After Starbucks, I head along the High Street to Eat Up where I order my second black Americano of the day. It's just the way I like it, strong with a thin layer of froth, and no tear-open sugar sachets, but cubes in Tate & Lyle treacle tins.

I've been in here before when the place has been heaving. This afternoon, however, all the tables are empty. I take a *Daily Mail* off the rack and open it. I see, to the *Daily Mail's* indignation, that the BBC is going easy on Lord Rennard and the Lib Dems, and George Osborne's recent performance in the House of Commons was 'like one of the Monty Python team acting a horseless knight.' Oh, and Britain has lost its Triple A credit rating because the Government hasn't cut back deeply enough.

On to McDonalds. I buy a burger, fries and coffee (they've never heard of an Americano), and have change from three pounds. I also have the entire hundred-seater downstairs dining area to myself. A worker in an apron is putting chairs on tables and sweeping the floor. Behind him rises a great sweep of Shrewsbury's medieval townwall.

This is not what you expect to find in your local McDonalds. These stones aren't polystyrene, you know. They're real, and part of Shrewsbury's history. There's even a woven tapestry on the wall.

The coffee in my polystyrene cup is terrible, an insult to the very word 'barista'. I struggle through half of it and leave the rest. A discarded copy of *The Times* tells me that Daniel Day-Lewis is the best actor ever, that Lord Rennard of the Lib Dems is in big trouble and that, according to George Osborne, the country's current Triple A downgrade shows he's been 'right all

Rumour has it that this is Darren Beddowes

along' (how can this be?). There's something about the cardinal too, but I can't remember what.

Out on Pride Hill, a man is playing a fandango on his guitar. It's wonderful. I head for home. Shrewsbury has plenty of other coffee establishments but I'm all caffeined-out. If you want it cheap (but in medieval surroundings) go to McDonalds. If you want to watch Shrewsbury sixth-formers catching up on their coursework and/or falling in love, go to Starbucks. If you want a really good cup of coffee, go to Eat Up (or I might add – though I didn't get there – the Shrewsbury Coffeehouse). Oh, and if you want to listen to the fandango, keep your ears open next time you're on Pride Hill.

STOP PRESS ON PRINCESS HOUSE

The word's out. The Secretary of State has spoken. The stopping up of pavement under Princess House has been approved. Brace yourselves for a lot less Square. Say goodbye to café culture. According to the report by the Secretary of State's Inspector, there are no overriding reasons on the grounds of public interest for not stopping up the highway. In other words, an ugly modern building in the heart of Shrewsbury will soon be even more in the town's face.

Strangely, the matter of ownership doesn't get a mention. The report refers to a 'loss' of land as though it was a pound in the pocket that had fallen out. But as far as I'm aware, the owners of Princess House haven't at any point offered to *buy* the disputed strip of land from Shrewsbury Town Council, nor has it been offered for sale. I find this weird. If I'm missing something here, perhaps somebody could explain.

MARCH

4th March
SIR SCALLYWAG & THE GOLDEN UNDERPANTS

Things have been a bit gloomy recently, so here's something to raise our spirits, courtesy of Giles Andreae and Korky Paul. Sir S and the GU is a picture book with a bounding storyline and glorious, in-your-face illustrations. It's naughty. It features kings and queens and bare bums. It has a giant who steals underpants (not just any underpants either, but golden underpants OF POWER) and a six-year-old hero who of course saves the day.

Several weeks ago, Sir S and the GU came to Shrewsbury School's Maidment Hall courtesy of musical group Ensemble 360, and now they're back by popular demand.

Ensemble 360, a flexible, eleven-piece chamber ensemble of five string players, five woodwinds and a pianist, was formed upon the retirement of the world-famous Lindsey Quartet. Music in the Round, with whom they collaborate, is an education group bringing high-quality music-making into the community.

This afternoon an audience of children and their families learned the Underpants Song and a series of key noises/actions required to bring alive the story of King Colin's tragic loss and Sir Scallywag's triumphant quest.

Tonight from Shrewsbury I can tell you that getting actions together with noises in all the right places was trickier than you'd expect. Eventually, however, the performance proper began, kicking off with Handel's Music for the Royal Fireworks.

'King Colin wasn't clever and King Colin wasn't bold,' the narrator narrated, 'but what made King Colin special *were his underpants of GOLD.'*

I'll spare you the rest. Some of the details now escape me. But what doesn't escape is the memory of Shrewsbury's little people (along with some of the great and good of the town), arms above their heads, doing the Golden Actions and singing the Underpants Song. They all loved it.

There were no actors on stage, just a handful of musicians, a screen, a few pics and a narrator. But for one glorious and magical hour, King Colin (and his bare bum) ruled. Or, at least, King Colin *tried* to rule – and very difficult it was, too, without his Underpants of Power.

For a three-year-old, what a fabulous introduction to the world of musicianship. Little people toddled out afterwards, their ears ringing to

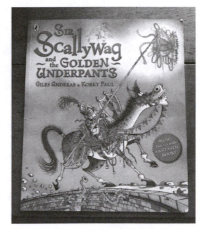

By Giles Andreae and Korky Paul

Rossini's *William Tell Overture*. For many, Sir Scallywag and the Golden Underpants will have been their first show.

6th March: ROBIN NOLAN & GYPSY JAZZ

Robin Nolan's rooted in the music of Django Reinhardt. The influence is unmistakable, but he's definitely his own man. 'You play a mighty fine guitar, Robin Nolan,' Willie Nelson said when he came across him playing on the streets of Amsterdam. And when George Harrison heard his gardener playing Robin's CD he invited him over to play at his Christmas bash.

From the Leidseplein in Amsterdam to Friar Park. Some jump. 'Friar Park was a fantasyland,' said Robin when we met at the Shrewsbury Coffeehouse. 'But George and Olivia were super-friendly, and playing before their famous friends wasn't as terrifying as playing before a gypsy audience at Samois-sur-Seine.'

The Samois festival, at the final resting place of Django Reinhardt, is the high altar of gypsy jazz. What with the music, camp fires, river and moonlight, Robin's first time there was a magical experience. 'I'm not a note-perfect performer,' Robin said. 'I'm imaginative with music. I use my sense of humour to get myself across. Yet they liked what I played.'

At Friar Park, they did as well. Robin may have been wide-eyed, but he knew that none of George Harrison's famous guests, including Eric Clapton, could play like him. It was the first of many gigs for the Harrison family. Robin played at Dhani Harrison's wedding. He even played at George's wake, when the sense of Harrison's spirit was palpable in the room.

'You were my father's secret weapon,' Dhani Harrison once said. 'He loved watching people's jaws drop when you began to play.'

With Shrewsbury's Chris Quinn on rhythm guitar and Arnaud van den Berg on bass, Robin is currently on a UK tour. Like Robin, Chris has honed his guitar skills on the streets – not in Amsterdam, but on Pride Hill. It was Chris who first brought Robin to Shrewsbury, and they've been playing together on Robin's UK tours ever since.

'The gypsy jazz scene has really opened up,' Robin said. 'Much of that is down to musicians going online, witnessing gypsy jazz being played by the tradition's custodians, then stamping the music with their own identity. The tango-inspired gypsy jazz of Argentina, for example, is very different to the young gypsy jazz scene currently taking place in France.'

Robin Nolan Trio

What were the names I should be listening out for, I wanted to know. 'Adrien Moignard,' Robin said. 'Guys like him are absolutely killing it. Listen out for Birelli Lagrene too.' And if I wanted to listen to Django himself? 'Minor Swing. 1937. It's the 'Stairway to Heaven' of gypsy jazz,' Robin said.

Over the years, Robin's performed his own brand of gypsy jazz all round the world, and headlined at all the major festivals. I asked if Christmas at Friar Park was his most outstanding gig, and he says that an Iceland gig stands out too - gale force winds and hail beating down outside whilst inside, in a warm fug heated by natural hot springs, Robin and trio played to a fantastic crowd.

What next, I asked. There'll be a new album, *Gypsy Blue*, out later this year, produced by Dhani Harrison. Then there are more tours, and Master Classes. Teaching is important to Robin. His tutorial books are recognised as an important element in the gypsy jazz renaissance in the US.

Tonight as I write this, the Robin Nolan trio will be playing Tenbury Wells. They're in for a treat. 'Robin Nolan is so amazingly good,' Bill Wyman once said in interview. 'As soon as I record something in the spirit of Django, I'll book him a flight and bring him into the studio.'

As commendations go, that's certainly one to add to the list.

11th March: 'WE ARE SHREWSBURY' IN HMP SHREWSBURY WITH GOVERNOR GERRY HENDRY

Getting behind the massive gates of HMP Shrewsbury is a complicated business. Even after securing an interview with its Governor, I have to be photographed, show my passport, be issued with a visitor's pass, buzz on doors, have my credentials checked and hand over my mobile phone.

Finally I'm escorted across a yard to a Georgian façade where a door opens a crack. A slice of face peers out. I'm ushered in. The door is locked behind me. By the time I've made it from street to Governor's office I've already forgotten how many locked doors I've been through.

Governor Gerry Hendry's office is large and light. His mantelpiece is packed with cards, which he readily shows me. *'Thank you for your thoughtfulness,'* I see in one. *'What can I say about a Governor like you?'* I read in another. *'It's taken a hard journey, and a change of lifestyle. Thank you for helping me get there,'* I read in another.

Shrewsbury Prison is rated amongst the best in the country, but it's being closed. It's a local prison, the majority of whose inmates are released into Shropshire and West Midland communities where they live in close proximity not only with ex-prisoners but staff too. Something the

Prison Service recognises as special about Shrewsbury, the Governor says, is the respect that staff and prisoners have for each other.

I see this in practice when Governor Hendry takes me onto 'A' Wing. By now there are only twenty-five prisoners left out of three hundred and fifty, but it's surprising the number who come up and shake the Governor's hand.

One man even shakes *my* hand. 'There's been a prison in this town for five hundred years,' he says, 'and when I leave next week I'll be the last prisoner. My name is Patrick Jackson. Don't forget it.' I assure him I won't.

'A' Wing is immaculately clean. We look into cells, including one with a heavy studded door left over from the early days of the Dana. It's small – toilet, basin, table, chair, bunk beds and telly packed in tight, walls and floors bare and tiny window grilled. It's as clean as a new whistle, though not as clean, I'm told, as 'A' Wing was before the cleaners were laid off.

Keeping 'A' Wing spruce, even in its last few days, is a matter of decency and personal pride. This is the prisoners' home, they say. It's all about treating it, and themselves, with respect.

During my morning in Shrewsbury Prison, I hear much on this subject. Whether running through departure information or just standing about, plainly upset, the way the prisoners interact with Governor Hendry attests to their mutual respect.

This is exactly the sort of prison that Governor Hendry has been working to create since his arrival in March 2005. *'Prisons are only as good as the staff who run them,'* he said, addressing his full staff. *'We have an absolute obligation to do everything we can to encourage reform... the decency agenda is about building relationships with prisoners based on knowing them and respecting them... It is about preserving the dignity of prisoners... about embodying values of integrity, honesty, confidence and good judgment ...'*

Now, however, HMP Shrewsbury awaits decommissioning by Order of Parliament, deemed too expensive to maintain, its inmates being sent to other prisons, including some that are privately-run. Interestingly, the Birmingham Chronicle recently reported 170 emergency call-outs to private prison Oakwood *in one month*. I ask Governor Hendry how many call-outs Shrewsbury has had. One, he says. In the last few years.

Here's the Prison Governors' Association on the subject of public v. private sector prisons: *'All the evidence suggests that smaller establishments meet the aims of the Government's rehabilitation revolution agenda.'*

Here, too, is David Cameron: *'The idea that big is beautiful when it comes to prisons is wrong.'* And Nick Herbert, until recently Minister of State at the Ministry of Justice: *'Huge prison warehouses are wrong. What's needed is a network of smaller local prisons with better integration with the local community and more focus on reducing re-offending.'*

HMP The Dana, Shrewsbury

Unfortunately, Cameron's words were spoken in 2009, before he became Prime Minister, and Nick Herbert's in 2008 when, as Shadow Secretary of State for Justice, he spoke against Labour Government plans for titan prisons.

For a non-politically biased view, here's what Professor Alison Liebling, Director of the Prison Research Centre, has to say in an Evaluation carried out by herself and colleagues from Cambridge University's Institute of Criminology:

'When they (ie. private prisons) *get it right they can provide decent and positive environments. But when they get it wrong, which seems more likely ... if they are run cheaply, they can be chaotic and dangerous places...*

'There are real risks in privatising prisons 'on the cheap' and in re-conceiving public sector prisons on the cheapest private sector model...

'At least two poorly performing private sector prisons in the UK have been returned to the public sector...'

A prison officer comes into the Governor's office to say goodbye. He's off to Stoke Heath after twenty-four years at Shrewsbury. Governor Hendry pounds his hand. He's not to forget what he's witnessed here, or drop his values to fit in.

I swear to God the officer's eyes are moist. He and the Governor are big men, but they're both visibly moved. The officer shakes hands with the prison chaplains too. As he leaves, one of them gives him a bear-hug.

The chaplains, David Farley and Bob Wiltshire, are here to tell me about Fresh Start New Beginnings, the charity set up within Shrewsbury Prison to work with problems of homelessness, unemployment, lack of education and support, the four root causes of re-offending.

This has involved a high rate of community interaction, encouraged by Governor Hendry. When David Farley first came to Shrewsbury Prison, the walls were high in terms of working relationship between prison and community, but mentors trained by Fresh Start New Beginnings have been coming in to help prisoners prepare for release, and to support them once they're released.

Another FSNB project has been the SORI scheme, an intense one-week course involving interaction with the wider community, including victims of crimes, aiming for a greater understanding of the ramifications of a crime, and a chance to learn and move on from it.

This truly innovative scheme, however, has now been stopped. The prisoners are dispersing, the prison about to close, even FSNB has closed. Governor Hendry and the chaplains have the unenviable task of dismantling everything they've created. There is no doubt how upset they are, as indeed is everybody I have met.

A week ago the chaplains held the prison chapel's last service, which was packed with inmates and volunteers. 'We Are Shrewsbury' was their watchword, and they could say it with pride, leaving behind a remarkable record of low re-offending, attesting to all their good work.

'Many years ago,' Governor Hendry says, 'when I was a prison officer in another part of the country, I sat in the cell of a particularly disturbed prisoner. We talked for a long time and he thanked me for listening. The prison authorities didn't listen to the inmates, he said. The whole system was wrong. Well, I shook his hand and promised that when I became a Governor, I would make a difference. I've never forgotten that promise. And here in Shrewsbury I *have* made a difference.'

In her 2011 Perrie Lecture, Professor Liebling said, *'We have found Shrewsbury Prison to be significantly better than its comparator prisons on everything.... It is possible that small is beautiful – or at least less cumbersome, complex and resistant. Our smaller, older prisons may have hidden strengths – relationships trump buildings in prisons like Swansea and Shrewsbury.'*

By the time I put up this post, all the prisoners will be gone and a small town within our greater town effectively have ceased to exist. It's time to go. We're standing at the door. On the wall hangs a board containing the names of all the prison governors back before the time when the Dana first became a public prison. The last name is Governor Gerry Hendry's. He shakes my hand. Earlier I shook the hand of the last prisoner in Shrewsbury Prison, and now I've shaken the hand of the last Governor. But if I'm here watching history being made, it's on your behalf as well as my own. Especially those of you who are residents of Shrewsbury. It's for you that I'm here today, getting behind yet another of our town's closed doors.

15th March: IT'S A NOMAD LIFE; A MUSEUM WHERE YOU CAN BUY THINGS

I'm staring at a row of arrows from Papua New Guinea. 'A museum where you can buy things' is how someone described this shop. Looking at its tribal artefacts from all around the world, I can quite see why.

Shrewsbury is renowned for its small independent shops. It's A Nomad Life, co-owned by Vicky Crooke and Sam Handbury-Madin, is one of its latest. Vicky studied History and Archaeology at St Andrew's, and Sam studied Archaeology at Bristol, then for four years worked for collector, author and art dealer Nik Douglas, who died last year in New York.

'Sam fought hard to go out to Anguilla and work with Nik,' says Vicky. 'And his persistence paid off. It was an amazing experience.'

After Anguilla, Sam worked in antiques in Vancouver, then returned to the UK with a view to building a business and opening a shop. Here in Shrewsbury he met Vicky, fund-raising for Build It International having previously worked for Barnardo's in London.

Both she and Sam have local roots, Sam through Shrewsbury School, Vicky having moved into town at the age of fifteen. She'd always wanted to run her own business and had accrued a wealth of interesting artefacts. 'I'm good at business,' Vicky says, 'and Sam's good at sourcing items.'

Provenance is important, so Sam sources mostly through personal connections. Whether it's the Nik Douglas family in the Caribbean, or trader friends in Bali, this means the bulk of antiques have been collected ethically and can be traced to source.

The ethical element is very important. Vicky doesn't say so, but I see from their website that she and Sam raise funds to support charity work overseas.

The Papuan Hornbill, native to New Guinea

How much interest, I ask, is there in Shrewsbury for tribal art? Vicky says I'd be surprised. The shop may only have opened six months ago, but sales have been really encouraging. Wyle Cop is a great part of town for independent traders. She and Sam have been made to feel really welcome.

I comment on a silver necklace in a glass cabinet. Engraved with a pattern of tiny rabbits and dogs, it's a child's necklace from Laos. Behind it is another, its rows of silver bands denoting all the stages of a woman's life from birth to motherhood and beyond. There are some lovely items in this shop. On the wall hangs a framed Fijian tapa cloth – a beautiful circle of fine, hand-pulped mulberry bark that has been painted with natural dyes.

Hardly surprisingly the shop is fitted with CCTV. Vicky gives me a tight, pinched smile. On their third day after opening they learned the hard way the need to be careful. 'This man came in. An older man, normal and relaxed. He spoke to someone on the way in. The shop was busy. We were only vaguely aware of him. A bronze Shiva stood on a shelf by the window. It was about twelve inches tall and heavy too, but the man picked it up, dropped it into his carrier bag and walked out. He did it in full view of people in the shop, in front of the window where anyone could see. Later the police found him on CCTV walking down Wyle Cop, but they lost him under the railway bridge. They said that type of theft was rare, and certainly nothing similar has happened since, but it taught us a lesson.'

What next, I ask? There are more auctions to attend, Vicky says, their website to maintain, and every month she writes about a particular artefact for the Love Shrewsbury website. Then, of course, there's a wedding to plan.

Vicky shows me her emerald and diamond art deco engagement ring. Over a year ago, Sam gobsmacked her with it at Aber Falls. 'Our families knew before I did because Sam asked my dad,' Vicky says. 'When I returned home with a ring on my finger I didn't need to explain anything.'

What a year, I say. Vicky nods. Bought a house. Got a dog. Opened a shop. Been robbed. Made new friends. Got engaged. Got the dress. Got the venue. Got the cars, the flowers, the cake. 'What a year,' she agrees.

18th March: MY TONIGHT FROM THE PREMIER INN

The man with the camera round his neck is from the *Shropshire Star*. I'm relieved to see him because I was wondering where I'd landed. Only a moment ago I was in Shrewsbury, but now I could be anywhere.

This is opening night at Shrewsbury town centre's Premier Inn. Newly-minted staff move across newly-carpeted floors, clearing away unscratched crystal empties, smiling at brand-new customers, putting new chairs back in place and generally keeping the place tidy. They look as if they've been practising for weeks. I ask the barman for a pint of milk. 'Would that be with ice?' he asks without batting an eyelid. I set up a tab. Who knows how many milks I'll have downed before the night is out.

From an empty sofa by a window, I watch cars go by. Voices in the dining room are discreet, much to my relief. I once had the misfortune to go into a Premier Inn in another part of the country, which was packed with screaming kids. Nothing like that here.

Photographing the Shropshire Star photographing the opening of the new Premier Inn

It's time to eat. I order food. I wait. I'm served by friendly staff. I eat. I drink more milk. I go to the loo. Nice toilet – grey slate floor, raised white hand basins, lots of aluminium trims. Afterwards I ask to see a room. Not that I want to stay, you understand, simply because I'm curious.

Everything turns out to be immaculate, as you'd expect on a first day. I view a mattress that's not been slept on yet, bed linen awaiting its first human contact, a bath that doesn't know what it's like to be filled. The nice man who's shown me the room tells me about breakfast deals, eat-as-much-as-you-can deals and weekend breaks. Already the hotel is fully booked for this coming August's Flower Show. In a couple of weeks too it will host some regimental air force reunion. So there you have it. Shrewsbury's Premier Inn is off to a flying start.

22nd March: BIFFO

I wanted to write a post on dogs in Shrewsbury's history, but have only found the talbot (credited to be the ancestor of the modern beagle), named after the Talbot family who were Earls of Shrewsbury. A tenuous connection, I know, especially as the family isn't reckoned to have lived in Shrewsbury, so I'm writing about one of Shrewsbury's top contemporary dogs instead.

His name is Biffo. As far as he's concerned, Shrewsbury belongs to him. His legs mightn't be long but you can tell by his strut, and the swing of his tail, that he's not a dog to be messed with.

When there's a camera around Biffo's a bit of a Brad Pitt. He can even be a bit of a Princess Di when it comes to looking up from under his eyelashes. But he's not as young as he used to be.

Burger-littered pavements on Sunday mornings are amongst Biffo's favourite things. Sticks are favourites too – and the bigger and heavier the better. Biffo is a dog with attitude. Favourite walks include under the railway bridge, Castle Walk, the Quarry and the cricket ground.

Biffo's favourite person is his thirty-year-old partner in crime, Idris Davies, who may look like an adult male, but he and Biffo know better than that. The nearest Biffo ever comes to total happiness is when Idris plays on the floor with him, the two of them rolling about like little kids.

Biffo

The nearest Biffo has come to death was when he walked into the River Severn at the bottom of St Mary's Water Lane without noticing it was there. Fortunately help was on hand in the person of his long-suffering owner, flat on her stomach, grabbing the tips of Biffo's ears (all she could reach) and yanking him out.

Biffo may be going blind, but he still runs like the wind. If you see a small brown dog with pinned-back ears, legs like pistons and a manic grin, you'll know it's him. And if you see a tall, white-haired woman chasing after him, you'll know it's me.

28th March
ONE A PENNY, TWO A PENNY, HOT CROSS BUNS

It's just gone 4.00am, and I'm down Castle Gates in the Shrewsbury Bakehouse, sipping coffee and trying to wake up. Dominic Schoenstaedt has been here since ten o'clock last night and his apprentice, Nick, had been in since three.

I sit on the stairs, keeping out of their way. A complex ritual is taking place that I don't want to interrupt. Dom likens running a bakery to playing chess, and I can quite see why. I photograph loaves coming out of the oven and buns going in. Dom and Nick have only been working together for three weeks, yet I marvel at the way they move around without bumping into each other.

Nick says he's the oldest apprentice in Shrewsbury. Previously, he spent six months as a Cornish fisherman. Dom started out on Sheila Sager's baking course learning the long fermentation process that makes Shrewsbury Bakehouse products so distinctive, was offered a job by her and within three months had become Head Baker. Since taking over the Bakehouse he's doubled its output. Nowadays he has Nick, as well as help from sister Vicky, but to begin with he was working alone, seven days a week, sometimes sixteen hours a day.

What makes a good baker, I ask. Hardly surprisingly Dom says stamina. That and discipline. Not cutting corners. Doing things right. Endurance too – the work's not hard, Dom says, but there's lots of lifting and bending and hours spent on your feet.

Nick's managing the mixer now, easing dough away from the sides. Once out he shapes it into rolls while Dom checks the temperature of the oven and sets the timer for the next batch to go in. Nick cleans the work bench and scales. He loads the dough for tomorrow's bread into plastic trays.

This morning's bread is ready to go to restaurants all over town. The ordering system is pinned to the wall. Dom does one 'special' a day. Yesterday was mango and cashew. It's fig and apricot today.

Dom fires up his computer to show me the programme he uses to calculate quantities. I ask if there's any equipment he lacks and he says another refrigerator would mean producing more bread. Good grief, I think, *more bread*. Given what's in the fridge and prover-retarder, in the boxes of mix, in the oven, waiting for the oven, out of the oven or piled up in baking stands leaving not an inch of space in the shop, surely this is bread enough. According to the programme in front of me, the Shrewsbury Bakehouse produces over 861 loaves a week at 800g each. And that's before starting on the buns, rolls and pastries.

It's 6.15am. Soon the first customers will be peering through the steamy windows, wondering what's available. Time to get the croissants out of the oven. The pastries need to come out too; Dom dresses them with juicy red fruits, then puts them back to finish. He sweeps the floor. The oven belches out steam. Nick moves a fresh batch of dough from mixer to box, then stacks it up with all the other boxes to go in the fridge until the following night.

6.40am. Some bread has been taken away, some put in the window along with stands of pastries. Outside the sky is filling with light. Here in the kitchen it could be any time. This kitchen is ruled by the seasons of the dough rather than the seasons of the sky.

6.45am. Small tin loaves have gone into the oven, sprinkled with oats. They are beautiful little works of art.

7.10am. A customer comes in on her way to the station. She buys a croissant. There's a bit of chat. After she's gone, the loaves in the oven are checked to see if they're baked. They are, come out, and bakewell tarts go in.

7.20am. Dom's decorating pastries with an icing-sugar-water paste. I ask which bread he eats. He says he goes for rustica. Nick says he's working through them all.

Shrewsbury Bakehouse hot cross buns

7.30am. The next customer comes in, wrapped in a heavy coat, its collar turned up. I listen to the rustle of a paper bag as bread is dropped into it. The ping of the till. The jingling of the door bell and the sound of the door scraping closed as the customer leaves.

7.45am. A couple more customers come in. One takes away a whole tray of bread. The other wants Dom to run through what he has available.

8.00am. The shop is filling up. The window is fully stocked and labelled. In the kitchen Dom bashes a half pound of butter with a rolling pin. I watch eggs being beaten with a whisk for tomorrow's hot cross buns. It's nearly time for fruit to go into the mix, but first the window-pane test has to be applied.

Dom takes a small piece of dough and stretches it between his fingers until light shines through. Only when the dough has reached this state of smooth elasticity can the fruit go in, otherwise, he says, it would be like dropping cold stones into the dough.

8.25am. Nick's wiping down and stacking trays. Vicky is dressing pizzas. The shop bell keeps going. Dom's hot cross bun dough is ready to be left until tomorrow night's shift. At what point, I wonder, does he stop saying tomorrow, and recognise that tomorrow has become tonight?

8.30am. The kitchen has totally changed shape since I arrived. Sitting on the stairs I can scarcely see the work bench now for all the boxes stacked up for tomorrow night. The speed at which these bakers work is astonishing. The skill's astonishing too. Even the easy bits are difficult, as witnessed by Nick who's struggling to roll out baguettes the way Dom does them.

When you buy a supermarket loaf, only the smallest proportion of cost goes into production and most of what you pay is mark-up. With an artisan-baked loaf, however, most of the cost goes into the bread, and only the smallest amount is profit for the bakery.

It's 8.45am. The shop is packed. Everybody's chatting. Dom peels out of his gloves. I say I'm going home, and he says he will soon too. Presumably at some point he'll catch some sleep. A girlfriend gets mentioned. I'm astonished that he can maintain any sort of life outside a working regime like this.

I buy a loaf. The 'staff of life' bread's called. Into the bag it goes. Then I'm out though the door, blinking in the sunlight of Castle Gates. In all the hours I've been here Dom and Nick have hardly stopped. I leave behind a shop full of bread. There is no end to this.

29th March: TOOT SWEETS CHOCOLATES

Julia Wenlock is the chocolatier behind Toot Sweets Chocolates. She's been in business for five years and already she's a national award-winning chocolatier, securing a gold star for her lavender white truffles and two gold stars for her dark butterscotch.

These are as near to Shropshire chocolates as it's possible, given that the source product comes from a narrow region ten to fifteen degrees wide around the Equator and the chocolatier is a Shropshire lass.

Sourcing ethically is central to Julia's business. Many chocolates nowadays are made with palm oil, but she insists on using cocoa butter. When it comes to buying couverture, she can tell you to the farm where it's from. All her couverture is single-source, giving her finished chocolates their rich, interesting flavours. And her other ingredients are locally produced, including lavender from Newport.

How did Julia get into chocolate? One of her earliest memories is of her mum buying chocolate chicks for Easter. She was always an inspiration, Julia says. However, around the time Julia went to university to study TV and Radio Production, her mum was diagnosed with cancer.

Julia moved home in 2006. At the beginning of 2007 her grandmother

Julia Wenlock

died, followed two months later by her mother. Not long afterwards, Julia opened her first shop. The timing wasn't good, not least with the recession beginning to bite. Faced with high rates and rent, Julia failed to see a return for her inheritance. Finally she decided to she move her centre of operations to Shrewsbury's indoor market – and she hasn't looked back since.

Recently Julia won Silver from the Academy of Chocolates, along with one of the UK's most famous artisan chocolatiers, Paul A Young. Then last September, she won a bursary providing a stand at the Good Food Show. The experience was invaluable. Julia was photographed for the *Good Food Magazine*. She gave daily talks in the NEC to VIP ticket holders, introducing them to her company and teaching them how to taste chocolate. Because she'd won a couple of awards, people came by to taste the product for themselves.

In other circumstances Julia's stand would have cost thousands of pounds, but it came for free, generating so much trade that Julia is booking to return this year.

I've tasted some of Julia's chocolates. Her chocolate slab with pistachio, cocoa nibs and flakes of smoked salt explodes like a firework, and I could eat her two-gold-stars award-winning butterscotch creams *all night*. She has an interesting white chocolate infused with cardamom, a delicate violet cream which leaves a subtle after-taste, and then of course there are the award-winning lavender creams.

It's interesting to interview Julia having just spent time in the Shrewsbury Bakehouse. The products might be different, but the lifestyle's much the same. So, too, is what Julia and Dominic are trying to achieve. Here are two young Shrewsbury people working to create local products of real quality. Like Dom, Julia's up in the night. After her day in the market she's experimenting with flavours and making chocolates until two in the morning or in some cases even staying up all night.

So let's support her. Let's support Dom with his bread, and Julia with her chocolate, and all our young people who are working to make Shrewsbury work for them. I've heard so much about young people in Shrewsbury moving away. But that's *so* not the case.

30th March
A HISTORY OF LIFE IN SHREWSBURY MARKET
by Janet & Peter Heighway
long-standing Market Traders – retiring today

'We have traded in Shrewsbury Market for forty-three years. We have always found it to be a very friendly environment, both for traders and customers. Our early married years were spent in Harrow, North London where we enjoyed gardening and grew our own fruit and vegetables. We attended courses in horticulture and both passed the RHS examination. We joined the local Horticultural Society, and Peter joined the committee, helping to arrange lectures and produce shows. We even entered classes ourselves – and won some, much to our surprise and the dismay of some of the old-stagers!

'After five years in London, we moved to a more rural setting, nearer to Peter's roots and to his recently-widowed mother. We both had 'proper jobs', but worked hard to develop our newly acquired house and land, both of which required a lot of reclamation and reconstruction.

'We had inherited a large number of old fruit trees, but had no idea of their varieties, so arranged a visit from a Ministry of Agriculture, Fisheries & Food adviser, who identified most of them. We had about a dozen damson trees and were determined to pick their fruit. We ended up with boxes of damsons, but nearly everyone locally had similar quantities so Peter toured the greengrocers with them, close to where he worked in Harborne and Selly Oak.

'There was an initial show of disinterest. Obviously the greengrocers were desperate to have the damsons, but wanted to give the impression of 'doing us a favour'. The price we got for a 12lb box was four shillings (20p in today's currency), equivalent to less than 2p per pound, which was better than allowing them to go to waste.

Janet and Peter Heighway

'Within a year, we planted a lot more fruit trees, including plums, together with gooseberry bushes and raspberries. Many of the original trees have either died or blown down, as we have had some terrific gales. On one occasion we returned home to find that a huge twenty-five foot damson tree had been lifted over the hedge without touching it, landing in the neighbouring field. We have continued to replace trees, but at our time of life it's not worth investing in new ones.

Our Introduction to the Market

'In September 1970, we thought we would try taking fruit to market. Peter's mother was still living at the family home in Madeley, so Shrewsbury seemed the obvious place, particularly as Peter had memories of visiting the market as a child.

'In those days the market was really thriving and every stall was rented out, but we managed to hire one yard of bench for a Wednesday afternoon. We found this so satisfying that we continued doing it more regularly, but it was only possible to take the occasional day's leave from work. After a while, however, we were allocated a permanent two yards of bench on Saturdays, so we started coming weekly, and have continued ever since.

'Many customers and fellow traders will remember the way the market was organised in those days. The man collecting the tolls and keeping everyone in order was Bill Cooper – a very amiable gentleman with lots of experience, who seemed to be quite fair and rigorous. In the Pannier Market, there were rows of benches marked in yards so that every stallholder knew the boundaries of their pitch. For years we had two mid-bench yards, with Mrs Morris on one side, with fruit, vegetables and flowers from her cottage garden, and Mrs Duddleston with her eggs on the other.

'Between the rows was a sturdy rail, which stallholders could lean against back to back with the people on the bench behind – so you soon got to know each other. Behind Mrs Morris was Mrs Morgan, also with a single yard for her pannier. Both left during the morning to catch their country buses home, and Peter was often called upon to carry their baskets to the bus station on Barker Street. Also backing onto us were Mr and Mrs Griffiths from Ford with items from their extensive garden, and they too became good friends.

'In those days, the Saturday market was exclusively produce (including flowers and plants), plus poultry and eggs – except for the four corners, which had other people such as Midda's clothes, Dave with his carpets and Angela Butler with cakes and biscuits. The competition from all the large stalls with fruit and vegetables must have been immense, but everyone seemed busy as there were more customers then, before the supermarkets started drawing them away.

Becoming More Established

'Eventually Mrs Morris and Mrs Duddleston gave up due to age and infirmity, so we were able to expand from two yards to four. We kept in touch with Mrs Morris and joined her 90th birthday celebration in June 1992.

'Across the aisle from us we had Mr and Mrs Crowther from Nesscliffe and when they finished years later we took over their few yards of bench for small bay trees and pots of herbs. These proved very popular, but eventually we scaled them down rather than compete with other stalls for whom plants were the main occupation.

'That part of our bench backed on to Paul and Roger Amess from Hemford, with whom we have always had a very happy association. In the other direction was Ken Walters from Ford, who will be remembered by many who are trading today. Usually some of his many children would be helping out, and we were privileged to be invited to some of their wedding ceremonies. His poultry and vegetables were much sought after, and he always seemed to be busy. Sadly he died soon after giving up the market and we attended his funeral in January 2008.

'There were many unique individuals in the market. We clearly recall the legendary Nora Lee whose stall happened to be near us. It was somewhat untidy and she never appeared to be unduly busy. She could often be seen trimming vegetables and fruit that were past their best, to make them look more appetizing.

'The permanent stall near us, now devoted to Gluten Free Living, was once the Pet Stall run by Gwen Parkes. Following her sudden death it was continued by her daughter, Annette, whose memories of the market go back a long way. Fortunately we still see her when she serves at Corbetts near us.

'As we all know, the appearance of the market changed markedly in 2003 when the management was temporarily taken over by the company LSD, with Tony Davis as local manager. All the old style benches were discarded together with the solid rails that separated them, traces of which are still visible in the floor. The present canopied stalls were introduced and we all had to apply for a place.

'The change was very controversial at the time, and we feared the effect it would have on us as we were allocated less than half the length of bench we'd had previously. However, on the day of the changeover we were told that we could have some extra space after all, and this was a relief.

Impressions

'Unfortunately we are unable to remember the names or faces of all the traders that we have seen, and in any case it's impossible to mention them all. After all these years, however, it is the friendliness and sense of family that stands out.

'Having occupied our stall for over forty-two years, the decision to retire does not come lightly. We hate disappointing loyal customers, who are also our friends. We will miss you all, but intend to continue visiting Shrewsbury, so hopefully will keep in touch. Thank you for your unswerving support and for being such good friends.'

APRIL

1st April: BELLS AND FIRE
– an Easter Vigil at St Alkmund's Church

I'm glad I went. I've had a busy few days and St Alkmund's Vigil was the perfect antidote. I only had to walk through the big doors at the back of the church and catch the scent of lilies, and something dropped off me like a weight.

A fire had been lit outside by Resident Priest, Richard Hayes, for the part of the Vigil called the Service of Light. Richard produced the Paschal candle and traced on it the sign of the cross and the Alpha and Omega, signifying Christ as the fulfilment of all things. He lifted it aloft to signify Christ as Light of the World. Then we lit our own candles from it and processed up St Alkmund's aisle.

St Alkmund's Churchyard

When I'd arrived, there'd been some light left in the sky. Now the church stood in darkness. We could have been a choir of monks processing up that aisle. Holding our tiny lights, everything felt, well, medieval, I suppose.

'By his holy and glorious wounds,' intoned Richard Hayes, 'may the light of Christ, rising in glory, dispel the darkness from our hearts and minds...'

All over the world people would be meeting around this same form of words, tracing Easter's story back to its roots. I sat in the chancel with a sense of history as the Liturgy of the Word began, starting with the words *'In the beginning',* culminating with the Gloria, upon which St Alkmund's organ burst to life and so did we, ringing handbells in a moment of fabulous chaos and cheerful disharmony.

I love it that a centuries-old liturgy has a place in it for chaos and diversity. Everybody's bell with its particular tone, and every ringer's own unique style of ringing was welcome. This was a Gloria in the truest sense of the word.

After the bells came the third part of the Vigil – the blessing of water and renewal of baptismal vows. This took place around the baptismal font into which water was poured from a great brass jug. 'At the dawn of creation your Spirit breathed on the waters...' announced Reverend Hayes. 'In the waters of the Jordan, your Son was baptised...'

The Paschal candle was lowered into the water as a symbol of death. 'Have mercy on us,' Richard Hayes said. 'Cleanse us from sin in a new birth of innocence by water and the spirit.'

After being sprinkled with water and wishing each other God's blessing of peace, we found ourselves at the heart of the Vigil. The Eucharist.

'The Lord is risen,' announced Richard Hayes. 'He is risen indeed,' we replied, and from thereon the liturgy unfolded - the Eucharistic Prayer, the Lord's Prayer, the Agnus Dei, the wafer and the cup, the body and the blood. Have mercy... have mercy... grant us peace. Lamb of God... bearer of sins... redeemer of the world.

Afterwards, I went home, dug out some chocolates and settled in front of the telly. Either I could watch Kate Mosse's *Labyrinth* – or a documentary on Bach. A single voice rising out of the *St Matthew Passion* like a bird on the wing helped make the choice for me. It was hair-on-the-back-of-your-neck stuff. Yet even after composing this amazing piece of music, Bach wrote to a friend, 'I see no future for myself.'

If he felt that way, what hope was there for any of us? An extract was played from the B Minor Mass. For a man who found reality baffling, its sense of consolation was nothing short of a miracle.

'Bach helps us hear God's voice in human form, ironing out humanity's imperfections in the perfection of the music,' said the narrator, and suddenly I was glad I'd chosen Bach over the mysteries of the Labyrinth. Glad I'd made it to the Vigil too. For me, its ancient liturgies were mystery enough.

4th April: THE BIG BUSK
– HAPPY DAYS IN SHREWSBURY

This event originated as a tribute to Ben Bebbington, a friendly and much-loved busker round town, who was tragically murdered last September. His music and poetry was of vital importance to him, and his sisters, Anne-Marie Bebbington [now Hambley] and Karen Higgins, have arranged for proceeds from the Big Busk to go to the Shrewsbury Ark, as it's where Ben's artistic endeavours received so much encouragement and support.

Beth Prior (with guitar), with Jayne Carpenter, Tim Compton, Clive Beasley, Karen Higgins and Anne-Marie Hambley

'Ben always felt less lonely when he busked,' they said. 'Saturday 6th April is his birthday, so we intend to fill the town with music for him.'

The event, which has the full support of Shrewsbury Town Council and town-centre businesses, starts at 10am. Acts performing on Shrewsbury's streets will include folk, opera, instrumental, acoustic, storytelling, magic and dance.

From 5pm – 7pm, Jim Hawkins will be doing a set at The Coffeehouse. Other evening sets will start at 7pm and continue until late in Frank's Bar, Morgan's, Ashley's, the Wheatsheaf, and the Hole in the Wall.

8th April: 'BEGGARS CAN'T BE CHOOSERS – WHY NOT?'

Those are the words that greeted me with when, inspired by the Big Busk, I visited the Shrewsbury Ark. 'I hate that phrase,' said Manager, Tim Compton. 'Why can't people have choices just because they've hit hard times?'

The Shrewsbury Ark is situated opposite the railway station. For many it's a lifeline, a place to turn to when the wheels of life start coming off, even an adoptive family. 'The Ark is a bit like a local without alcohol,' said Tim. 'Some people are just passing through, but the Ark definitely has its regulars.'

Work with the town's homeless began in the 1970s with the Christian Centre, initially based at Old St Chad's. Accommodation in the Old School House at the Welsh Bridge became available later, then moved to Castle Foregate in 1997. However, in 2006 government funding dried up and this night shelter had to be closed.

Aware of the need to provide for rough sleepers and others, Shrewsbury & Atcham Borough Council bought the Ark's building to be run by the Christian Centre Association, which pays it rent. Its doors opened in March 2008. Eighteen months later Manager Tim Compton joined the team, with a background in mental health and supported housing for the homeless.

'I wasn't looking for a job,' said Tim. 'But this one came along and ticked all the boxes. Not, you understand, that I'm a box-ticking type.'

Tim definitely didn't come across as a box-ticking type. As we talked, he showed me around. Showers, a laundry, sitting rooms, a clothes bank, a food bank, a kitchen, computers, a designated phone line for clients' medical/social/benefits/ housing etc use, an outdoor smokers' area, a lift for wheel-chair users – it was amazing how much Shrewsbury Ark's tiny building had packed into it.

In the kitchen, Deputy Manager Amy Parkes was cooking lunch and a volunteer was collecting a client's medication. 'When I first came here,' said Tim, 'I could see that we needed to raise the level of engagement. There's now a strong emphasis on welcoming. We act as hosts. People aren't just left to their own devices when they come through the door.'

The Ark isn't just a place for boiling up a kettle for a brew, however, or providing a lunch. It's a place where staff and volunteers care about the people who come through the door, and will take time to establish a dialogue with them. They're not naïve about human nature – they're aware that the picture people present may need exploring, and that offering help won't always be straightforward. But they'll do what they can.

What was the worst thing about the job, I asked Tim. Bureaucracy, he replied. He understood the processes that local government, say, or the Department of Works & Pensions insisted on going through. But it was frustrating to keep crashing into barriers and feeling so powerless.

And the good things, I asked. 'When an individual achieves what they've been striving for – that's pretty good,' Tim replied. 'A number of people can now look back and say *I can't believe I am where I am today.* It's great to see a former rough sleeper coming back from his first day in a proper job.'

The Ark provides a postal address to enable homeless people to apply for jobs, as well as clothes for an interview and shower facilities for sprucing up. The team visits people in hospital. They've even been known to find a home for the occasional dog.

On one memorable occasion, Tim was asked to be an ex-client's best man. He agreed on conditions. 'No Amsterdam stag do, and no stripping anybody and tying them to lamp posts,' he said. In fact he ended up being chauffeur, photographer and master of ceremonies

Tim Compton

– and since then has become godfather to the man's daughter. 'It was a privilege,' he said.

Did the Ark attract trouble, I asked. Not often, Tim replied. There was the odd bit of attitude. However it was rare for anyone to really kick off. 'Generally speaking, the Ark is a respectful environment,' he said.

In 2010 Rowan Williams, then Archbishop of Canterbury, visited the Shrewsbury Ark. Some regulars couldn't believe that a man like him ('he's friends with the Queen') was really going to visit them. The occasion was memorable, not least because the Archbishop wasn't to be rushed, taking time and talking to everybody. When he left, he remembered all their names. People were important and he made that plain.

Tim picked on that when I asked about volunteers. What qualities did they need, I wanted to know. 'They need to be people,' was his reply.

Plain and simple. No more than that.

How would Tim like to see Shrewsbury Ark's work developing? Shrewsbury needs a night shelter, he said. Homeless people shouldn't have to go to Telford for a bed. Also he'd like to extend the Ark's work county-wide. 'There's a need right across Shropshire. And definitely a need for us to provide support outside 'office' hours. But then we'd need more staff and volunteers.'

Back to that again. You can't talk about the Ark without volunteers cropping up. Tim is deeply grateful to the Ark's many volunteers, but says they could do with more. 'All people have to do is get in touch,' he said. 'It's as easy as going on the website or picking up the phone. Holding fund-raising events, donating clothes, providing food – cooked lunches, snacks, cakes and biscuits – all of this is helpful.'

Time to leave. Any final words from Tim? 'I'd like people to realise how very much they've got in life,' he said. 'And I'd like them to think before judging, and not make assumptions based on appearance and manner. A person in need is as human as anybody else, and requires respect. I remember once somebody saying *Why do so many homeless people have dogs?* Well, why does anybody have a dog? For company, security, friendship. Homeless people are no different to anybody else.'

13th April
WORKING MAGIC WITH AUTHOR PETER MURPHY

'I've never been into such a beautiful library. Thanks for inviting me.' Peter Murphy stood before us, book in hand. He was a slight man, dark-haired and pointy with whiff-beard, silver earrings and something steely about his eyes that belied his tousled appearance. Over the next hour, he promised, he'd endeavour, whether on books, libraries, rivers or mythologies, to speak coherently and with interest.

The venue was Shrewsbury's Castle Gates Library and *Shall we Gather at the River* was the book. If we hadn't known before why Peter Murphy's publishers had included Shrewsbury in his book tour, we quickly found out:

'On the first day of November in the year of '84, that enduring river

turned on the town of Murn.... The current picked up speed and the river swelled to the lip of its banks...Local radio issued flood damage updates on the hour.... Everywhere was besieged and soaked as that bloated old river conquered the valley slopes and threatened the town's worried heart...'

This was a book of rivers and floods. And we in Shrewsbury understand rivers and floods. 'In their dreams the townsfolk do not speak. Because they do not wish to rouse the river', read Murphy. And carving its path around our town was a force of nature that we, too, don't wish to arouse.

After his reading, somebody wanted Peter Murphy to talk about the sense of harrowing in the book, driving men to the river. 'I wish you'd been around five years ago,' the author said. 'I could have written what you just said. You could have saved me a lot of time.'

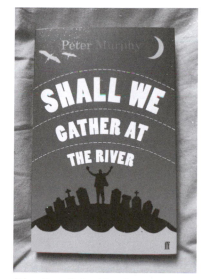

People talked about the book's emphasis on shadow forces at work. Self-sabotage Murphy called it. 'Aaah,' growled an old man. 'I always says when sumoon falls in the Severn there's a lot a reeds in there. There's not much hope for 'em.'

By author Peter Murphy

'Reminds me of Robert Mitchum,' Murphy said. 'A scene in *Night of the Hunter.* He's murdered the mother and she's lying in the bottom of the river, her hair entwined amongst the weeds.'

Later, when the event was over and everybody had left, I interviewed Peter Murphy. He lives today in Enniscorthy, the town he wrote about in his latest book. Educated by the Christian Brothers, he made it through primary school and two years into secondary education before being thrown out for not wearing uniform. Back in those days, it was music and comics that grabbed his attention. And books.

'Going to the library was a ritual,' he said. 'It was something we as a family always did. It was just a bare room too – a strip light and shelves of books. I used to pick the action adventures. Alistair McLean. Stephen King. James Herbert. Typical boys' stuff. Then John Steinbeck – my first truly literary writer, I suppose – then the Beats, Hunter S. Thompson, Raymond Carver and James Kelman.'

There are moments in *Shall we Gather at the River* that seem pure Raymond Carver, the story literally hanging between the lines of words. Some writers are just storytellers, but Peter Murphy is a craftsman. Where did he learn to write, I wanted to know.

At 17, back in school, Murphy won a national essay-writing competition and was sent off on a European Union sponsored trip. This was the first time he saw the world outside his small-town Irish life. Interestingly, the essay itself hadn't particularly engaged him. More engaging was drumming, and rock 'n' roll.

'For nine years I was a drummer in a rock band,' Murphy said. 'It was a full-time commitment. I enjoyed playing – but it didn't provide a living and I had two small children to support.'

Murphy remembers submitting features about Stephen King or Motorhead to magazines, certain this would pay more than drumming. The magazine Hot Press took everything he sent its way. It didn't pay much but he kept his head above water. It was a self-betterment exercise, too. 'One thing led to another,' Murphy said. 'Soon I was doing major interviews and working on radio and TV, a regular guest on RTE's arts review show, The Works. For six or seven years I worked this way, and might have carried on, but in one single week two things happened that changed my life.'

In 2001 Murphy's father died. Then, within a couple of days, his youngest daughter, Grace, was born. A month after that, he started writing fiction. Within a year he'd started his first novel, *John the Revelator*, which took six years to write but was published to great acclaim.

There was an emphasis on collaboration in writing John the Revelator, Murphy said, and again in *Shall we Gather at the River*. 'I shared my work with a group of writer friends. 'We'd meet to talk about each other's work. Openness and collaboration was important. In particular I felt close to the writer Sean McNulty. I trusted him.'

Shall we Gather at the River is more complex than *John the Revelator*, drawing on suicide legends, flood mythology from Christian and pre-

Christian eras, the strange nature of obsession and the Gaia theory of nature as a living entity that both gives and devours. It inhabits familiar territory to anyone who has read the novels of Flannery O'Conner.

Indeed, it was from O'Connor's *Wise Blood* that Murphy took the name Enoch (along with Enoch in the Gnostic gospels – the only mortal taken without dying to heaven). It was a form of homage, he said.

Was Murphy a religious man, I wanted to know. It was the spiritual, Murphy said, that interested him, especially the how, when and why of spiritual manifestation in philosophy and ideas. We talked about the power of religious language, and of words used to locate members of one's tribe. 'Certain words have incredible power,' Murphy said. 'They speak a sort of code.' Writing was all about weeding out the mamby pamby words, and getting to the juicy, high protein stuff. 'Like the pots of stuff my dad used to cook up for our dog,' Murphy said. 'Writing's a bit like getting a gumbo going, reducing it down to a pure stock.'

Currently Peter Murphy's time is divided between doing book readings and performing with his band, the Revelator Orchestra, about whom one reviewer wrote, 'Imagine music that sounds like Tom Waits on drums and Lightnin' Hopkins on a battered hollow-body thumping away down in the cellar while Murphy reads. The Revelator Orchestra combines the weirdness of Poe with the coolness of the Beats over a soundtrack that might have been created by the Velvet Underground.'

What next for Peter Murphy? He didn't know. He'd have to write another book to find out. I loved that for answer. I never know what I'm up to when I commence a new book. This is my sort of writer.

It was getting late. There was a girlfriend at the door, a dog and car outside and the Holyhead ferry waiting to take them home. 'Thank you,' I said. 'You put stories together, characters, words on a page, and magic happens,' Peter Murphy replied.

16th April

BABIES, BARISTAS & BOOGIE NIGHTS – JESSICAH KENDRICK & THE SHREWSBURY COFFEEHOUSE

Jessicah doesn't know the sex of her and Chris's baby. Finding out is going to be part of the excitement of the birth. If it's a boy, she says, Chris is keen on Django, but she's not so sure.

Chris is the musician Chris Quinn. Jessicah is Jessicah Kendrick, the zippy founder-come-manager of the Shrewsbury Coffeehouse. She's a petite, wiry woman with an elfin face and big smile, and she's smiling now, telling me that Chris reckons a baby won't change their lives. It's going to be easy, otherwise people wouldn't do it – that's what Chris says.

I'm not saying anything, and I don't need to. Jessicah is the oldest in a family of five. She remembers her dad driving off into the night accompanied by crying babies. She knows it won't be easy, but reckons they're ready for it.

All of this is conveyed in a soft American drawl. The family arrived in Shrewsbury when Jessicah was a young-for-her-age, tree-climbing thirteen. 'I had to adapt,' Jessicah says. 'I started wearing cooler clothes and hanging out with the popular girls. It wasn't until SCAT that I got to be myself again.'

After SCAT (Shrewsbury College of Arts and Technology) came Middlesex University and a Fine Arts degree. As well as art, Jessicah was interested in sociology. Back in the 80s, everything had seemed silver-lined, but it wasn't like that now and she wanted to know why. How had *Sex in the City* turned into *Desperate Housewives*? Why were so many women no longer willing to call themselves feminists?

After university, Jessicah returned to Shrewsbury and worked in Starbucks. She became involved with Platform Alteration, a monthly arts and music event held in the Old Post Office pub. Was that where she met Chris, I ask. No, she replies. Ten years before, there had been a few casual dates. Then they'd got together again a few years ago. Then suddenly there was this moment when Jessicah thought, 'If I don't really go for this I might lose it.' And they've been together ever since.

'We're good together,' Jessicah says. 'Both of us are work focused.

Both get on with people, both want the same things. Some people might find a musician's lifestyle hard, but I'm an independent person. If Chris is off gigging, there'll always be other things I want to do or I'll be off round to Mum's.'

Jessicah's mum is the artisan baker Sheila Sager. If her daughter likes a bustling life, it's because that's the family way. 'When I was a child you'd come to the table, and fifteen other people would show up. In the UK, I discovered it wasn't usual to go round to people's houses unless you were invited. But in the States I'd knock on any number of doors and it would be *Hi Jessicah, does your mum know you're here, do you want to stay to supper?* I guess we brought that with us when we moved to Shrewbury.'

Jessicah Kendrick

Jessicah has brought that spirit to the Shrewsbury Coffeehouse. What she wanted was a home from home. A place to pitch ideas, to share stories, play games, chat and hang out. 'Someone said the one thing Shrewsbury didn't need was another coffeehouse,' she says, 'but they were wrong and I knew it even then. I felt as if Shrewsbury was craving for something and the Coffeehouse has filled the void. Over fifty per cent of our customers come in on an almost daily basis. Two years down the line, I feel as thought it belongs to its customers, and we owe it to them to keep it what it is.'

The Coffeehouse grew out of Jessicah's 'quarter-life crisis', going in five directions at the same time but not knowing what she wanted next. Creating a mind map was how she sorted herself out. What did she like doing? She listed it all down. What was she good at? That went down too. Was there any common ground? Jessicah looked for connections and came up with – *a coffeehouse.*

Jessicah says that she enjoyed the Coffeehouse from the first day of construction onwards. She envisaged the sort of ramshackle college-run coffeehouse that crops up in university towns – ramshackle in a good way, she emphasizes. What she didn't envisage was how successful it would be. She's surrounded herself with a great team. There's Simon, who does ordering and accounting, Richie who's in charge of food and drink and she's in charge of events.

If the Shrewsbury Coffeehouse has taken off, it's partly due to these events. To begin with Jessicah used Chris's contacts to book live acts, but slowly word got out that a Shrewsbury Coffeehouse gig was worth having. The place would always be packed. The audience would be appreciative. The venue allowed for the sort of intimate atmosphere that show-cased jazz, folk, swing and roots music at their best.

Jessicah's been pulling in big names too. Last year the Coffeehouse hosted Fapy Lafertin, the godfather of gypsy jazz. Then they had Dick Gaughan – he of the legendary Boys of the Lough. Then John Etheridge, Stephane Grappelli's long-term guitarist, performed – and that night was so popular that he's coming back this week to a Shrewsbury Coffeehouse event at the Lion Hotel.

To be able to bring to Shrewsbury musicians of this calibre is quite a feat. But in the coming year, the Coffeehouse has booked Tim Kliphaus, the Dutch virtuoso violinist who trained with Stephane Grappelli; Clive Carroll; John Doyle, who played for Barack Obama at The White House on St Patrick's Day; and Catfish Keith, American acoustic blues singer-songwriter/steel guitarist.

Jessicah loves it that people of all ages come to these events. She also loves it that other groups use the Coffeehouse. There's a book club, a thriving poetry group and other groups too. 'If the Coffeehouse is open anyway, why not? The space is there to be used.'

Jessicah would love to get specialists in to talk about their different fields. She'd love a New Scientist magazine club for talking about the latest articles. If someone set it up, she'd give it her full support. However, with a baby ten weeks away… Jessicah's voice trails off.

When that baby comes, I'll let you know. We'll hang out bunting and raise a glass. For now, however, it's time to say goodbye. Today's Jessicah's 'day off', but already she's been into the Coffeehouse once, and now she's heading back to find its diary and book an event.

I say I hope she doesn't stay. What she should be doing is going home and programming in a bit of rest. If you see her doing anything else, tell her straight. But will she listen? Will she hell.

20th April: SECRET SHOPPING WITH MS X

We've had babies, Batman and bakers, chocolate makers, market stallholders and a prison governor. But we haven't yet had a secret shopper.

Ms X agreed to do the job this week. We nearly didn't make it to the shops because our trip started in SHREWSBURY ABBEY. We tried out pews for size and sang Baa Baa Black Sheep very loudly in the choir stalls. Ms X was particularly keen to look for knights, but when she found one, he turned out to be made of stone, bigger than she'd expected, with a scary expression.

Ms X

Next up were SWANS. Half way across the English Bridge, Ms X was riveted by a swan on an island in the river, building its nest. She wanted me to photograph it, which I did.

INFINITY & BEYOND. Miss X was disappointed to find this shop/café closed because through the window she could see framed superheroes on the walls.

BELLINI'S ICE CREAM PARLOUR. Here we faced the disappointment of no credit card machine, which meant tiny tired legs trailing all the way to the Square to find a cash machine. But the journey there and back was worth it. Miss X chose strawberry ice cream which she ate in a sundae glass, during which time it did not escape her attention that I wolfed down an ice cream sundae AND a piece of cake. Ms X would like to visit Bellini's Ice Cream Parlour again.

THE ANTIQUES CENTRE. Ms X started out our day by saying *Let's go and have adventures,* so a secret cave underground where treasures are waiting to be discovered was the obvious place. In a state of high excitement, Ms X ran so fast from stall to stall that I could scarcely keep up and there were moments of sheer panic when I thought I'd lost her.

First there was a hand-painted German rocking cradle that she liked. Then a tin toadstool music box, a yellow dress with feathers, a flamenco dancing doll and an embroidered Chinese suit. There was a skateboard which Ms X said she'd be happy if I'd bought, a vintage Mickey Mouse and a paintbox which I *did* buy because it was called 'Treasure Trove'.

THE WORKS. Here some multi-coloured windmills on sticks caught Ms X's eye, along with sherbet flying saucers and Haribo Strawbs. A fancy face-mask caught her eye, but we bought paint brushes instead, to go with the paintbox from the Antiqus Centre.

At the top of Pride Hill, we went into WAITROSE. Ms X selected pasta for lunch, and pasta sauce. Outside we stopped for a short tree hug, then it was home to paint. Enough secret shopping had been done for one day. Ms X told her mum she'd had a good time.

23rd April: CARTOON FESTIVAL WEEKEND

A sunny Saturday morning, and I was off to the Square for Shrewsbury's 10th Annual International Cartoon Festival. I arrived to find it heaving

Pauline Fisk by Helen Pointer

with artists, boards, brushes, pens, happy snappers and curious questioners. A band played while children and adults alike queued to have their portraits drawn. By the following day, most of the cartoonists' enormous canvasses were filled with colour. In the distance I made out the flash of a red beret, which I knew meant that illustrator Linda Edwards had joined the throng.

Linda told me I'd find more artists in the indoor market. Usually it's closed on Sundays, but today it was open, lights on and most of the weekday stalls doing business, every conceivable spare corner filled with cartoonists and friendly faces.

You can't go far in Shrewsbury without bumping into friends. For a while there I thought I'd walked into the pages of *My Tonight From Shrewsbury*. Alison Patrick greeted me, whom I'd last spoken to in the Unitarian Church. Then there was Market Hall Manager, Kate Gittins, Julia Wenlock the chocolatier and Town Clerk, Helen Ball, whom I last saw speaking at the Public Inquiry in defence of the Square.

It was lunchtime by now, so I took myself off to Mirage Mezze and settled into one of their huge gilt, velvet-padded thrones. Up in the gallery, the *Bridgnorth Ukelele Band* almost made me want to dance. Instead I had my picture drawn by a lady cartoonist in a red top hat. All the way through my sitting, she kept laughing. This made me laugh as well – something I realised was a ploy when I saw the final drawing.

26th April: GHOSTS IN THE LOGGERHEADS? SURELY NOT

Liz and Nick have been running the Loggerheads for long enough now to get to know the ghosts. They've had a busy time with all those ghosts. To describe the place as small and dark with sloping floors, tiny bars and booth-sized rooms called 'Poets' Corner' and 'Gents Only' merely scrapes the surface. Atmosphere is what the Loggers is all about. It isn't the oldest pub in town, but it certainly feels like it.

Nobody knows how many times the Loggerheads has changed hands, but it's a matter of public record that on 9th May 1822 it was bought at auction from one Thomas Williams, and ten years later it was advertised to let after its landlord auctioned off his household furniture, brewing vessels and 140 gallons of ale.

By 1900, the Loggerheads consisted of three public and nine private rooms, including accommodation for ten people in three bedrooms. At some point it hosted a brothel, and Liz has seen ghosts queuing up for it on the staircases, beer in hand.

Liz has been Landlady now for fourteen months. She and Nick took on the pub as untrained novices. When they opened the door at 11.00am on their first day, Valentine's Day 2012, there were seven ex-licensees outside, and three of the town's current licensees, as well as somebody wanting to celebrate their 70th birthday with friends. They all piled into the front bar and sat with arms folded, waiting to see what would happen next. Liz and Nick stared at them. They stared back. Then Nick laughed. 'Go on,' he said. 'What do you want? Which glasses? You're going to have to tell us. We don't know.'

A book was run on Liz and Nick's sticking it out. It was only thanks to YouTube that they learnt to do the cellar. Some people were horrified to see ignorant first timers in charge of Shrewsbury's most precious pub. The only way they got by, according to Liz, was by asking questions. And the help they had was fantastic. 'We couldn't have put it all together and made it work without an incredible amount of support.'

Ghosts in the Loggerheads?

Marsdens is the brewery that owns the pub, but the Loggerheads provides a selection of ales from a number of other breweries. Banks and Pedigree are available all year round, but annually there are fifty other ales too. This is a proper pub, Liz says. A drinking pub. A local. She doesn't see herself as its owner. She sees herself as its keeper. It's up to her to preserve what's good about it, 'to keep it nice,' as she puts it, and to respect it.

Refurbishments have taken place over the last year. Taking advice from locals, Liz and Nick have installed an extra pump for mild to be available all the time. Then, without removing any of the ancient benches, they've made them more comfortable with cushions. Fires have gone into every bar. There's a newly set up darts team, a poker night on Wednesdays, live music at weekends and a Tuesday night slot for younger musicians in Gents Only, as well as the long-standing one on Thursday nights. There's wine on offer too, as well as ales.

And there's a refurbished menu. All of it's what you'd call comfort food – Sunday roast, local steaks from the grill, sausages and mash.

The pub's not used exclusively as a drinking hole.

Liz works in the pub from eleven in the morning until three the following morning. It's a long day, especially with a growing-up son. 'But people look out for you,' Liz says, 'and they look out for your children. I've moved around a lot in my life, so have never really had a proper base. But I've got one here. The friendship here is a powerful thing.'

By day the central bar is very much an inner sanctuary. It's the place to be, for yarns and company. It isn't a bar for drinking on your own. That's more likely to happen in Poets' Corner or Gents Only. And then, of course, there are the ghosts.

Liz is aware of them at all times of day or night. There's the lady who comes into the lounge dressed all in black. Then there's one with two children who wakes Liz up at night. There's a gentleman who opened the door and walked in one day dressed in a long green velvet coat, white socks and a three-cornered hat.

And then there's the noise. Lying in bed at night, Liz will say to Nick, 'Can't you hear the chattering along the top landing?' But he can't. She's been out onto the landing and seen it as it must have been in the old days, all the walls dark, the wood work unpainted, men crowding the landing and stairs. She's asked them to cut the noise – and they have. But another night she'll wake up and they'll be at it again.

A good night for seeing ghosts is Tuesdays, Liz says. She's no idea why, but if you're thinking of going for a pint and a bit of a thrill at the Loggers, she reckons Tuesdays are your best bet.

28th April: THE RAILWAY BRIDGE – AND OTTERS

I was down by the river a couple of days ago. The waters had gone down and the towing path was high and dry, if a bit muddy. Over the river loomed the massive bulk of the railway bridge. The cobbled path beneath it was dark, which meant that the sudden flash of a torch's beam really startled me. What was going on under there?

As I drew closer, a shadowy figure came into view, leaning over the railing, directing a beam into the swirling waters between the pillars of the bridge. 'What are you looking for?' I asked, imaging dead bodies or contraband [I'm not a novelist for nothing]. 'Otters,' he replied.

I've only seen otters in the River Severn twice. First time, back in 1997, was the night I moved into town. I walked down St Mary's Water Lane in the dark and watched the black river flowing under the bridge. Up popped what I thought, in a moment of weird disorientation, had to be a seal. Quickly, however, I realised it was an otter. It ducked and dived. I was transfixed.

Under the railway bridge

Then, a couple of years ago, dog walking between the Castle Walk footbridge and the railway bridge, another otter appeared, swimming against the flow of the river, keeping abreast with me until we both reached the steps at the bottom of St Mary's Water Lane, where I lost sight of it.

The railway bridge is one of my favourite places in town. Despite the graffiti, the slippery cobbles and the pigeon poo (maybe because of them?) it fires my imagination like almost nowhere else. It's not just one bridge, but three – two made of iron girders, the third an arched stone bridge sandwiched between the two.

At the right time of day, you'll get sunlight reflected off the river onto the bridge's grimy walls, even reaching into its darkest recesses. Trains rumble overhead. Its acoustics are fantastic. Whether it's the hrmm-hrmm of pigeons, the slap-slap of water or the notes of a jazz saxophone improvising under the girders on a quiet night, the quality of sound is remarkable.

The first time I heard that saxophone was around the same time I first saw an otter. A white veil of mist came off the river and this wonderful music came out of the darkness. I couldn't see who was playing it, but often after that I'd go down at night and the phantom saxophonist would be there. I should have introduced myself. I wrote the saxophonist (indeed the whole bridge) into a novel instead, creating Abren and the street boy, Phaze II, in my book, *Sabrina Fludde*, providing them with a home up amongst the girders of the railway bridge – where I believe they live to this day. Having invented these children I look up for them all the time. Even today, years after writing *Sabrina Fludde*, I can't stop believing – just like those elusive otters – that I'll see them one day.

MAY

3rd May: JIM HAWKINS IN THE EVENING, AT FRANKS

A while back I wrote an Open Studio piece about illustrator, Linda Edwards, which I entitled *On the Sunny Side of the Street*. Now here I am on the sunny side again, interviewing the owner and director of Jim Hawkins Ltd, otherwise known for his BBC Radio Shropshire *Jim Hawkins in the Morning* show. This is a man who couldn't be more sunny if he tried. Is it something in the water, I ask myself. Is it in the air? Why are so many Shrewsbury people so upbeat?

Jim can't answer for the rest of Shrewsbury, but for himself, he says, he made a decision years ago to stop being a 'pint-half-empty' type and become a 'pint three-quarters-if-not-brimming-over' type instead. 'I can't see the point of not being positive,' he says. 'Life was so boring the other way. And negativity's corrosive. On a personal level it eats away at you. And it's not good for society either.'

Jim's definitely not the sort of person you'd find saying 'there's no such thing as society'. Life for him is all about interacting. He hates it when people view each other with suspicion, and he hates the way the media plays a role in this.

Jim has worked in radio for over thirty years, starting with a university radio station, then 'moving with a bunch of us to a commercial station opening up the road'. Over the years, he's witnessed radio being bland at one extreme, and playing devil's advocate at the other, with a tendency towards bullying. 'How often is radio journalism sword of truth stuff, and how often is it just a matter of wanting to start a fight?' he says. 'People are encouraged to judge each other. There's a real lack of empathy sometimes.'

Jim gave up newspapers over a year ago – and he hasn't missed them. They're bad for his mental health he says, and he's not joking here. Jim has a twenty year history of mental health issues and now knows to remove all obstacles, be they news stories, online articles or indeed negative and angry Facebook and Twitter followers, that might be a bar to his continued good health.

'Once I used to be a three-newspapers-a-day man,' Jim says. 'I told myself I liked to be well informed, but reading the news was upsetting me. So often the world it described wasn't the one in which I live, where people care about one another and take time to make a difference. Then one time somebody said to me *look for the good*, and I started to see things in a more balanced way. *Seek out the celebratory*, they said. *Look for the inclusive.* And those words made sense. They shifted something inside my head. Since then my tectonic plates have fitted together in a new and better way. Initially living that way involved an act of decision, but not for long. Quickly it became a way of life.'

Jim Hawkins

I'm enjoying talking to Jim. We're in Frank's Bar on Frankwell and the sun's shining outside. It's the end of the day – time for feet up, a drink and a good yarn. We get onto the wealth of community ventures around town. Jim mentions the Street Pastors who go out at night to help people in difficulty around the pubs and clubs. Then there are the Food Banks, of which there are now two in Shrewsbury, as well as ones in Telford, Market Drayton and Bridgnorth.

We talk about the Severn Hospice, and the thousands of families whose lives it's touched. Jim tells me about the Telford Hospice, for which an appeal was launched bringing in five million pounds. Jim was at the sod cutting ceremony. He says it was very emotional. There's a spirit of generosity about, he says. Again and again he's seeing people caring for each other. He's definitely of the opinion that people are mostly good, and that they definitely deserve to be regarded as such, unless they prove themselves otherwise.

Jim was born in Romford, and moved to Shrewsbury ten years ago for the Radio Shropshire job. I say something about radio being his platform, and he corrects me. Radio's a portal, he says. His shows aren't about him as presenter. They're about the listeners. To make his point, Jim quotes radio guru, Dan O'Day. *Radio actually doesn't matter. You've got to love your audience and the people you're talking with.* 'It's not a matter of coming into people's homes and saying *here I am,*' Jim says. 'It's a matter of saying *there you are.*'

So who stands out in ten years of people featuring on the show? Jim mentions the two Bens – Ben Bebbington of Big Busk fame, and Ben Hughes, a man with a life-limiting illness whose bucket list includes campaigning to get people on the organ donor register. 'Both these men have stories that are engaging and make us all think,' Jim says. 'I've been accused of not caring for Shropshire society, meaning Society with a capital S. But these two are true Shropshire society. If I've had anything to do with persuading people to pay them attention, then that's great.'

I like this man. He's full of stories about people – and we haven't even started, yet, on The Bench. Do you know about Jim Hawkins and the bench? It's over five years now since, equipped with a hand-held recorder, Jim first headed off across the county to sit on a bench and see who'd come and talk to him. He's been doing this ever since, which means more than two hundred and fifty benches, unless Jim returns to certain benches more than once. All weathers he's to be found out around the county, at all times of year.

'Why?' I want to know. 'Because of the power of storytelling,' Jim replies. 'I stroll down a street, I sit on a bench and I see what happens. People come along and we start to chat. So many people have stories to tell that may not be regarded as newsworthy, but they're worth hearing all the same. And this is my way of getting to hear some of them.'

All sorts of people come along. The other week in Newport, Jim met Cintia from Brazil who told him about the long journey that brought her to the UK. Then another time, elsewhere across the county – on a rainy day Jim will never forget – he met an old man from Manchester who last saw his wife alive the day the doctor came for a home visit. That doctor was Harold Shipman. There's a story for you.

Plainly not everyone's as good as Jim would like to think. But that doesn't dent his faith in human nature. I ask whom a one-year blog on

Shrewsbury shouldn't leave out, and the answer he gives me is as long as his arm. One of the first things he noticed when he moved to Shropshire was how generous local people were. 'The county's beautiful,' he says. 'But its people make it particularly so.'

On the subject of Shropshire people, have you seen Jim's photographs? These are every bit as positive as the man himself. Then there are the nights when he's to be found in local venues playing music for people to chill or dance. 'Taking music for a walk' he calls it. His Sunday Socials are at Eighty-Six'd, in Ironbridge, and his Saturday Socials at The Coffeehouse in Shrewsbury. Plainly Jim enjoys seeing people enjoying themselves.

It's time to go our separate ways. Last calls for anything Jim wants to say. 'One in four people will experience some level of mental health issue during their lives,' Jim says. 'It's great when people hear about this on my show, and get the point that's being made. If there's anything I can do to remove the stigma surrounding mental health then I will.'

6th May: NOT A DAY FOR STAYING INDOORS

The suggestion was to walk the river loop. It sounded like a good idea, but I'd no idea we'd be out all day. We set off with weekend guests Kate (a Londoner) and Idris (Shropshire born and bred). Down St Mary's Water Lane we walked, through Traitor's Gate, then along the river and under the English Bridge. On one side were terraced gardens with moorings, on the other allotments in the shadow of the old town wall.

We walked beneath an avenue of trees. Our dog Biffo rushed about like a small brown bat out of hell. We stopped to talk to Andrew Bannerman, our local councillor, and wife Annie, out with their dog too. The Quarry lay ahead of us with its sloping lawns and graceful avenues of trees. We passed the Pengwern Boat Club on the far shore. A blind man

Mike Willmott on fiddle and Mike Penny on accordion.

came along with a bounding black dog. He stopped to chat, but his dog went racing on and the man hurried after him, clutching his white stick.

One week from today the regatta will be happening on this stretch of the Severn. There'll be crowds lining the bank and tents up on Beck's Field on the opposite shore. The river will be full of teams of rowers and the boathouse bars full of drinkers. Let's hope the weather's as good as it is today.

When we reached the Quarry we found it full of families strolling in the sun, children on bikes, kicking balls about or on the swings and slides. It was a perfect day for sitting over a coffee watching the world go by. However, the Quarry's only café (attached to the swimming pool) turned out to be shut. Why would anybody close the only café in the Quarry on a sunny Bank Holiday Monday? I can't answer that.

Back in town, we sat in the garden of Cromwell's Hotel, overlooking rooftops, chimney pots and the tower of St Alkmund's Church. Swallows flitted about. Soaking up the sun, Idris and Kate began to have serious regrets for having booked a midday train back to London. Another round of drinks was ordered and lingered over. Then it was a race to Waitrose to buy rolls and ham, and suddenly we were all legging it to the station, and the train was gone and Dave and I were on our own again.

We walked down to the river, unwilling to return home. The new town theatre came into view and we imagined spinning out the afternoon over drinks on its balcony. Inexplicably, however, we found the theatre closed. The busiest, sunniest day in town since I don't know when, but in yet another major town-centre outlet, everything was closed. Weird.

Help was at hand, however, up on Belmont Bank. Here in the bright sunshine we found a maypole ready to be danced around, samba drums playing and Chris the Piper giving it his all, standing on the wall of Old St Chad's. The street below the wall was heaving with children buying candyfloss, having their faces painted and their hair braided. Radio Shropshire's Jim Hawkins was out and about taking photographs. In the Hive Arts Centre, which was hosting the event, we found Julia Wenlock selling chocolates. The courtyard behind her was full of rabbits and exotic birds. We bumped into Joanne Bloodworth, the Shrewsbury-based dress designer, off to India soon on behalf of Nottingham Trent University. Lucky her.

Eventually, to the strains of a fiddler and ukulele team, we slipped away. By now we'd been out all day. The sun was still shining on Pride Hill as we passed the high town cross. As I write this, it's still shining now. Through the open window I can smell food being cooked. Where's it coming from? I've no idea. Seven thirty in the evening, and life in Shrewsbury feels pretty good.

10th May: MEET MICHAEL MORPURGO

Michael Morpurgo, ex-Children's Laureate, National Chancellor of the Children's University, multi-award-winning author of the highly acclaimed *War Horse*, was in Shrewsbury last weekend for the Children's Bookfest. Backstage at Shrewsbury School's Allington Hall, he and I talked about his own childhood. Its highlight was being read to by his mother, he said, but the rest of his childhood in post-war London was incredibly bleak. 'The war had a lingering effect. The grown ups were all traumatized. But I did have an incredible degree of freedom.'

Back then city children rambled freely or simply played together in the streets. 'There weren't so many cars in those days,' Michael said. 'I remember bombsites, and other kids out, and all of us roaming about.'

School, on the other hand, was regimented. And now, Michael feared, we were returning to that sort of thing. 'Back to the tests,' he said. 'Back to words counting for nothing but punctuating and spelling. All the lovely stories and poems are out. Instead of listening and dreaming, we have learning and reciting. And everything's a competition.'

The one thing Michael learned in school, he said, was how to fail. His schooldays were dominated by fearfulness. School was a place for punishments, humiliation and fear. At seven and a half, he became a boarder. Succeeding became even more important. 'I discovered that I was good at sport and singing,' Michael said. 'But something died inside of me. The art of survival – that's what growing up was all about. You either had to fight, or go along with things and keep your thoughts to yourself.'

Back at home too, with his mother and step-father, Michael recognised that succeeding was important. His family was different to others, he said, but he couldn't have explained why. In public they were 'the Morpurgos', but his mother was divorced and her children had different fathers. 'We were a family full of secrets,' Michael said. 'It wasn't until I was twenty-six that I met my real father. 'The Morpurgo family', as presented to the world was a myth.'

Even so, Michael spoke with respect of his parents. He didn't want to judge anything they did. They were brought up in different times, he said. His mother came from a Christian Scientist family. There was great pressure on her to become an academic, but she became an actress instead. Then there was her marriage failure, and her desperate struggle to hold everything together for her children as well as herself. 'It was an interesting childhood,' Michael said.

What was it, I wanted to know, that Michael most wanted to give children when he wrote for and talked to them? In the last couple of months, this was Michael's second visit to Shropshire, and on both occasions tickets had sold out.

'What I want for children,' Michael said, 'is what I didn't have myself – a sense of being of worth. If a child's contribution isn't recognised, it's alarming the speed with which anger and alienation can start building up.'

Having started his working life as a primary school teacher, Michael plainly knew what he was talking about. It wasn't until his late twenties that he began to write. He wasn't one of those writers who knew from the word 'go' what they wanted to be. 'But one should be able to find one's own pace,' he said. 'Life's not a rush.'

Outside, the buzz of a growing audience could be heard. Faces popped round the door, then disappeared. But even here, with only a few minutes before going onstage, Michael plainly felt that life wasn't to be rushed.

'Back in my schooldays,' he said, 'I was told I didn't have an imagination. I wasn't sure back then what imagination was. But I was lucky. When I needed it, the right support came along.'

As National Chancellor of the Children's University, Michael knows that many children still need that support. Did he have a message for the children of Shropshire, I asked. For the longest moment this most eloquent of men sat in silence, then he leant forward and said, 'It's important to find your own way in life. The Children's University can take you on a long walk. It's the long walk of education, and you'll discover your path that way. Sometimes the walk will take you uphill and your legs will ache and you'll become tired and breathless and not want to go on – but you should. Then sometimes there'll be wonderful days, the sun will be out, everything will be lovely – but that's not the end, because you and I know that it'll rain again. But you have to keep on walking. You have to make that start. You've got to get out and walk.'

12th May: SHAKESPEARE & SHREWSBURY

The grand finale of one of Shakespeare's plays is set in Shrewsbury. Not many people know that. The play is *Henry IV Part I*, and its dramatic climax recalls one of the pivotal moments in English military history, not least because it's the point at which the longbow finally came into its own.

All the key political figures of the day featured in that play. King Henry IV rode out from Shrewsbury Castle along with his son and heir, the hapless Prince Hal who was about to have a personality transplant and become the Henry V of Agincourt fame. The scion of the ambitious Percy family, Harry Hotspur, lined up for battle too. Lord Edmund Mortimer was there, descendant of Edward III, tied by marriage alliance into the Percy family. Even that great Welsh hero, Owen Glendower (who according to Shakespeare called 'forth spirits from the vasty deep') was briefly there, before seeing the lie of the land and turning back.

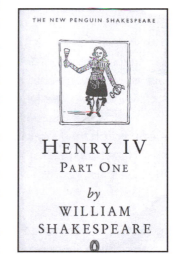

THE NEW PENGUIN SHAKESPEARE

HENRY IV
PART ONE

by
WILLIAM
SHAKESPEARE

And Sir John Falstaff was there. The same Sir John who, alongside Hamlet, is reckoned to be one of Shakespeare's greatest characters. Imagine it, a character of that stature in the works of Shakespeare – and connected to our town! That's something worth shouting about, but does anybody know it [I bet the people of Elsinore know about Hamlet]? *Not as far as I can see.*

The battle in question is the Battle of Shrewsbury. I'm no historian, as I'm always saying, but here's the run up to it. Back in 1399, Henry Bolingbroke usurped the throne of England from his one-time playmate and cousin, Richard II, becoming King Henry IV. Fairly quickly, however, his one-time allies, the powerful Percy family, started planning rebellion, pulling together an alliance of lords that included Owen Glendower and the underage Earl of March whom they wanted to crown king in Henry's place.

Complicated? Well, you should see Henry IV's family tree! His great, great grandfather was the mighty Edward I, his father John of Gaunt, son of Edward III. His uncle was the Black Prince, and his grandfather started the Hundred Years War. And that's only a small handful of the *men* in the family. There were more queens, princesses, ladies, lords, kings, princes, rivals and coups in the making in the Plantagenet family than there are stalls in Shrewsbury Market – and I'm not exaggerating here.

There are those who believed Henry IV seized the throne by starving the legitimate king, Richard II, to death, and those who reckoned, given the number of other family members, that Henry's claim to the throne was very weak indeed.

In the summer of 1403, forces gathered against Henry in Cheshire, with a view to marching on Shrewsbury, which was garrisoned by his son, Prince Hal. The king headed north-west to intercept them before they could join forces with Owen Glendower. A race for Shrewsbury took place, which the king won, isolating the Percy family's famous warrior son, Harry Hotspur, on the north side of the town with the Severn and the king's army between him and any hope of Welsh reinforcements.

For a day or so, a stand-off took place, neither side seeming keen to fight. The abbots of Shrewsbury and Haughmond attempted to mediate, but with King Henry unwilling to back down, the battle finally commenced with only two hours of light left.

Consequently, Shrewsbury was short – but it was savage too. By nightfall the battlefield was so strewn with bodies that the ground could no longer be seen. For the first time English longbow men had turned on each other and the result was that even the Percys, by the end of the day, had lost their famous son.

The Battle of Shrewsbury secured the family line of Henry Bolingbroke. However, most important in Shakespeare's dramatist's eyes, it was a precursor to Agincourt. In the course of battle, Shakespeare transforms Prince Hal from wastrel son to his father's rightful heir. Not only Harry Hotspur's body is placed at Prince Hal's feet at the end of the battle, but Falstaff's too. Here we have Hal's old drinking partner and alternative father-figure pretending, like the coward he so often was, to be dead to avoid having to fight.

Ten years ago, before an audience of Shropshire schoolchildren, I conducted 'Parkinson-style' interviews with all the main protagonists in the Battle of Shrewsbury. The venue was Battlefields Church. One after another, Hotspur, Henry IV and the other main 'players' in the battle came clanking out of the green room (ie. vicar's vestry) in full armour to be quizzed about the part they'd played on the day. At the end of the interviews the whole lot of us trooped outside, lining up with the Henrys on one side, the Percys on the other, to charge each other armed with rubber truncheons and let battle commence.

It was great. The best event for children, said the Battlefield Conservation Trust, that they'd ever done.

I'd love to see the Shakespeare play. I know that the BBC filmed it as part of their *Hollow Crown* series, but unfortunately I missed it. Shrewsbury College of Arts & Technology made a film of the play too, in conjunction with the British Youth Film Academy. It was premiered in Shrewsbury this January but, would you believe it, I missed that too.

15th May: SHINY, SHINY GREAT GATSBY FLAPPER-GIRL FROCKS

Baz Luhrmann's *The Great Gatsby* premieres in London tonight. Even as I write, Leonardo di Caprio fans are awaiting his red carpet moment. But behind the Luhrmann film lurks the Robert Redford one, and behind *that* lurks F. Scott Fitzgerald.

I love the writing of F. Scott Fitzgerald. I even love *Tender Is the Night*, which I've heard described as 'about nothing'. I particularly love Fitzgerald's long short story *The Diamond as Big as the Ritz*, but I love *The Great Gatsby* too, with its cool, pared-back style and classic tale of jazz age glamour and greed.

I'm guessing that interest in Twenties clothing will soon be booming – which is just as well for Emilia Jones. I was in her St John's Hill shop,

Jazz Age Glamour

E.A. Jones, today, looking at her 1920s dresses, jackets and coats. Some are for sale, others come from her private collection.

Emilia showed me one of her favourites – a beaded, flame-orange dress from the early '20s which she bought at a Christie's auction when she was just fourteen. The purchase of that dress was a defining moment for her as a collector. When the parcel arrived from Christie's, beautifully packaged with layers of tissue paper, it started something that carries on to this day. 'Thanks to that dress, I fell in love with the 1920s,' Emilia said.

E.A. Jones is the perfect treasure trove. Rifling through dresses, skirts, blouses and coats, all carefully labelled with period details, I wanted to know how Emilia decided what to buy. 'I buy what I think Shrewsbury people will like,' Emilia said. 'I've been here long enough to know what that might be. But I'll also buy things of special interest, like a 1780s dress I saw last week, and the lovely New Look coat on the rack over there.'

As she spoke, Emilia took items off rails to show to me. One was a velvet coat (the shocking pink made famous by Schiaparelli) trimmed with a hint of fur. Trying it on felt like drowning in warm milk – a surprisingly agreeable experience. I imagined the stir it would cause if I swanked into Waitrose wearing it. Oh, for a bit of glamour in our lives!

Out of tissue paper emerged a black dress, as light and fine as gossamer, decorated with beads and tiny dots of silver. Its hemline was scalloped, beaded and embroidered, its sash hung down lopsidedly, creating an asymmetrical effect. Emilia explained that this dress belonged to the late 1920s when designers were moving on from the tape-chested androgynous look, waistlines rising and dresses becoming more feminine.

On and on the items came shimmering after each other. A beaded flapper-girl dress; a light, white, sleeveless dress beaded with silver; a black-fringed shawl covered in snow-white silk embroidery that shone like moonlight on a midnight lake; a velvet evening coat decorated with tiny flowers; a heavy black cloak smothered in the most intricate silver embroidery. The word shimmering didn't do it justice – it was hard to believe this piece wasn't exhibited in the V & A.

The 1920s was such an interesting time, Emilia said. A time of dramatic change. Hemlines shot up, arms and legs appeared, everybody wanted shiny, shiny clothes. 'Lots of glass, beads, sequins and metallic thread,' Emilia said, bringing out a series of head dresses beaded in silver and crocheted in gold. 'But not everybody dressed like the flapper-girls. Even more imaginative clothes were being designed. This black evening dress with a scalloped edge, for example, isn't a typical flapper dress, but it's very much of the period.'

Some of Emilia's clothes come from auctions in the UK, some from France and others from the US. A 1940s American blouse, she said, would be more extrovert than a 1940s British one. 'The US was more confident,' Emilia said. 'The war hadn't bitten so deeply there, and it showed in their clothes.'

Emilia knows sellers all around the world, and in return has made a name for herself as someone who sells exquisite, interesting things. H & M, eat your heart out, and M & S. E. A. Jones, is to clothing what Shrewsbury Market is to fish, meat, fruit and veg. In other words, this is the real deal – and I'll be back.

Oh, and F. Scott Fitzgerald, I've just started re-reading *The Diamond as Big as the Ritz*.

17th May: DAN CASSIDY, THE FIDDLE PLAYER

The first time I met Dan was in Poets' Corner in the Loggerheads pub. I sat with members of my family in one corner, and this solitary man sat opposite looking in a bit of a fug. Slowly he was drawn into our conversation, which was about American country music. We had made a new friend.

An American himself, when we met recently in the Loggerheads Dan said he grew up with a guitar on the wall, introduced to folk songs by his banjo-playing father. Very quickly his sister, Eva, emerged as somebody who could carry a melody. She and Dan were very close. She stood by him when he headed off to Germany with an English outfit, the Bobbie Barnwell band. Their father reckoned what Dan needed were qualifications, but Eva Cassidy encouraged him to keep going.

Eva was a year older than Dan. He describes her as a person of great courage and unswerving instinct, who achieved great things, though she didn't at that early stage have his confidence for public performance. When Dan left the US for a second time, determined to go it alone and make something of himself, she remained behind in suburban Maryland.

Dan headed for Iceland, a country he'd gigged in after his stint with Bobbie Barnwell. All he had was a one-way ticket, his fiddle and $500, but he succeeded in infiltrating the Icelandic music scene as the only electric fiddle player doing it his way. 'Everybody wanted Dan Cassidy playing on their albums,' he said. 'I found opportunities that wouldn't have been available anywhere else.'

This was Dan's second teenagerhood. Iceland was a place for hard drinking – and he drank hard. People lived fast lives. Reykjavik was a party capital – a regular free-for-all. Back in Washington DC Dan had worked as a courier eight hours a day, playing part-time in bands after a daily three hour commute. Now he was making a living out of what he loved.

Dan's home base is Iceland to this day. He's married and has a little daughter, Eva, who is seven years old. 'The day she was born was the day I laid off booze,' he said. 'Drugs, the lot. I cleaned up my life. And it's been that way ever since.'

Dan teaches, plays in Iceland and tours Europe with his swing quartet. Sometimes he works on TV. Sometimes he collaborates with other musicians. Sometimes he plays alone. But every year he comes to Shrewsbury.

'It was Bobbie Barnwell who brought me here,' Dan said. 'I was with her band for three and a half years before returning to the US to that job as a courier. Every six months she'd come back to this country for a short period, and because Shrewsbury was where she hailed from, that's where I'd come too.'

These were difficult years. Dan had constant money problems and frequent immigration issues. He had trouble connecting with people too. '*I was a troubled young man*' is how he describes it. He remembers trying to work his way into the local music scene. St Patrick's Day in the back room of the Seven Stars in Coleham is one occasion he won't forget. 'It was a folk gathering,' he said. 'I had this weird home-made electric violin, and Bobbie's brother-in-law Cedric and I played some bluegrass together. It wasn't what people were used to hearing. At the end somebody went *yeeehaaaa.* I didn't get the sense that it was meant kindly.'

Dan Cassidy in Poets' Corner at the Loggerheads

After that Dan was on a mission to prove how versatile the violin could be. 'I wanted to be Dan Cassidy the Fiddle Player, not Dan Cassidy the Eejit,' he said. 'In pub sessions, on TV and radio, doing rock stuff, Hendrix and all that, doing country & western – I was not an ordinary violinist and I was out to prove something.'

The friendship with Bobbie, Cedric and their families has grown over the years. Now Dan says Shrewsbury feels like a third home, and the Hickman/Barnwell clan an extended family. Since 2004, Bobbie's nephew James has been playing in the Dan Cassidy Swing Quartet, and Dan and James play together too. Dan has watched James turn from a little kid to a hulking six foot man. He's seen him take up the guitar, learning from his dad and, as Dan puts it, '*take the ball and run with it*'.

Currently Hickman & Cassidy are on a six-week tour of the UK. They're in the South-West next week, then Scotland the first week in June, including a concert on Skye. Their music is a mixture of swing, bluegrass, blues and folk. They're writing their own material too.

Dan has always loved the combination of violin and acoustic guitar, the one so lyrical, the other with its percussive element driving forward the beat. 'I find that blend intriguing,' he said. 'And when you add in someone like James, who can really sing, you've got it all. With Eva, I was used to working with a real high-calibre singer. And what James and I have today is built on the foundation of that partnership.'

Eva was uncomfortable with gigging. She honed her skills in the recording studio, Dan said, rather than the rough and tumble of live performance. 'There's a lovely film coming out about her,' Dan said. *"Timeless Voice – Eva Cassidy'*. It'll be on the Sky Arts Channel and eventually out as a DVD. All sorts of people are on it talking about the impact of her music at that very highly commercialised time in the business. And there are some lovely clips of her singing, of course. You know, she came to see me in Iceland a couple of times. People were mesmerised by her. Not only did they sit in silence while she sang, they wouldn't even touch their drinks until she'd finished each song. She had such presence. Her voice commanded attention.'

A moment's silence fell between us. But Dan's a natural talker in his own quiet way, and it didn't take much for him to be off again, telling me about the masterclasses he runs, teaching classically-trained musicians how to play by ear.

'Some day, if I live long enough,' he said, 'I'd like to change the way people think about learning stringed instruments. I'd like to see them borrowing from the best of jazz, folk, classical, pop. Teaching and performing go hand in hand. There's a golden opportunity, via performance, to inspire young musicians. And inspiring young musicians is what I want to do.'

But wherever Dan goes, he'll always return to Shrewsbury. 'There are lots of chapters in my life,' he said, 'and in between them all is Shrewsbury. This is the place where I chart my development as I strive to prove my salt.'

Eva would have loved it here, Dan said. 'She never wanted the big stage. She would have loved singing at one of the music nights in the Loggerheads. It was my dream to bring her over here. In fact in her last letter to me she talked about coming to Europe. But she never did.'

21ˢᵗ May: WHAT'S GOING ON IN THE MUSIC HALL? HERE'S YOUR CHANCE TO FIND OUT

Last week, courtesy of Tim Jenkins, Heritage Project Manager for Shrewsbury's new museum, I had a chance to sees behind the scenes at what's going to be our new museum. Just a few short months before it's due to open, I can tell you it still looks like a building site. For two hours I picked my way through vast open spaces slowly being turned into galleries housing everything from the county's prehistoric collection and its Roman artefacts to the modern day. An education suite is being built, sponsored by the Walker Trust. At first floor level, looking down upon the Square, a gallery is being created to house national and international touring exhibitions.

This is all very exciting. Add to it the restoration of Vaughan's Mansion, a 13th century mansion of national importance, and it's even more exciting. Early in the building process it was discovered that Vaughan's Mansion had dislodged itself from the main body of the Music Hall and was tilting dangerously in the direction of the Benbow pub.

Now it's been rescued, and even its courtyard will be open to the public, as part of the museum's coffee shop.

How much do you know about the Old Music Hall? The original building was positioned between two higher parts of Saxon Shrewsbury, separated by the town pond [see my post A Bog, A Square and One Big Stink], built on what was once an ice-age kettle hole.

Shrewsbury's new Museum & Art Gallery under construction

In the 13th century the pond was filled in, the adjoining slopes terraced and the Square turned into a market place. Vaughan's Mansion was built circa 1290 at one end of this new civic place, though hidden behind the street frontage.

The classical frontage we now all see was built by the Haycock brothers in the Georgian period. Behind it, to the left, stood the early Victorian Assembly Rooms. Then, right across the building, the Victorian Public Rooms were installed. In the cellar at the front of the building was a coffee house. And running through it all was what was once known as Fire Office Passage, with fire service ladders hanging along the walls.

It's amazing to see these old spaces coming back to life. In particular I was delighted to see the ceiling of the auditorium – once a murderous shade of red – restored to its original colours. It's an incredible ceiling, and the auditorium beneath it looks pretty incredible too. Soon it will house the museum's main collections.

So, what's my lasting memory after picking my way through it all, kitted out in jerkins, goggles, hard hat and hobnailed boots? It's hard to choose. It certainly was exciting to get a glimpse of the 1960s nuclear bunker that has always been a bit of a Shrewsbury urban myth. And the art gallery overlooking the Square is going to be fantastic. And so is the timber work of Vaughan's Mansion.

But for me it has to be the auditorium, light pouring in through windows that for years have been blocked up. Beyond these windows I could see the rooftops, ridges and chimney pots not only of Vaughan's Mansion, but of much of our town. Shrewsbury's a museum too – albeit one with a thriving contemporary life. I feel privileged to live in such a fabulous place.

26th May: THE BOYS FROM THE BIRD'S NEST

People are always talking about the boys from the Bird's Nest. They've done great things for the market… We're so lucky in our town to have them… They're great guys… When am I going to interview them?

So, sitting in the Bird's Nest café earlier today, I suggested fixing up an interview. What's wrong with now, said co-owner Victor Deng.

Nothing I could think of, so we retreated to a cosy corner which just so happened to be the Bird's Nest's original site, with seating for twelve. 'And now look at us – the Bird's Nest seats sixty,' Victor said.

The Bird's Nest has only been in Shrewsbury Market for two and a half years, but it's very much part of market life. At any one time you'll find students, young mums, families, shoppers and old market regulars at the sprawl of tables and sofas. The market's never had anything quite like it before, but the Bird's Nest and the market fit together like a hand and a glove. So where did the original idea come from?

The Bird's Nest Café'

Victor and fellow-owner, Aaron Brown, had wanted to start a business for some time. They'd both worked in the food industry and were keen to branch out on their own. They had the cash to get started and a café seemed a good idea. Aaron's girlfriend came up with the Bird's Nest concept, and it was whilst trawling the region for the right location that Victor and Aaron discovered Shrewsbury.

'We both live in Birmingham,' Victor said, 'but couldn't afford Birmingham rents, so it was a matter of finding somewhere within commuting distance. We knew as soon as we arrived in Shrewsbury that we'd found what we wanted.'

That was back in December 2010. Victor says they fell in love with Shrewsbury. Now all they needed was to find a location for the sort of café they had in mind. High Street rents were correspondingly high, and the market seemed more exciting anyway.

It was a time of change. Some old stalls were closing and new ones opening up. The word went out that there was a new coffee house in the market, with good food too, and people started coming in.

Everybody loves the Bird's Nest's food, which comes in daily from its central kitchen in Birmingham. And the cakes too, courtesy of Fabulous Joe Cakes, Birmingham, and Cherry Bakewell in Wem. My favourite is the beetroot and chocolate cake, and the pavlova is as pretty as anything you'll ever see sitting on a plate.

'We couldn't have done it without help,' Victor said. 'Everybody got behind what we wanted to create. We were made so welcome here in the market, and had so much support.'

Shrewsbury's indoor market has a long history, but I'm guessing that Victor Deng and Aaron Brown are the first market traders to have held an Africa Day with live music, including a drumming workshop, African poetry and an African menu, which they served all week.

Victor told me that live music was always part of the plan. Africa Day was a huge success, and so have been the twice-monthly Bird's Nest Matinee Sessions that include the spoken word and poetry. In addition, on 12th June, Victor and Aaron are bringing a choir from Malawi into the market. This is most definitely an event not to be missed.

I took Victor's pic. He called the girls together and I took their pics. Then he called over Vincent and Alex and I took all their pics, laughing and looking like they enjoyed what they were doing. Click, click, everybody was laughing by now, and people were looking on, the Bird's Nest chirruping, the whole place abuzz.

'We're so grateful to everybody who comes and likes the place and comes back,' Victor said. 'We're just two young guys from somewhere else, and the market has embraced us whole-heartedly and the people of Shrewsbury have too.'

29th May: THE OLD SHREWSBURY SHOW

On the 6th March 1878, using powers afforded him by the Fairs Act of 1871, the Home Secretary abolished the Old Shrewsbury Show, which had been held annually at Kingsland every second Sunday after Whitsun, recurring like a force of nature since before Elizabethan times.

The celebration had its roots in the Festival of Corpus Christi, but had lost its religious component by the time of the Reformation. Trade guilds erected arbours between what's now Ashcroft Road and Beehive Lane and their masters, journeymen and apprentices processed up there to entertain the Mayor and Corporation.

However, the writing was on the wall for the Old Shrewsbury Show. By 1866, Headmaster Moss of Shrewsbury School (citing support from all 'right-thinking people', including 'moralists, parents and educationalists') suggested moving the Show's location. The eyes of the great and good of Shrewsbury – including those at Shrewsbury School – had fallen upon Kingsland as a site too valuable to waste on what the Chairman of Shrewsbury's Quarter Sessions described scathingly to the Home Secretary as a *pleasure fair,* attracting a lower sort of person and resulting in much drunkenness.

This was the voice of Victorian England speaking. Until then the police had turned a blind eye to the excesses of the Show. However, now battle lines were drawn up. On one side were the companies and guilds, on the other the great and good of the town, including the clergy (especially Julia, reformer wife of Revd Charles Wightman of St Alkmunds). Even the Shrewsbury Chronicle got in on the act, describing the Show as a 'ridiculous pageant' with its 'usual array of drunken kings and factory queens promenading the streets'.

Heading for Kingsland

In its glory days, however, the Show was a grand institution. Its procession included the Mayor and Corporation along with burlesque figures wearing huge comic heads. Crispin and Crispianus escorted the shoemakers, Vulcan the smiths and Rubens the house painters. Henry I always appeared, having granted Shrewsbury its initial charter. Cupid led the tailors, the Stag led the skinners, Henry VIII was in charge of the builders, the Black Prince led the cabinet makers and hatters, Elizabeth I the hairdressers and bakers and the flax dressers were led by Katherine of Aragon.

A contemporary record describes Kingsland as a 'tented field of glorious pastimes in all its enticing forms'. These included 'fun shows', 'shindies of every sort', shooting, wines, cakes, comfits, beef and ham sandwiches, coffee, brown stout, beer and 'backey'. 'Slapbangs' were also on offer.

Even as late as 1831, not only the Mayor and Corporation attended, but so did eight guilds, two County MPs and the Earl of Powis. However when the Municipal Corporations Act of 1835 stripped the guilds of their legal status, there was no longer a formal obligation for the Mayor to attend – and that year's Show saw only the Butchers' Guild attending, along with a random assortment of apprentices.

The Show's fortunes briefly changed in 1849 when the railway came to Shrewsbury. For a few years, boosted by cheap trains from Chester and Stafford, visitors poured into the Show. In 1850, the Shrewsbury Journal described the railway station being 'besieged all Monday morning by crowds of people to view the ancient pageant of the Shrewsbury Show.' Every mode of conveyance, from carts to steam engines, was employed in transporting the punters out to Kingsland. One train alone is credited with carrying 2,900 passengers. Is that possible? Have I read this right? I read the figures again. Yes, I have.

So how could such a popular Show come to an ignoble end only twenty years later? A press report of 1870 describes it as *this once famous Show*, celebrated with *mimic pomp*. Another recorded 'just' four thousand people coming in by train. Yet twenty years previously trains had been bringing in as many as 32,000 – an extraordinary figure.

The Victorians were as successful in running PR campaigns as we are today. Then, as now, they knew that people could be easily swayed. The campaign against the Show began as soon as it began to show signs of revival. In 1849, the town's clergy attempted to persuade people against going to Kingsland, and the Mayor was taken to task for encouraging 'beastly intoxications, horrid Sabbath desecration and tremendous oaths and cursing'.

Though the Show was now held on a Monday, Sabbath Day observers were offended by stallholders travelling to the Show and setting up on a Sunday. An Evangelicalism that wasn't just local, but nationwide, had the town in its grip.

This wasn't just a religious crusade though; it was a social one, targeted against the lower classes. The Show was too unsophisticated and tawdry for refined tastes. Desperate attempts were made by its organisers to introduce novelties. Traditional burlesque figures were joined by contemporary ones from popular songs. However, nothing could halt the Show's demise.

In 1882, Shrewsbury School left its town-centre location, where it had been housed for over three hundred years, and moved out to Kingsland – with its brand-new bridge – where it still stands today. Headmaster Moss had finally got his way.

Well, I've always reckoned that I know my Shrewsbury history, but plainly there are some gaps, and this is one of them. Until recently I'd never heard of the Old Shrewsbury Show. Thanks to the sterling work of Patti Price and Barrie Trinder, however, I now have – and so have you.

[For more information, see 'Victorian Shrewsbury - Studies in the History of a County Town, by the Victorian Shrewsbury Research Group editor Barrie Trinder.]

JUNE

3rd June: THE BEN BEBBINGTON TRIAL

On the night of 6th September last year, two boys encountered a drunk man on Ditherington Road. They made derogatory remarks and when he headed off down Old Canal Lane, trying to get away from them, followed him, pushed him down a flight of steps and launched an attack.

The man was Ben Bebbington. In the darkness on the lower path, he was kicked in the chest and stamped on the head. His screams could be heard over music coming out of a local pub. It's not known at which point he was fatally injured by a boot-blow to the head, but he made it to the upper path, where he collapsed. He was discovered by a cyclist at 1.10am and taken by ambulance to the Royal Shrewsbury Hospital. C.T. scanning revealed serious damage to his skull and he was transferred to Stafford where doctors discovered that surgery wasn't able to help him.

Ben's life-support was switched off at 8.35am, and he was pronounced dead. The marks of two trainers on his head were photographed. A post-mortem on 8th September found that Ben died of an acute subdural haematoma. Extended injuries were mentioned, including two lacerations to Ben's scalp, which could have been caused by a glass bottle.

Ben's attackers were Shrewsbury boys. I was in court yesterday to hear the sentencing at their trial. The morning after the attack, round at one of their houses, they attempted to burn their trainers in an oil drum and wash their clothes in a washing-machine. Then the boy whose house it was put pressure on his mother to drive him into Shrewsbury to buy an identical pair of trainers to present to the police as the ones he'd been wearing on the night in question.

Accompanied by other family members, she drove to Lyth Hill, where her son hid the charred remains of both his and his friend's trainers in a hedgerow. Later the same day, the two boys went to the police to tell a concocted story about having been attacked by Ben and pushing him down steps to defend themselves.

All this I learned in Birmingham Crown Court last week at the sentencing of Stuart Doran and Bradley Davies. Their barristers presented a variety of mitigating circumstances, including finally coming clean in Doran's case, and youth and naivety in Davies's, and the fact that there had been no intention to kill.

Ben Bebbington didn't know the young men who attacked him, and they didn't know him. For them, what happened was a matter of random violence. For Ben, it was a matter of death. I don't know why young men might be angry enough to kill a stranger on the street, but last Friday in Court 5, after the barristers had finished speaking for the boys, this is what the Judge had to say:

Ben Bebbington was a man aged forty-three, who had never done any harm and had led an at times sad and at times full life. He had touched many people for good. On the night in question, he had been at a low point in his life. He was drunk, and not in a good way. For anybody meeting him, there had been two ways to deal with the situation. One was to show compassion and try to help. The other was the thuggish option, taking advantage of Ben's condition and attacking him in a violent way.

Ben Bebbington on Haughmond Hill

Stuart Doran and Bradley Davies had taken the latter option. Their offence was one of murder, and it was compounded by there having been two of them, and by the gratuitous level of the violence, using their feet as weapons and launching not just one but two separate attacks. Not only that, but next day, along with members of Davies's family, the boys had attempted to conceal evidence, and concocted an untrue account of what happened and presented it to the police.

'I am asked,' said the Judge, 'to find no intent to kill, and in the strictest terms there was none. However, the behaviour of Doran and Davies was so sustained, and the level of gratuitous violence so great that the degree of mitigation can only be small.'

On this basis, Stuart Doran and Bradley Davies were both sentenced to life. Taking into account Doran's having pleaded guilty, he would serve sixteen years and whether he'd be released at that point would depend on the parole board and on his own behaviour.

Stuart Davies was sentenced to fourteen years. He gave his family a thumbs-up as he was sent down.

After this, Bradley Davies's mother, cousin, half-brother and one other person were placed in the dock, guilty of perverting the course of justice and making false witness statements. Their barristers presented mitigating circumstances on behalf of each of them. The Judge, however, ruled that the serious offence had taken place of deliberately misleading the police in the face of murder. He sent the mother down for two years (shock waves around the court, sobbing in the gallery) along with a half-brother whose loyalty to his family had in the Judge's words 'crossed a moral threshold'. Another family member received a Youth Rehabilitation Order and a further family member received a suspended sentence and two hundred hours of unpaid work. 'If you fail to complete these, you will go to prison. Do you understand that?' the Judge said.

Since last September, the Bebbington family has been living in a parallel universe. Ben's death, and the manner of it, has become their life. The police have been the constant in that life. 'They have been wonderful,' Ben's sister Karen told me when we spoke afterwards. 'But it's been like living in a bubble. The rest of the world is normal, but we in Ben's family are in the bubble – and the awful thing is that it's happening again. Another family is starting out. The family of Georgia Williams in Telford. Our hearts go out to them. We know exactly where they are. Then there's the random murder at that cash machine of another local man, Robert Barlow. What's happening in our society to make young men so very angry?'

None of this was the Shrewsbury Karen knew, she reckoned. Her Shrewsbury was a lovely place, full of good and kind people. Even amongst the communities where Doran and Davies lived, the Bebbington family had found nothing but kindness and support.

I sat in the sunshine afterwards taking it all in. All those rows of barristers, those files and mountains of paperwork, all that police work and all that grief. None of us, I guessed, were any wiser as to what was really happening here, or why. But an attempt had been made to uncover the truth. Details matter in a court of law – and thank God that they do.

More than anything, that's what I carried away. It wasn't so much the sense of courtroom drama that impressed itself on me, but the forensic determination to be fair, to take every last detail into account.

Back home, I found a message on my phone from Ben's other sister, Anne-Marie, and a recording of Ben in conversation with Radio Shropshire's Jim Hawkins. Though I knew Ben by face as a busker on Pride Hill, this was the first time I'd heard his speaking voice. He was reading one of his poems. This is how it ends:

'There are those who have convictions,
only want to drag you down, though you're not around.
Still the light is fading out,
and the sun can take the
dream train out of here.
To fade out of here,
across the hills and silent trees.
Across the hills, and free.'

6th June: VIVAT REGINA

There were no fanfares, trumpeters or cries of Vivat Regina in Shrewsbury last Sunday, but the organ was in good form, and the choir had plainly practised to within an inch of its life. The occasion was the 60th Anniversary of the Queen's Coronation, and the Service of Thanksgiving was held in that ex-wooden small Saxon church later upgraded by Roger de Montgomery in order to be buried in it.

I'm talking about Shrewsbury Abbey, an imposing building by anybody's standards, but a small reminder of a grander past as part of a Benedictine monastery that had jurisdiction over one of the main entrances to our town. Tolls were levied on traders. The Abbot served on embassies, inspected the local militia, guarded hostages, acted as a Justice of the Peace and sat in Parliament.

The glory days were over, however, by the time of Henry VIII's dissolution of the monasteries. After 1539, all that remained was the Abbey's church, and that's where a packed congregation met last Sunday to pray for that person referred to in the order of service as 'Our Sovereign Lady, Queen Elizabeth', thanking God for her long reign.

I remember watching the Coronation from underneath a table (don't ask) in a relative's house. Like many others, I was seeing telly for the first

Outside Shrewsbury Abbey

time. All I have now are distant memories from a bygone age when I thought that queens wore crowns, jewels and glittering robes and were impossibly glamorous every single day.

The service began with vicar, Paul Firmin, recalling Shrewsbury Abbey's long history of proclaiming God's love. A processional hymn brought choir and clergy to their appointed places. This was followed by a Bidding Prayer (ie. a prayer telling the congregation what it needs to pray for – in this case the Queen), followed by the Lord's Prayer.

This was followed by a hymn taken from the Coronation, followed by a huge chunk of liturgy sung by the choir. The congregation variously sat or stood their way through Preces (short petitions sung as versicles) Responses, Psalm 122, the Te Deum Laudamus ('Thee, O God, We Praise') and the Jubilate Deo (on Google I found this described as 'Snoopy's happy dance' but you could have fooled me).

In between, we had readings by Councillor Pate, Chairman of Shropshire Council, and Councillor Murray, MBE, Mayor of Telford and Wrekin, extolling us to 'submit ourselves to every ordinance of man for the Lord's sake,' (according to the Apostle Peter), and 'Render unto Caesar the things which are Caesar's, and unto God the things that are God's,' (according to Jesus Christ). There was an opportunity for the full congregation to say out loud the Apostles' Creed ('I believe in God, the Father Almighty, Maker of Heaven and Earth'). Then the choir was off again. Suffrages were sung (prayers offered for the repose of the souls of the faithful departed), Collects (other prayers) and the Choir Anthem (surprisingly short).

After this, the congregation sang 'I Vow To Thee My Country' (by Cecil Spring-Rice, British ambassador to the US in 1912, a career diplomat who wrote hymns on the side) and listened to a Sermon by the Bishop of Ludlow, Right Reverend Alistair Magowan.

Upon the Queen's Coronation, he said, she'd not only been equipped for the occasion in a Norman Hartnell frock, but equipped heart and soul for a life of worship of God and service to others. Church and State were brought together in her Coronation Oath. Her taking Communion upon that occasion had been an expression of her need of God's grace. Since then she had done her duty as Queen joyfully. Not only that, but her Christian service was a matter of public record.

Even before she became Queen, speaking as heir to the throne, the Queen had said, 'I can truly say that the King and I long to see the Bible where it should be, providing comfort to the nation. From my own experience I know what it can be in a personal life.' Indeed, 'Here is the most valuable thing the world affords,' were the words pronounced upon handing the Queen the Bible in the Coronation ceremony. It was a book that gave freedom and a way of life that all could follow.

The final hymn was the 'Old One Hundred' – 'All People That on Earth Do Dwell, Sing to the Lord with Cheerful Voice'. It was followed by a special prayer read by the Lord Lieutenant of Shropshire, Algernon Heber-Percy, a Blessing by the Bishop of Shrewsbury and the National Anthem. The vicar dismissed us with the words, 'With the risen life of Christ within you, go in the peace of Christ. Alleluia, alleluia,' to which we all replied, 'Thanks be to God.'

14th June: THE HEADMASTER'S HOUSE

Five years ago, Stephanie and Graham gave up country living, a horse and ten acres to move into the Headmaster's House in Shrewsbury's town centre. It's a building with a history, and they're proud of it and of its connection to Shrewsbury School.

Shrewsbury School was established by charter in 1522 by Edward VI. By 1562 two hundred and sixty-six boys studied under the Headmastership of Thomas Ashton, who achieved a national reputation for the school. By 1586, situated in the building now occupied by the Castle Gates Library, Shrewsbury School was known as 'the best filled school of all England'.

Despite his massive contribution to the reputation of Shrewsbury School, however the initials on the gate to Stephanie and Graham's house aren't TA for Thomas Ashton, but SB for Samuel Butler. Butler was the Headmaster who rescued Shrewsbury School from a long period of decline. One by one he acquired houses for boarders. A new chapel was built. The old Headmaster's House was upgraded, its Jacobean frontage replaced with a pseudo-Tudor facade.

Stephanie and Graham's hall has oak panelling left over from the days when boys (including Charles Darwin) lived in it. Their cellar has old passageways once leading underground to the main school building next door. Between their hall and kitchen they have an arched tunnel in what has reliably been established as the old town wall.

Once the houses opposite were school buildings too, and the ones further along the lane were part of the old town gaol. Now they're all domestic residences.

'We love living here,' Stephanie said. 'Every day there's something new and interesting to see. We eat out a lot. The town's full of great restaurants all within short walking distance, so it seems crazy not to.'

The Headmaster's House is five thousand square feet and five storeys tall, with a view of Shrewsbury that hasn't changed much for the last few hundred years. 'You'd think we'd have a few ghosts,' Stephanie said. 'But it seems not.'

Even so, one particular story about the Headmaster's House merits a ghost. In 1608 the town Bailiffs attempted to remove a master who was suspected of being a papist. A 'notorious riot' took place outside the house, extending over a period of four days and three nights. When one of the Bailiffs attempted to enter the building to remove the master by force, a timber beam was thrown down at him which, according to Stephanie and Graham, killed him outright.

We were on the roof terrace, up among the chimney pots, when

Stephanie told me that story. I looked down. Beneath me I could see the yard of the old Shrewsbury Gaol where the leader of the notorious Red & Green Gang escaped from his own hanging. Beyond that was all that remains of the picturesque black-and-white house once famous as the home of Palin, maker of the Shrewsbury Cake, which was medieval in origin. Then, crossing the top end of Castle Gates, was the café and well-being outlet, 'Serenity', housed in what Graham described as 'that amazing French chateau-style church' – in other words the ex-St Nicholas's Presbyterian church. Beyond that stood the half-timbered magnificence built by Sir Francis Newport on Dogpole, moved to its present site outside the castle by his grandson, Lord Bradford, in 1696. Beyond that was Shrewsbury Castle and beyond that, crossing the road again, the Castle Gates Library, formerly Shrewsbury School.

Stephanie and Graham inside the Headmaster's House

What a panorama. Talk about time travel. This was like another world – but Marks & Spencer's food hall called me back to the 21st century. My fridge was empty and there was supper to shop for before closing time.

Farewells were made outside the Samuel Butler gate. 'You should see the house in the snow,' Graham said, looking back up at it. 'You could easily believe you were in Dickens' day.'

17th June: WINGFIELD'S TOWER – A SAFE STRONGHOLD

In 1086 the Domesday Book described Shrewsbury as a town of 252 houses and four churches. No mention was made of any defensive wall, but the old name for the town, 'Scrobbesbyrig', derives from the words 'scrub' and 'fortified place' suggesting *some* sort of protection. Maybe this was the natural protection of the River Severn but in the 9th century

Shrewsbury was granted a royal charter giving it the status of a 'burgh' – and this word too suggests a fortified place.

The construction of the town walls as known today is dated between 1220 and 1242. In 1215, the town had fallen to the forces of Llywelyn the Great and Henry III was determined that this wouldn't happen again. At the start of the 14th century, Shrewsbury Castle was rebuilt and strengthened by Edward I, followed by a further rebuilding and repairing of walls a century later, courtesy of Henry IV.

Wingfields Tower on Town Walls

Nowadays none of the town's gate-houses on its old medieval bridges survives. Nor, apart from the archway on St Mary's Water Lane, does it appear (as far as I'm aware) that any of the old gates remain. However, parts of the old walls remain, and amongst them is one of its original towers, now gently leaning with age.

I'm talking about Wingfield's Tower on Town Walls. After ceasing to be required for defensive purposes, it was leased to a big wool merchant family called Waring. A ground floor crossbow slit was blocked up when a fireplace was installed, but other arrow slits still remain.

The battlements are reckoned to be a later addition. The tower's slate-roofed lean-to was added in the 19th century as a privy. When it became known as Wingfield's Tower, or why, I've no idea.

By 1816, the tower was the workshop of the watch-maker, John Massey. In the 1860s it was converted into a dwelling, and provided accommodation for the coachman at Swan Hill Court, whose gates lie opposite to the tower to this day.

In 1930, Rachel Hunter of Swan Hill Court made over the tower to the National Trust. It was occupied until the 1980s, first from 1937 to 1954 by Mrs Janet Mitchell, then from 1954 to 1967 by Mrs B Curtis, then from 1968 to 2012, it was leased to Mr and Mrs Hector and then from 2012 to the present day by Shrewsbury High School.

Over the years, Wingfield's Tower has fascinated me enough to feature in my novel *Sabrina Fludde*. However, I'd never been inside until today's Open Day courtesy of the National Trust.

The interior of the tower is tiny, but surprisingly habitable. Fireplace, gaslights and panelling were added when it was made a dwelling in the 1860s. The glazed windows were fitted at this stage too, but the pavement outside the tower, installed to keep traffic at bay, didn't arrive until 1991.

You can clearly see this tower on the Burleigh Map of Shrewsbury, currently housed in the British Library. According to Phil Scoggins of Shrewsbury Museum, though this was a Tudor map the layout of the town will have been unchanged from medieval times.

I love it that our town was once walled, and that some of those walls remain. When I come home after being away, I have a wonderful sense of being enfolded by the town as I walk up Castle Gates. It reminds me of that old Reformation hymn by Martin Luther, 'Ein Feste Burg', 'A Safe Stronghold'. That's how I think of Shrewsbury. Long may it remain.

20th June: FLASH FICTION SHREWSBURY

Short, short stories have been written for a long time. Kafka did it, so did Chekov, and Hemingway's *'For sale: baby shoes, never worn'* has been quoted to death. The phrase 'flash fiction', however, is believed to have been coined back in 1992 as the title to an anthology of very short stories – and it's a name that's stuck.

Today flash fiction is being written, and read, all over the world. People have different ideas about how long flash should be. 1,000 words? 50? *10?* Ten's pushing it, I reckon. The good people who met at the Shrewsbury Coffeehouse last night to celebrate National Flash Fiction Day settled for 500.

Last year, Shrewsbury had the honour of launching the first National Flash Fiction Day on May 15th, Flash Fiction Eve. It was a huge success. People didn't just read their stories, they wrote them on the night, sometimes collaboratively, and in some cases with complete strangers. 'I haven't written a story since I was in primary school,' somebody said.

And she and others were back this year, raring for more.

In just one evening, we heard about Gabriel Rossetti's obsession with exotic animals; window-cleaners encountering ghosts; an annunciation

Shrewsbury Coffeehouse

for a new Virgin Queen; a couple of murder mysteries, one told from the point of view of the corpse; trench life in the First World War; the experience of being mum to a dysfunctional family; running away to join the Foreign Legion and much, much more. The stories were as diverse as the people who attended.

Also during the evening, the Flash Fiction Shrewsbury website was launched. The town already has its own Flash Fiction Shrewsbury Facebook page, but now here's a place for Shrewsbury's flash fiction writers to post their work.

At the end of the evening, 'Snow' by Julia Alvarez was read from the book 'Flash Fiction - 72 Very Short Stories', edited by James and Denise Thomas and Tom Hazuka. Here was a true master of flash at work. An inspiration to us all. *'Each snowflake was different,'* the story ends up, *'like a person, irreplaceable and beautiful.'* And that spoke for the whole evening. All those people, all those different takes on life. Shrewsbury has so much talent to offer.

21st June: MIDSUMMER NIGHT ON BECK'S FIELD

I remember one Midsummer night in South Shropshire, climbing a hill and finding fox cubs playing in a hayfield under a full moon. That was pretty special, but this Midsummer has been special too.

This morning, it was raining but I headed off for the allotment, calling in on Chris Quinn and Jessicah Kendrick on the way, proud parents of newborn Baby Austin. Yes, the Shrewsbury Coffeehouse baby has arrived. Even eight days into night feeding, Jessicah looked radiant. Today's her birthday. Baby Austin was celebrating the occasion by being asleep.

On the allotment, I found roses in bloom. I could smell them everywhere, courtesy of the rain. I spent a few happy hours on my knees pulling up armfuls of weeds, then filled a box with gooseberries and rhubarb and headed back home.

By this time the sun had come out. I strolled along the river at a leisurely pace, still smelling roses. Back home I found I couldn't bear to stay indoors. I tried weaving. I tried cleaning up my kitchen. I tried writing at my desk. The hours ticked by. I couldn't settle.

In the end I went out again, mooching round town until hunger got the better of me. At my favourite restaurant, The Golden Cross, I treated myself to a dinner for one. During my main course I read Robert McFarlane's new book, *The Old Ways*, downloaded onto my Kindle. During dessert, I listened to happy Japanese tourists laughing together and singing snatches of songs.

River Severn from Kingsland Bridge

I came out to find the sun so bright that still, at half past nine, I couldn't bring myself to go home. I cut up Swan Hill past the Coach & Horses pub, crossed Town Walls, passed the Girls' High School and headed across Kingsland Bridge where I caught a snatch of music coming from the Quarry, saw boys and girls sitting on the grass and stood watching the river flowing past, as dark and ruffled as a silk scarf (though later, when I returned, it was like mirror glass).

Finally I made it up here, to where I am now – Beck's Field, where the grass is long and tangled with buttercups. Beneath me on either side of the river I can see weeping willows and the tree-lined paths of the Quarry. Standing proud of them is the great dome of St Chad's Church.

I love it up here, overlooking the rooftops, treetops, towers and spires of our town. This is where you'll find me watching the fireworks on Shrewsbury Flower Show nights. And this is where I came a few years ago to witness a total eclipse of the sun. What better place to witness the wind drop and the birds fall silent, to see light bleaching out of the sky and the shadows of night appearing as the sun turns black?

And what better place, here and now, to watch the sun stay up like a naughty child refusing to go to bed. On the far side of the world the winter equinox is happening right now, black upon black. And here I am in Shrewsbury, basking in glorious light whilst the school bell tolls behind me, and St Chad's rings out the hour, and across the river kids go by on bikes, and looking down upon the town on this Midsummer's Night, I can't think of another place I'd want to be.

There's a path cutting through Beck's Field, weaving its way through long grass down to the river. Over dinner, my Robert McFarlane book talked about paths – walking them, and reading about them too. The compact between writing and walking was almost as old as literature, he said – 'a walk is only a step away from a story, and every path *tells*.'

I love that quote. I know exactly what McFarlane means. 'I can only meditate when I'm walking,' Rousseau wrote. 'When I stop, I cease to think.' His mind worked with his legs. I know what that means too.

23rd June: SHREWSBURY'S 1ST MARATHON

It's 7.00am, and I'm awake and limbering my writing muscles. Two hours to the start of Shrewsbury's first marathon, and am I going to have the stamina to stay the course? According to the *Shropshire Star*, thousands of people are going to be lining the streets, including the one just outside my own front door, to cheer on more people than joined up for the first year of the Edinburgh Marathon. Is that possible? 2,750 people running past my front door in only two hours time on a sleepy Sunday morning?

I head for the Quarry, which is where they're meant to start. At first the town appears its usual sleepy Sunday morning self, but as I get closer I catch snatches of music and then, yes, I swear I can hear a hum of voices.

Hum? By the time I reach the Quarry gates up by St Chad's Church, what I'm hearing is a muffled roar. I look down towards the river. 8.30am and *the Quarry is full of people.* There are numbered runners everywhere wearing evidence of origin or intent. I see a little group for Wrexham AC, another for Shrewsbury-based charity Medic Malawi, and here's a group running for the Teenage Cancer Trust.

Sophie and Amy Fewtrell lost their brother Adam to cancer two years ago. He was only twenty. Today Sophie and Amy, along with another Amy and Tilli are running in his memory, to raise awareness of the Teenage Cancer Trust. Adam spent much time in Birmingham's Teenage Unit, but the Teenage Cancer Trust would like to see a teenage ward in every hospital in every town and region.

Suddenly everybody's lining up to go. Down near the start line, I see a police team running in memory of Georgia Williams, the murdered teenage girl from Wellington in Telford. Music is booming out, courtesy of Radio Shropshire. People are queuing for last-minute loo-calls. All the organisers are waiting for now, apparently, is the all-clear from the town's cones-men, who are making some last-minute adjustments.

Shrewsbury Marathon, Castle Street

Whilst we're waiting for the off, I get talking to two runners, Anna Hughes and Emily Hunt, who are limbering up for the half-marathon which starts thirty minutes after the main one. They're sisters of BBC Radio Shropshire presenter Johnty O'Donty [O'Donnell], who does the Sunday morning Treasure Hunt. One of them is running with the Shrewsbury Runners, the other trains on the Peaks outside Sheffield, where she lives.

Suddenly it's lift-off time. The runners chant, 10,9,8,7,6,5,4,3,2,1... then, led by a team of cyclists, they're off. Not the fastest lift-off, but that's what pacing is all about, I guess. They've a long way to go.

I chunter after them, taking short cuts across town in the interest of keeping up with events. I see the first few runners reach the High Street. I pass a nice young man with an electric mandolin outside the Loggerheads pub. I pass three elderly ladies outside the bank, sitting on fold-up chairs, cheering on the runners.

Leaving the town centre, I head up to Kingsland and the marathon's turn-around point. By the time I reach Town Walls it's raining, but that doesn't seem to bother anybody. When I arrive at the turn-around point I find balloons hanging from trees, music playing loudly and a party atmosphere on the go, to keep up the runners' spirits.

Returning into town, I hear clapping and cheering everywhere I go. A crowd has gathered at the bottom of Wyle Cop to encourage runners as they head back over the English Bridge. I follow the route they're taking, along the river back towards the Quarry. A penguin plods past me and a man with a Shrewsbury Food Bank trolley. An older looking gentleman with terrible feet limps by. A woman drags herself along clutching a water bottle. 'You're looking comfortable,' a fellow runner encourages her. 'You can do it.'

An ambulance goes by. People make way for it. Down by the Start – which has been transformed into the Finish – Mayor Jon Tandy is preparing to present cups. The first few runners, I'm told, are in [Wayne Dashper, Tyson Dunning, Edward Hardy] and the rain is so heavy by now that it's running down the page as I attempt to write.

I walk away from the thick of the crowd around the Finish line. All around me I hear stories of triumph, fatigue and in some cases pain. Wounded runners wrapped in silver foil are attended to by physiotherapists. A woman is carried off the course. People make way for another ambulance to go by.

I pass a lady whom I saw running a couple of times in different places, each time looking as if she didn't know how to go on. Now she's finished. I have to stop to congratulate her. She looks so pleased with herself. I don't know your name, lady, because I forgot to ask, but if you ran the Marathon today and happen to live on Wenlock Road I might be talking about you.

26th June
FROM HEAVY METAL TO SHREWSBURY FOLK

It was the Severn Valley Railway that brought Alan and Sandra Surtees to Bridgnorth and it was Bridgnorth that originally housed what's now become the Shrewsbury Folk Festival. A small gathering of folkies was expected, but seven hundred happy campers turned up. By the time Robert Plant headlined on the fourth year, the Bridgnorth festival had outgrown its site.

'The Robert Plant thing,' says Alan Surtees, sitting in the lounge of the Lion Hotel, 'was a secret right until he went on stage. There would have been a riot if people had known who was about to perform.' 'He wore shorts,' Sandra recollects. 'He had lovely legs.'

The Band was billed as the Priory of Bryan. 'On they came,' Alan said, 'and nobody knew who they were. Then suddenly the penny dropped. We'd secured Robert Plant – knees and all – for one hundred quid. What a thing to have pulled off.'

Bromyard Festival is where Alan and Sandra first met, and festivals have been in their blood ever since. They both agree that Alan's the one for thinking big, and Sandra for scaling things down until they're do-able.

Sandra and Alan Surtees

'What we've worked to achieve is a festival with a good atmosphere, where strangers can talk to each other, children can play and learn in safety and people who see themselves as 'different' can fit in. All that, and good music too.' That's what Sandra says.

'The festival attempts to cater for everyone,' Alan says. 'Babies to eighty year olds. The music is really varied. People come to the Shrewsbury Folk Festival knowing that they'll discover new favourite artists every time.'

The Folk Festival has been in Shrewsbury since 2006, situated at the West Midland Showground. 'For a man who loves music, I'm now living the dream,' Alan says. 'Every year we get to pick the acts we like. We're not scared of trying something new. We like experimenting. We're not risk averse.'

This year 'not being risk averse' includes the comedy duo Doyle & Debbie, whom Alan and Sandra first heard in Nashville, making fun of the country music scene in the heart of the country music scene – and the country music aficionados lapped it up.

They've also booked big name bands, the Afro Celt Sound System, and Capercaillie with its Gaelic vocalist, Karen Matheson. They've secured a rare performance from Canada's Be Good Tanyas. Then there are the Oysterband, Eddi Reader, Heidi Talbot, and the Carolina Chocolate Drops, proving that it's not only wizened old white men from the Blue Ridge Mountains who can play real country.

'Artists get plenty of feedback when they perform at the Shrewsbury Folk Festival,' Alan says. 'In some festivals they get changed in the loos, go on stage, play, come off again and go home. Here we talk to them. We treat them well. We have a lovely reception area for them. We make them comfortable.'

Making people comfortable is key to what the Shrewsbury Folk Festival is about. It matters to everybody that children are safe and the facilities are good. John and Sandra put on a separate children's festival, its huge marquee providing workshops for children to make things like lanterns which they'll parade with at night.

What's the worst thing that's ever gone wrong, I want to know. Sandra remembers one headline band dropping out at only a day's notice, though they managed to find a replacement in time. However, when K.T. Tunstall's father died, she had to drop out on the day. No alternative headliners could be found, so Alan and Sandra put together a super group and had a folk slam instead.

Artists who'd never before played together piled onto the stage. Somebody had seen Maddy Prior about the festival in a yellow jacket with black polka dots – and the hunt was on to find that woman in yellow and black. Before the concert began, the excitement outside Marquee 2 was palpable. When the doors opened, people literally ran in. In thirty seconds the whole marquee was filled.

It's obvious that Sandra and Alan live, breathe and sleep the Shrewsbury Folk Festival. Sandra's been working on it full time since 1999. Alan retired from business three years ago, and is now full time too. What sort of business, I want to know. 'I had a steel fabrication company,' he says. 'From heavy metal to Shrewsbury Folk,' I think. 'Not a bad move.'

JULY

3rd July: LA VIE EN ROSE

Crossing St Alkmund's Square this morning, I caught a hint of perfume and found a delicate yellow rose. Then passing St Julian's I found flame-red climbers gracing the church wall. Then behind Old St Chad's, I came across blowsy pink roses growing up against the convent wall.

I love it that in a busy town centre with cars passing by you can still stop at the scent of a rose and look around to see where it is. Outside our house, a rose bush bought at one year's Flower Show is spreading across our old brick wall, scattering its blooms like stars.

I've been out this morning tying them back. Was this a particularly good year for roses, I wondered, or is it just that I was noticing them more? I ask Joyce of Lulu Flowers, and she reckons it's been a good year so far, courtesy of the rain. I'm in her shop, having a cup of tea, surrounded by beautiful blooms.

Joyce has owned Lulu Flowers for five years. It's a long way from her old life as a biker chick. She left Shrewsbury when she was young, thinking it had nothing for her, and became a member of the all-girl bike group, the Amazons. Her husband Terry was in a biker gang too. It was biking that brought him and Joyce together.

Joyce describes her biker days as a tumultuous decade awash with accidents, injury and ill-health. Some of the things she went through would set your hair on end, she says. She describes Terry as her rescuer, who brought her home when things got bad.

'Everything started going wrong for me when my mother died,' Joyce says. 'I was eighteen. Losing her, more than anything, was what loosened my connection with Shrewsbury.'

Joyce's mum grew up in Astley, near Hadnall, and worked for Silhouette. Her dad lived in Belle Vue. His memories included working at the Lion Hotel as a hotel porter. Joyce's nan worked at the Gala Bingo, and her grandfather was a train driver in the days of steam – his stoker was Terry's grandfather, which shows what a small world Shrewsbury is.

Joyce at work in Lulu Flowers

Joyce bought Lulu Flowers after her father died. A floristry shop seemed an ideal way of spending her inheritance. There was a magic moment, she says, when everything came together. The shop came on the market – and in a moment of madness she bought it.

'I wanted a shop that in some way reflected me,' Joyce says. 'I'm a very English girl at heart, I love the countryside and I wanted my shop to be English, flowery, natural and, I guess, feminine. But I wanted to mix things up a bit as well. I'm not a person who likes to keep things simple, so Lulu Flowers has a vintage side too.'

When Joyce bought it, Lulu Flowers was situated in School Gardens, tucked away behind Castle Gates. Now it's on Castle Street in a prime position on the other side of the street to Marks & Spencer's.

'Sometimes I'm overwhelmed with how pretty my shop is,' Joyce says, 'and absolutely thrilled at what I've achieved. Other times, I wish that I was tidier.' Behind the counter is an assortment of clipboards, notes, scissors, pots, bows, raffia and rolls of cellophane. Then mixed up with the flowers and plants is an assortment of vintage stuff – pretty tea and coffee sets, ornamental vases, pots and jugs, original paintings and interesting-looking sepia photographs.

What does Joyce do when she's not in the shop, I ask. She and Terry have a place in Criccieth, she says. She loves the beach and the open sky. She's done a bit of travelling in her time – Australia, the Far East, the USA.

Even here on Castle Street, Joyce feels in touch with the natural world. That's important to her. And so is returning to her roots. It's entirely fitting that she has a business in the heart of Shrewsbury. Joyce is a Shrewsbury lass through and through.

7th July: ANNIE COCKBURN, A.E. HOUSMAN & THOSE BLUE REMEMBERED HILLS

I've been thinking for a while about doing a *My Tonight From Shrewsbury* outside broadcast, and now here I am on the edge of the Long Mynd, in the garden of Annie Cockburn, specialist in play therapy with troubled children, occasional belly-dancer (Annie loves dancing) and long-time friend – and there couldn't be a better place for it than here.

The view from Annie's garden is world-class, facing two of Shropshire's most beautiful hills, Caer Caradoc and the Lawley. Sheep are grazing. Skylarks are singing in the air. From where I'm standing, the only road I can see is the sleepy little lane running down the side of Annie's house. Perfect.

Drovers would once have used that lane to bring sheep off the Mynd. Several times I've seen it filled with sheep, but those days are over now. All that's left are the cottages and farmsteads, and their barns as silent witnesses.

Annie's barn stores lawnmowers, garden chairs and a barbecue. Its upper section is used for parties and other social gatherings and its eaves house nesting swallows. Occasionally I've slept in it and awoken in the night to a scent in the air, lingering like the ghost of a long-forgotten harvest.

Annie decides that what we need is a walk round her garden. We head up her lawn, where hens once picked the dry earth beside her pond, vegetables grew in rows and goats in the pig shed waited to be milked. The dry earth is now a luxuriant green, the goats are no more and the hens nothing but a memory in the collective consciousness of the local fox community.

But the pond remains, willows hanging over it, turquoise damsel-flies cruising its surface and lilies opening out. It's surrounded by yellow irises, dots of forget-me-not and as many kingcups as I've ever seen in one place. Beyond the kingcups, a wilderness of monkey flowers – planted in the pond as just one single stem – tumble in chrome yellow profusion, dotted with pinkish grasses known in flowering time as Yorkshire fog.

This is the perfect month to be in Annie's garden. She's always trying to find ways of sharing it too. Sunshine only has to be predicted and she's on the phone. 'Why don't you come over? It's going to be a perfect day.'

We're back on the terrace now, sheltering from the sun under a huge umbrella, eating scrambled eggs and slabs of granary toast, washed down with home-made nectarine wine and strawberry ice cream. There's not a cloud in the sky. This is Shropshire at her most beautiful, wearing her summer colours, green upon green, the white of wild roses, the foamy cream of elderflowers, sunshine upon foxgloves, dots of yellow buttercups just about everywhere.

Caer Caradoc from Lower Wood

Every other year Annie's sons organise a little music festival on this land, bringing together bands and musicians who happen to be friends. This is a private event, no Glastonbury here, but tents will go up in Annie's fields, a bonfire will be lit and there'll be barbecueing and music. Annie's ex-husband Bob will perform with his guitar. Their son's band, The Seven Inches, will sing their own idiosyncratic, highly original songs, and my family's own small band will bring to life an eclectic mix of blues and folk with a bit of doo-wop jazz thrown in.

It's all fairly homespun, just people who like each other getting together – in some cases growing old together – and doing it in a spectacular landscape.

People drive through Shropshire, heading for Wales, no idea what they are passing by. For those who linger, however, the fundamental elements of the landscape are recognisably the same as when the poet, A.E. Housman, wrote wistfully about the county in his book of verse, *A Shropshire Lad*.

If Housman were to come back now, even though he'd find the way of life very different, this would still be his Shropshire – just as it's mine. I moved here forty years ago, a young woman without roots, raised a family and found a home.

11th July: AT MY WINDOW WITH A BROKEN WING

If you recognise the above quote, odds are that you belong to that generation for whom Bob Dylan speaks for a surprising number of situations.

Yesterday morning I found a bird on my windowsill. Upon closer examination, it wasn't the raven of Dylan's 'Love Minus Zero, No Limit', but neither was it an ordinary Shrewsbury pigeon. Dove-grey with a pinkish breast, it had an air of dignity – and that's not anything I've ever noticed in the local pigeon population.

Later in the morning, sunning myself on my front step, I noticed  the bird hopping about looking ever so slightly agitated. I propped a sunshade against the railings, and it perched in the shade. After that, the two of us sat side by side. I wondered what made it so comfortable with human company. It didn't look sick. Its wings appeared to work. It hadn't been shot.

On the off-chance that heatstroke was an issue, I put down some water. Apart from a quick flap, however, the bird's day ended where it had begun, back on my windowsill. Its feathers ruffled up, it tucked in it's chin and it hunkered down for the night.

Dove sheltering under fig tree

The bird was still there when I came downstairs today. Its eyes were open, but it looked asleep. I made some coffee, cleared up last night's meal. When I looked again, the bird had gone. Perhaps it had had the rest it needed and was heading home like all the other tourists who come to Shrewsbury and return refreshed.

17th July: AT THE PUB WITH SUSAN CAROLINE OF PENGWERN BOOKS

It's a warm summer evening, and I'm in the Dog & Pheasant on Castlefields with Susan Caroline, talking about Pengwern Books. Keeping an independent bookshop in business in the current climate has taken a lot of ducking and diving. Susan's doggedness is astonishing.

After starting life on Fish Street, Pengwern Books has had a variety of homes, not least being to the immediate right of the altar in St Alkmund's Church. At a time when it looked as though Shrewsbury's only independent contemporary bookshop might go down, this proved a refuge in a storm. These days, however, Pengwern Books is thriving in Shrewsbury's indoor market.

Susan talks about her lifelong love of books. From an early age she was a fast reader. The reps are astonished, she says, at the speed with which she can rattle through a book from cover to cover. One holiday she recalls heading out to Greece with 14 books, none of which (including Brian Keenan's *An Evil Cradling*) were light reading – and none of which returned unread.

I hardly ever pass by Pengwern Books without wanting to buy something. The shop may be small in terms of floor space, but it packs a powerful punch. Susan acknowledges how important her shop window is. She says she's never knowingly bought an ugly book. 'Design is important,' she says. 'The cover really matters. But when it comes to buying in stock I go on gut instinct. I know my customers. I have an eye for what they'll like. But there's no particular formula to it.'

Susan's choices don't come from reviews. She very rarely reads them, much to my surprise. The reps come in, ['I'm blessed with great reps'], and she goes through their lists saying *no, no, no,* then suddenly there will be a *hang on there*, followed by a *yes, I'll take that one.*

Price is a consideration. It's vital to stock books people can afford. Susan tends not to go for hardbacks, though she makes occasional exceptions, such as Matthew Sewell's lovely *Our Garden Birds*. 'People want books as entertainment,' Susan says. 'They don't all want Booker Prize winners. Good writing doesn't have to be unattainable. And just because it's populist doesn't make it bad.'

I ask Susan to name a few books she would recommend. Sophie McKenzie comes up first, with her novel *Falling Fast*. It's great for teens, Susan says, and anyone interested in the subject of growing up. The first novel by Annabel Pitcher, *My Sister Lives on the Mantelpiece*, is another quite amazing book, and Susan has a high regard for Dick Francis and what she calls 'his intelligent, respectful writing'. Then there's Susan Cain's *Quiet: The Power of Introverts In A World That Can't Stop Talking*. Then there's Raymond Feist's *The Magician*, which should definitely be in everybody's Top 100 books, and the list goes on and on.

Pengwern Books has amassed many loyal customers over the years. One used to ply Susan with chocolates on a weekly basis, and had to be stopped. There are others who'll come in for tea and a chat, and others whom Susan has met literally on the street outside her shop and persuaded to come in – and they've been coming in ever since. 'People either have to use their local bookshops, or they lose them,' Susan says. 'It's as simple as that.'

Susan is making an important point here. Without independent bookshops run by dedicated booksellers, reading will become blander – and writing will too. It's the independents who have nursed the career of many a writer through their troughs to their successes. Hilary Mantel is an author Susan mentions. Would her publishers have stuck by her, she asks, without traditional bookselling keeping her in the public eye?

All very well, but how can independent bookshops compete with the online market and the convenience of click-and-deliver shopping, especially for those who don't have time to rifle and browse? Susan has a cunning plan. 'Go to www.hive.co.uk,' she says. 'It's a massive online shop set up by Gardner's, one of the UK's biggest book wholesalers and the last of the independents. They've provided an online platform for purchasing books. All you have to do is set up an account, just as you would with Amazon, select your local bookshop as your nominated store and that shop will reap the benefit as if you'd shopped in it personally. You can buy online to your heart's content, and have deliveries to your home, but you're not doing down your local independent. In fact, you're helping it.'

You have to be ingenious to sell books these days. Susan has kept Pengwern Books alive for nine years. Helping her have been her son, Ben Draper, and Lorna Godwin, whom she describes as having 'forgotten more than I'll ever know'. Then there are Andrew Johnson and Hilary Hannaford, who both worked with Susan for many years.

Andrew brought a knowledgeable breadth of history, politics and current affairs to the mix sold by Pengwern Books, and Hilary was brilliant at customer relations and the actual business of selling. 'People think you can just set up and sell books and press the till,' Susan says, 'but there's so much more to it than that. Even in my tiny shop I have room for an armchair and a kettle. You have to get to know your customers in this business. And Andrew and Hilary understood that. They were a joy to work with, and I'd have them back in a flash if I could.'

Susan Caroline in Pengwern Books

So what about the future, I ask. Susan recalls a ticketed author event she put on a few years ago involving Alan Titchmarsh. People queued for half an hour beforehand in order to get a good seat, and even those without tickets waited on the street to catch a glimpse of the great man.

'I wouldn't mind doing a few more events like that,' Susan says. 'I dream of having a café and gallery, too. I'm always thinking about ways of diversifying. Working the way I do is bloody hard sometimes, but I'm proud of Pengwern Books. The written word is so important. I love what I do.'

Susan's dedication to Pengwern Books is second to none. Extrovert and friendly, she's a real presence in her shop. Recently she had a short trip to hospital but, within hours, was planning tomorrow's tasks and how quickly she could get out. 'That's what it's like,' she says, 'when you're running a business. Sometimes people can be a real help, but there are some things only you can do for yourself.'

21st July: SIMON BARFORD'S PORTRAITS

Simon Barford is my hairdresser. He's great at cutting hair, and even better at painting portraits. At the end of the day, after work in Toni & Guy, and spending time with the family, his time is his own to paint. One day he'd love to paint full time. To earn his living from it – and why not? Already Simon's work is selling, and he's only been painting for the last three years.

A couple of days ago, Simon brought over a few canvasses for me to photograph, and told me his story. His painting life began three years

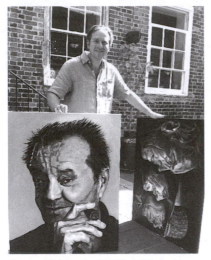

Simon Barford with Jack Nicholson and Clint Eastwood

ago when a friend turned forty. On his present list was a reproduction of a George Ioannou painting of Michael Caine. Simon took one look and thought *I could do that.* It was his eureka moment.

Simon had never much cared for art in school, but then as a dyslexic he'd never much cared for anything. Inspired, however, he bought a canvas and a small set of acrylics and set off, producing a painting that everybody told him was indistinguishable from the Ioannou original.

Certainly, as fortieth birthday presents went, it was a hit. Suddenly friends wanted portraits of other subjects. Simon was in business. Clint Eastwood? He'd give him a go. Steve McQueen the same. Jack Nicholson too, and Desmond Tutu. Somebody even wanted the minis from '*The Italian Job*'.

Just like that, Simon had discovered what he wanted to do with the rest of his life. There's no bigging up about him, no fuss. He knows he has a lot to learn, but he loves what he's doing. 'I'm a copyist,' Simon said in matter-of-fact fashion, 'but I reckon I'm good at it.'

On his father-in-law's sixtieth birthday, Simon wanted to give him a painting of his favourite corner of the Lake District. This was a departure from the portraits he'd produced so far. Simon looked at the work of William Heaton Cooper, found a photo of the appropriate landscape and painted it in Heaton Cooper's style. When his father-in-law saw it, so convinced was he that Simon had bought an original that he scolded him for spending so much money. Simon owned up – but the present was no less appreciated.

Simon's criteria for embarking upon a commission is very simple. He has to feel a sense of urgency about doing it, and he needs to come up with an unusual angle to work from – maybe a photograph, definitely something that rings a bell, tells something about a person or has its own particular quirk.

'Each painting takes about fifty hours,' Simon told me. 'And most of them will be painted big. I've no idea if I'm doing it right because I've never been taught, but all my paintings start the same way.'

Simon wants his paintings to tell a story. 'It's important not to overwork them,' he said. 'I think I've developed a sense of when I should stop.'

Simon is full of ideas. At the moment he's fascinated by magic of the sleight-of-hand variety. He'd love to do some paintings showcasing conjurors' hands in the process of performing tricks.

He'd paint all the time if he could, he told me. Then he packed up his paintings and went back to work.

23rd July: BLOOMIN' SHREWSBURY

My favourite entrance to Shrewsbury is beneath the railway bridge from St Michael Street, which isn't the prettiest street in Shrewsbury, but when you come out the other side the view is so dramatic and surprising. Nothing prepares you for the railway station's crenellated roofscape, or your first glimpse of the castle, or the cluster of little shops on Castle Gates – the artisan bakers, the coffeehouse, Pomona the greengrocer, its wares spilling out onto the pavement – as the road winds uphill, steep and narrow to what looks like another castle (the Castle Gates Library) at the top.

I mention this in passing because this is the way I came into town this morning after a stint on the allotment, only to find girls in period costume in the library garden selling posies, and gardeners leaning on their hoes, looking as if they were waiting for something special to happen.

Andy, Jake and David were the gardeners' names. I asked what was going on, and was directed over the road to the castle where Shrewsbury Drama Person Extraordinaire, Maggie Love, was in period costume too, and the town's Youth Theatre was having a Pyramus and Thisbe moment from *A Midsummer Night's Dream*.

Maggie McKean

Today was Britain in Bloom Day, Maggie explained, and, even as we spoke, the judges were on their way.

I rushed home, dug out my favourite floral waistcoat – which felt like the least I could do in the circumstances – and spent the rest of the morning ducking and diving around Shrewsbury in the wake of the judges.

There was plenty of other dressing up to be found. Outside St Mary's Church I encountered Lady Penelope Penhaligon looking for the Raven Hotel [long-since replaced by H&M]. Outside St Alkmund's, I met a small group of council officials, including Town Clerk Helen Ball wearing a hat. Outside Bear Steps, I met Lady Christine and her maid, whose costumes I mistook for ladies of the night. They were not impressed.

At the top of Grope Lane, I encountered the real ladies of the night. One told me she was Sarah Salisbury of the late 16th century, born in Shrewsbury, but died in London. She might have told me more, but a man appeared and she had to break off for a bit of cat-calling.

I carried on down Grope Lane into the Square, which was full of dancers performing what may or may not have been quadrilles. The town crier was in full gear (is it something in the water that gives Shrewsbury the tallest town crier in the country AND the tallest MP?) and a couple of hecklers/scutchers/spinners from the Ditherington Flax Mill were in action.

The Square was packed, the press of people added to by an exodus from the Job Centre, courtesy of a fire alarm. Don't these things always happen just when you don't want them to?

I left them all to it, heading for the quiet calm of the judges' final destination – the Dingle in Shrewsbury's Quarry. Here I found Margaret, daughter of Percy Thrower, standing before her famous father's bust. Once she and her family had lived in the black-and-white house by the Quarry gates. In fact her two sisters had been born upstairs. Now used by the Horticultural Society, it had been Percy's house when he was Head Gardener.

How did Shrewsbury fare in the judging stakes? I've no idea. All I know is that there were flowers everywhere, and even some vegetables thrown into the mix. Shrewsbury looked a picture. But then when doesn't it? You tell me.

27ᵗʰ July: STOP PRESS – THE ANGEL AWARDS

A couple of days ago I dropped into St Alkmund's Church, attracted by the wide open doors and pinpricks of candlelight burning before the altar. The ends of the pews were decorated with white gauze bows for a wedding, but they made the church look like something out of Swan Lake.

I only meant to stay for a moment, but with sunlight pouring through the church's clear-glass windows, I couldn't tear myself away. I took a photograph of the ornate gold work on the dove-grey organ. I photographed a plinth of flowers before the altar, and the painted lady in the window behind it. I photographed the pews, the aisle and the west window of the church, through which yet more sunlight was streaming. I felt as if I'd stepped out of ordinary life into a place where time, well, was just *different*.

Just as I was thinking this, up popped Resident Priest, Richard Hayes. Richard is an enthusiastic man at the best of times, but even by his own standards he was fizzing. Had I heard the news, he wanted to know, big grin on face (and when Richard grins, his whole face lights up)? St Alkmund's had been short-listed for English Heritage's prestigious Angel Awards.

I hadn't heard – not of the short-listing, nor in fact of the Angel Awards, which Richard explained were sponsored by the Andrew Lloyd Webber Foundation and supported by the *Daily Telegraph*. There to celebrate the efforts of local people to save historic buildings, the judging panel is chaired by Andrew Lloyd Webber, and this year's judges include English Heritage Chief Executive, Simon Thurley, Charles Moore of the *Telegraph* and the Bishop of London, the Rt Revd Richard Chartres.

Reverend Richard Hayes in gardening kit

No wonder Richard was smiling. The criteria for winning extended beyond buildings being at risk to communities cherishing and working for their restoration. The judges were looking for vision in the restoration work, and a sense of inspiration and imagination.

For St Alkmund's to have made this short-list was a real feather in its cap, but should it win, the feather will be in Shrewsbury's cap too. St Alkmund's is an integral part of town-centre life. Surrounded by fine old trees and ancient buildings, it's at the heart of the town's shopping and business district, standing on a site that has housed a church since around 900AD.

The restoration of St Alkmund's has included re-roofing, installing subtle, near-invisible photo-voltaic panels, re-glazing windows with handmade, clear glass (matching the 18th century originals), re-decorating walls, restoring the painted East Window, installing a kitchen and toilets and generally bringing the building into a good state of repair. This has been a massive project for St Alkmund's congregation to undertake.

The finals [sorry, 'glittering Awards Ceremony' is what it says on the website] of the Angel Awards will take place on October 21st in Westminster Theatre. A small group from St Alkmund's will attend. Richard and I made our farewells and I headed home, leaving behind long shafts of sunlight pouring through the windows – and one happy priest.

29th July: LILY'S RIVERSIDE TEA GARDEN

Ms X and I decided to take afternoon tea (in her case strawberry milkshake) in the sunshine of Lily's Riverside Tea Garden. Where else in Shrewsbury were we likely to find stuffed monkeys hanging from trees, lantern-lit grottoes, swans gliding across mirror-glass lakes, a fairy castle, a naked doll sun-bathing on a doll-sized park bench and hedges stuffed with soft toys?

Exploring was irresistible. Most of our visit was spent with Ms X running full-pelt around the maze of paths, making extraordinary discoveries in the realm of gnomes and fountains, me hurrying after her, worrying that she might trip on something, pitch into the river or simply disappear.

If you've never been to Lily's, you're missing a treat. It's on Smithfield Road, opposite the bus station. Lily has lived there for twenty-five years. When she moved in, her garden had no privacy. People were continually looking over the wall at its view of the river, so Lily started planting trees and tall shrubs for shelter. She started building arches too, and creating nooks and crannies that gave her endless pleasure. Then she thought *why not let other people enjoy this instead of keeping it to myself* – and that was the start of Lily's Riverside Tea Garden.

'I have it open for six months of the year,' Lily said. 'It doesn't make a fortune, but I like having it, and it covers its costs.' She's very matter-of-fact about things. Like the flooding. Over the years, Lily's grown accustomed to the Severn's floods. 'Just by looking at the river I can guess what I'm in for,' she said. 'Then everything has to be moved up higher. Sometimes I lose things. I'll leave something behind, reckoning the river won't budge it, but I'll be wrong.'

Nothing daunts Lily for long. In the early days her garden was a mass of brambles, but now everywhere you look her love of gardening shows. Her husband's no gardener, she says, but her dad and brother have both been gardeners, and as a carpenter her husband has shaped the garden in other ways. 'We didn't plan this,' Lily said. 'It all just happened bit by bit.'

Over the years, Lily's had her share of problems. When it rained she used to have trouble with paths coming up. Then her wall collapsed into the river, revealing a methane problem in the culverts beneath her garden.

It took three years for Severn Trent to put this right. Eventually they rebuilt Lily's collapsed bank with steel, but the council forced them to do it again with brick. For several years, there was precious little garden – and definitely no tea – but now everything is safe, secure and thriving again.

Visiting Lily's garden is like looking into a person's face. Lily declined

Ms X exploring

to be photographed, but she didn't need to be – her garden speaks for her. Where did all the grottoes, golden Buddhas, swans, Shivas, children's toys and Chinese lanterns come from, I wondered.

Lily said she and her husband used to be licensees of the Albion Vaults. One Christmas Lily decorated its windows for a competition, which the Vaults won. At New Year she did it again. Her regulars liked it. She did it for Valentine's Day and then, almost without thinking, the changing window decorations became a feature of the Albion Vaults.

Recently Lily has handed over the day-to-day running of the tea garden to her daughter, Dirrie. Lily and her husband have four children, three boys and a girl. Sometimes Lily's daughter-in-law helps out too, and her granddaughters have worked as waitresses.

There's a distinct family feel about the place. While I was there, people kept coming in who were either regulars or family and friends. 'Afternoon, Chris...' 'Hot enough for you, Jim...' 'Dirrie, there's a family down by the corner, haven't been seen to yet...' Lily may no longer be in charge, but her eyes, I noticed, didn't miss a thing.

AUGUST

2nd August: SPEAKING UP FOR THE STEW

In the early Middle Ages, the ford in the River Severn between Shrewsbury and Frankwell was one of the town's few crossing points. Then the fortified (and partly inhabited) St George's Bridge was built in the mid-12th century, linking Frankwell to the end of Mardol. This bridge became known as Welshman's Bridge in the 13th century.

A number of buildings in Frankwell show evidence of development in medieval times. By the 16th century, Frankwell was a prosperous area, adjoining a thriving river port-of-call. The Anchor pub, still standing today, stood in line to the old Welshman's Bridge. That bridge came down, however, and was replaced by the present Welsh Bridge in the 1790s.

Nowadays there's not much left on the Quay to remind us of those distant days when the Welshman's Bridge spanned the river with its towers and jumble of dwellings. But the very last vestiges of that bridge were found as recently as the

On Frankwell Quay: The Stew and the Guildhall

building of Shrewsbury's theatre, and not far from them is The Stew, which, remaining as it does from those old days, is part of the reason why Frankwell Quay is a conservation area.

If you're wondering which building I'm talking about, it's the fenced-off, abandoned-looking building immediately adjacent to the Guildhall, which you may have walked or driven past and thought *why doesn't somebody do something about that place?* Well, its owner wants to. Over a period of years, the building has fallen into disrepair, and he's put in for planning permission to have it demolished and a boutique hotel built on the site instead. He doesn't reckon The Stew is worth saving. But there are people who do, and I'm one of them.

The Stew may currently look a bit of a wreck, but it's a repairable wreck with an honourable history, rooted in Shrewsbury's trading past. Once our sleepy River Severn was the second busiest river in Europe. As river highways went, it was the motorway of the 18th century, giving legs to the Industrial Revolution – and one of its thriving ports was here in Shrewsbury.

The early 16th century was when river trade really kicked off in our town. Mardol Quay was where much of the action took place, but Frankwell Quay, built in 1607 by Roland Jenks, soon became important, with all the appendages of a busy port – storehouses, chandlers, warehouses and, in the 18th century, on the site of a much older building, The Stew.

If you live in Shrewsbury, go and take a look for yourselves. Photographs don't convey the imposing nature of the building. Part of it used to be a fine old merchant's house, of the same date and with the same sort of dressed stone, as the Old Guildhall on Dogpole. It doesn't take much imagination to see what it could be restored to, and the impact that would have on Frankwell Quay.

So significant a building is The Stew that the current Guildhall was designed around its features, in an attempt to complement them. This is a conservation area, and rightly so. With a decision looming on the future of The Stew, this is our chance to speak up. Let's work to save this landmark building on historic Frankwell Quay.

5th August: BRITANNIA IN BLOME

How about this as a description of Shrewsbury:

"The Severn is navigabale to Schrosbery. At the entrance there is a suburb, the church of which appears to me to have formerly belonged to some fine abbey.

"I ascended from thence to the town; which is mounted on the platform of a rock, scarped on almost every side, which renders its situation naturally strong. Besides which, the wall that encloses it made it difficult to be scaled.

"The environs consist of large woods, and high mountains. Nevertheless, the town is filled with people and rich shopkeepers, who dwell in two large streets, one leading to the market-place, and the other turning towards the left. Near which are the Great Church, the Exchange and Town-hall.

"They are in a street called Aystrit, which is so broad, that it seems a long market-place, terminating at one of the ends of the town, where stands the Castle and commands it ; being more elevated and by so much the stronger, environed on one side by broad ditches, closed with good walls, and on the other there is no approach, on account of the steepness of the rock. But it has been ruined by the late wars, insomuch that, excepting a few towers, and some lodgings within, I see nothing remarkable."

Inside Candle Lane Books

Read this too:

"For largeness, neatness of buildings, both publick and private, variety of streets and populousness, [the town] may be ranged in the number of cities of the first rank.

"It is a town of good strength, as well by nature as by art ; being fenced about with a strong wall; besides another bulwark ranging from the Castle unto, and in part along, the Severn; through which there are entrances into the town: on the East and West, by two fair stone bridges, with gates, towers, and barrs: and on the North by a strong gate, over which is mounted the Castle, once exceedingly strong.

"It is a place of great resort, and well inhabited by the English and the Welsh, who speak both speeches: and enjoyeth a great trade for cloths, cottons, frizes and a variety of other commodities: this being the common mart between England and Middle Wales."

Both these accounts are from H. Owen and J.B. Blakeway's *History of Shrewsbury*, published in 1825 – which I've just bought in first edition from Candle Lane Books. The first is a piece of 17th century travel writing published in Paris in 1672. The second is taken from Britannia of Blome, a geographical description of the kingdoms of England, Scotland and Ireland, with the isles and territories *'thereto belonging, enobled with illustrations, the like never before seen'.*

Richard Blome was active as a seller of maps and books in the late 17th century. The Britannia was his principal work, though it was described by some as plagiarism, and said to include poorly drawn and sketchy maps. I've seen his maps, however, and they don't look sketchy to me. Google him. He's worth looking up.

8th August
OPEN STUDIO – NATHALIE HILDEGARDE LIEGE

Nathalie is a tall woman with sharp eyes behind her specs and a long dark plait. Today she has a flower tucked into her hair. She claims not to be naturally talkative, especially about her work, but sharing is obviously very important to her.

Nathalie grew up in the suburbs of south-east Paris, the daughter of a computer analyst father and seamstress mother, who made the wedding dress for the Russian bride of Prince Michel Magaloff. 'I regret that I don't remember it,' Nathalie says. 'I was in the womb when that dress was made and only a few months old when the wedding took place in the Russian Orthodox Cathedral in Paris.'

Nathalie studied Fine Art at the Sorbonne where the concept of plastic art was stretched to include poetry, theology, psychology and ethnology. Afterwards she worked in the Pompidou Centre, where she was influenced by the work of Louise Bourgeois, which she saw at close hand. 'There was something in it,' she says. 'Half-serious, half-naughty. Something very French.'

Nathalie came to the UK in 1995. In France she'd found stained-glass designers and manufacturers functioning in two separate worlds. In the UK, however, the two were brought together, which was what she wanted.

Initially Nathalie attended the Swansea Institute, but she left after the first year, disappointed by the course and put off by a neighbour's being stabbed. 'I had to rescue him from a bath of blood at four in the morning,' Nathalie said. 'It was the final straw. I moved to Wrexham University, where I was much happier.'

Nathalie graduated in 1998 and received the Worshipful Company of Glaziers and Painters of Glass Journeyman's Award for 1998–2000. To begin with her studio was in Ironbridge, but she's now situated in the English Bridge Workshops in Shrewsbury. Here she produces stained glass for private commissions as well as public and worship sites.

Nathalie Hildegarde Liege

Currently Nathalie is working on windows for St James's, Ryhill in Yorkshire, in memory of parishioner June Mary Cooper, based on the theme of Our Lady of Walsingham. Concurrently she is working on a series of fine art pieces whose source are the words *Enter into the rocks and hide in the earth,* taken from the Bible – Isaiah 2 v.10.

For a number of years Nathalie battled with lymphoma, of which she is now clear, but having cancer changed her perspective. 'Before, my work was very different. I was searching for something, but I couldn't make it into one whole. I'd been on a long journey since the age of ten, moving from a position of atheism to one of belief. I finally became a Greek Orthodox Christian in the year 2000.'

Nathalie says that her spiritual life is of prime importance in choosing ideas to develop into pieces of art. 'We're called to be humble towards things, but so often we're far from humble towards nature and what is given to us. This is something that I want to get across,' she says.

Many of Nathalie's images, based on ideas she's been developing for years, involve recycled or reused items. Before the lymphoma, her focus was different. Now the narrative drive of her work 'just keeps going, keeps going.' She sees her work as a form of storytelling.

I'm fascinating by one image on the studio wall – a head drowning in a sea of grass. Nathalie relates it back to her cancer, when her mother was ill too, slowly dying from an incurable illness. This difficult time, Nathalie now says, was 'an evolution in who I am'.

Nathalie's second name, Hildegarde, is her Orthodox one. Becoming Orthodox is plainly a big thing for her. She grew up typically French Catholic, baptised as a baby but unlikely to enter church again except for her wedding day. This non-activity to the point of unbelief, she feels, impacted on the way she worked, tied to deadlines, a slave to the notion of slogging it out.

Now, however, she is more flexible. When she feels that something is happening that shouldn't be lost, she will say 'no' to whatever gets in its way. She's more finely tuned to the life of the spirit working in her, on behalf of others. She feels that what she's learning, and is able to create, shouldn't just be kept for herself. 'Why not share more?' she asks.

Many of Nathalie's pieces speak of silence, everything stripped bare except the layers of self, one inside the other, interconnected mutely, as she puts it, by 'the mystery of who we are'. A sense of change runs through her pieces, a sense of what we on earth can hope to aspire to, and what change can do to us, 'as bitter sometimes,' Nathalie says, 'as it is sweet.' I notice a fascinating mix of control and lack of it in some pieces. Nathalie smiles. 'That's life,' she says with a half-shrug.

In recent years, Nathalie has been writing. Poetry at the Sorbonne had for her been an intense experience, 'two years of smoke-filled rooms' is how she describes it. Her poetry began as personal, not for publication, but encouraged by the poet Liz Lefroy, Nathalie now writes in French and translates into English, reads at poetry events in Shrewsbury and also writes occasional pieces of fiction.

On the back burner is an idea for a series of small books giving voice to the complex emotions lodged in a child's heart in the face of illness. This voice draws on Nathalie's having been ill herself and losing her mother at the same time, experiencing everything stripped away except the little child inside.

'The aim is to speak words of truth in clear, simple language whilst the adults speak mysteries in long words to do with chemotherapy and drugs regimes. *Mummy loves you*, the voice inside translates. *You are her little darling.* These are the words the child needs to hear.'

I like the way Nathalie puts things. To me, much about her voice harks back to Louise Bourgeois being 'half-serious, half-naughty, very French'. 'Days are ongoing creations,' she says. I like that. And I like it when she says, 'When I present myself as an artist, before and beyond anything else I'm Nathalie Hildegarde, a manifold being, *touche-à-tout.*'

10ᵗʰ August: SHREWSBURY FLOWER SHOW

In 1857, Shrewsbury's Carnation and Gooseberry Show changed its name to the Flower Show and moved from Frankwell to a marquee in the town centre. It continued until the First World War, then was revived in 1920. By the Second World War, it was held in the Quarry, Shrewsbury's main park. Except for the years when the Quarry was dug over for allotments as part of Shrewsbury's war effort, it's been there ever since.

And now it's Flower Show time again. All the usual pageantry (military band, Mayor and entourage etc) has taken place, and people are jostling to get in through the main gates to the strains of a steel band playing 'You Are My Sunshine'.

I'm amongst them. I know the Flower Show won't spring many surprises, but I'm not here for surprises. I'm here for the marquees, the fireworks in the evening and to see a few friends.

Inside the Judging Tent, Shrewsbury Flower Show

The Flower Show is a great place for meeting people. Before I'm even through the gates I bump into Karen Higgins of The Big Busk. Then, inside the Showground, I bump into ex-councillor and good friend Bill Morris, then Helen Ball, Town Clerk, in a pink flowery hat, then my old friend, artist Penny Timmis, holding court amongst her canvasses in one of the hospitality suites.

After stopping to chat, I head down to the river where the oldest working narrow-gauge steam engine is huffing up and down. There's a real mix of stuff down here – stalls with fluffy toys, garden furniture and Orthotic Works, whatever they might be. A man is attempting to sell the Light n' Easy Eco Deluxe Steam Mop ('I'll be honest with you...' his sales patter begins). Another is selling Gnu Airers. *What are they?*

In the distance I hear a male voice choir singing Men of Harlech. Following the sound to the bandstand I bump into my Welsh friend, Dai – no mean singer himself. For a few minutes we listen together, then I'm off again, heading for the main marquees, where the competition-class fruit, flowers and vegetables are to be found.

Here I wander from marquee to marquee, past the smoothest potatoes I've ever seen, the biggest onions and carrots so exquisitely tapered that it's hard to believe they're real. I find cabbages with elephant ears, cauliflowers with hearts as big as dining-plates and gooseberries as big as apples (well, maybe crabapples).

Some marquees celebrate the produce of local gardeners and gardening clubs, others showcase the market leaders in the horticultural industry. I walk between banks of feathery grasses, a riot of carnivorous plants and a mind-blowingly colourful display of bougainvillea. Outside I even come across a scarecrow competition – and the best 'man' most definitely has won.

I head down to the showground to find white-helmeted motorbike riders making way for show jumpers. 'It's Tim Davies on Salome II,' says the voice over the sound system. 'Smack on the time. That's a clean round. Tim Davies on Salome II leading by five seconds ex-act-ly...'

In the evening, I'm back for Bellowhead, where seats and blankets are not an option and any right-thinking person is on the hallowed turf, bobbing up and down waving their arms. The best fun's to be had right in front of the stage within breathing distance of the band. These boys and girls certainly know how to work a crowd.

After Bellowhead, the turf is cleared and spotlights come on. It's nearly fireworks time, but first there's 'Land of Hope And Glory' to get through, followed by 'Jerusalem', 'Rule Britannia' and the English and Welsh national anthems (I have to come clean, Englishwoman that I am, and say how much I love Land of My Fathers – now *that's* an anthem).

The Flower Show fireworks are a Shrewsbury institution. Never mind the 50,000 people who'll watch from inside the Showground – on the bridges, in pub gardens all over town, on the streets and up on Beck's Field, with its view of fireworks reflected in the water, it's party time.

With the first bang, we're all lit up, courtesy of Reverend Ron Lancaster's Kimbolton Fireworks, our faces raised before a night sky full of exploding stars – little kids again, gasping and wowing as the fireworks go off, bang, bang, bang.

Then darkness falls. For fifteen dazzling minutes we've been drawn together by a bit of magic, courtesy of gunpowder and fire. Now we head for the exits, the Flower Show over for another year, and suddenly there's a sense of summer on the wane. A lone piper pipes us out to 'Scotland the Brave'. The man at the gate says, 'Thank you,' and 'Goodnight' as if each of us was his personal guest. A typical Shrewsbury gesture, that.

14th August
THE EXTRAORDINARY HISTORY OF THE STEW

Forgive me. I'm back on The Stew again, but its history gets more exciting the more I look into it. The earliest mention of a building on its site goes back to 1405 when James Callerode (also known as Dyer) conveyed The Stew, comprising land, a croft and dovecote to his son Thomas. It's described as being immediately upstream from the St George's Bridge [later known as the Welshman's Bridge].

Some years later, in an agreement designed to resolve debt issues, a group including Edmund, Earl of March – joined later by Richard of York, the Earl's powerful heir – were invested with possession of The Stew as a freehold estate. These were the days of the Wars of the Roses, when two powerful Plantagenet lines, both descendants of Edward III, fought for the crown of England. Richard of York had a claim to the throne of England on the Yorkist (ie. white rose) side, and the Lancastrian (red rose) side was represented by Henry VI, son of Henry V, who became king at the age of eighteen and developed a well-earned reputation for being easily swayed.

In 1433 Richard of York signed a release on the Dyer lands, including The Stew. However, in 1445 a new agreement was drawn up, and again his name was included on it. The word used for this agreement was an enfeoffment – an old English word with Norman origins going back to feudal society, but also used in property law.

Despite this enfeoffment still being in place, the heir of Thomas Dyer, Hugh, decided at his death to pass on rights pertaining to The Stew and the body of land around it to Sir John Talbot, a Lancastrian supporter, later to become the Earl of Shrewsbury. In Dyer's will his brother William was made his heir, and in 1452 that William released any rights he might still have on The Stew to the same Sir John Talbot.

Confused? Believe me, this is simple compared to the mass of detail documented in the Drapers' Archives. These were complicated days, with kings fighting for, and losing, crowns, in a continual state of deposition and reinstatement. And it was the powerful Yorkist side of this wrangle that appeared to have the strongest clout regarding The Stew.

The Drapers became involved in the story of The Stew in 1462 when, as a means of resolving the legal wrangles, King Edward IV passed onto them the Dyer lands by Royal Charter, because, it stated, there were no other claimants.

That's not the way, however, that the family of the staunchly Lancastrian Sir John Talbot saw it. Having become Earl of Shrewsbury, he was killed at the Battle of Northampton in 1460, fighting on the side of the Lancastrian king, Henry VI. During the two-year period when Henry VI was reinstated on the throne, Shrewsbury's widow Elizabeth, Countess of Shrewsbury – famous in her day as 'the old ladye of Shrowesburie', though not to be mistaken for that other old ladye of Shrowesburie, Bess of Hardwick – seized her chance and sent in her steward, Alan Stury, to seize The Stew and adjoining lands by force.

In 1471, however, the Yorkist Edward IV was back on the throne, and Henry VI was executed. This was the perfect moment for the Drapers to act. The king was petitioned, the Countess of Shrewsbury being described as 'a gretely manace', and Alan Stury was called before his Council by Edward IV. Whatever was said, the Drapers retained possession of lands and building, described as *'a croft called le Stewe, croft with the pond there in Frankwell, next the chapel of St. George, between the land of John Colle, called Colle (apple) orchard, and the bank of Severn.'*

Never mind the Battle of the Roses, which still had a way to run. The battle of The Stew was finally over, and the Drapers free to lease The Stew without dispute. The Countess of Shrewsbury died in 1473 and was buried in Shrewsbury Abbey. Whoever would have thought that a property in Shrewsbury was once the source of so much strife – and amongst the great movers and shakers of their day too?

At some point The Stew and adjacent property came into the ownership of the Scotts of Betton Strange. It was subsequently exploited as a large-scale maltings and brewing enterprise. The Scotts held land around Frankwell Quay throughout the 18th century, but a deed dated 1713 puts The Stew in the ownership of John Astley, a 'yeoman of Little Berwick'.

The Stew

An agreement of 1728 mentions John Astley too, along with his son and heir Thomas, as owners of 'a messuage and malthouse' called 'The Stew in Frankwell' [the word 'messuage' meaning a dwelling, together with its outbuildings and adjacent land appropriated to its use]. It's believed that he was the builder of what we currently think of as The Stew, which in its day was a merchant's house of high quality with cut stone quoins, most of which are still intact.

So a long and noble history attached to the site, and a building from the early 1700s that's robust and simply in need of repair according to Peter Napier, to whom thanks for pointing me in the direction of the Archive of the Worshipful Company of Drapers (it's Peter Napier, the Royal Institute of Chartered Surveyors' accredited building surveyor who surveyed The Stew along with Structural Engineer, John Avent in 2006 for Shrewsbury and Atcham Borough Council.)

'The building is solid.' That was the message Peter wanted to convey. It might not look like it to the untrained eye but there's nothing fundamentally wrong with it. 'It has an amazing roof,' he said,

'constructed out of Baltic pine, which in its day would have had to be brought up from Bristol by barge. The building needs to be given a modern use, but despite its current state of disrepair both myself and John Avent, current Chairman of the Institute of Structural Engineers' accreditation scheme, concluded that it was robust. The roof could be repaired. The only crack in the building hasn't moved in thirty-five years. In the owner's application to have it demolished, he describes The Stew as derelict. But it's not.'

Peter Napier's not the only one to speak out for The Stew. In the last few days, English Heritage has come out and said that it should be saved, and at the time of writing that's the view of the County Ecologist as well, Shrewbury's Civic Society, local residents, and Shrewsbury Town Council.

Frankwell Quay is important in the town's history and The Stew is an important part of Frankwell Quay. What's needed here is not only to save it but to find a good use for it. And a fine example of this kind of transformation isn't far away.

Today the Cinema in the Square, housed in the beautiful Old Market Hall, is an important part of Shrewsbury life. Once most people had never seen inside it. Now it houses a cinema and attractive café/bar. Everybody loves and uses it. It's at the heart of Shrewsbury town life. Its restoration has been a huge success.

There's a word I've heard bandied about recently – the Italian word 'centro storico', meaning 'historical heart'. In this respect, Frankwell Quay and The Stew are every bit as much a part of Shrewsbury's centro storico as the Old Market Hall, and should be preserved as such.

SEPTEMBER

6th September: C.R. BIRCH & SONS

I've been shopping in Birch's since I was a young woman who'd just bought her first home. That's forty years ago, and to me it hasn't changed a bit. But that's not how Margaruite Birch sees it.

'The day the cattle market closed,' she said, 'the whole town changed, including Birch's. We had the exit to the market opposite our shop. The farmers wives would come in and leave their baskets with us, then go up Pride Hill to enjoy themselves. At the end of the day, they'd collect their baskets and go round the back of the Raven Hotel to meet their husbands and get lifts back home.'

Back in those days, C.R. Birch & Son primarily served the farming community. Its tanker went round the farms selling tractor vaporising oil, diesel and paraffin. In the shop it sold hay forks, pig troughs, soft soap in buckets, mothballs (for keeping mice out of the combine harvesters and protecting the leather seats of vintage cars) brummocks (look 'em up on Google if you don't know) and thistle podgers. It also sold leather horse gear and saddlery.

Charlie Birch bred champion trotting horses. In the Birch's inner sanctum at the back of the shop the walls are dotted with photographs of him and his horses. His favourite, Countess Dewey, became Champion of Great Britain for three years, 1933–35, and over twenty years later, in 1957, Charlie won the GB championship with Miss Azoff on a trotting race-course near Edinburgh. [For many years, the magnificent winner's silver cup resided in the front of the shop for Birch's customers to see.]

Charlie, known in the family as Pop, started C.R. Birch & Son in 1909, a staggering 104 years ago, renting the redundant blacksmith's business of Messrs John and Thomas Jones (which went back to the early 1800s). By 1922, his business was so successful that he was able to buy the property outright, and it's remained in the family ever since.

Sons Richard and Gordon joined Charlie in the business. Then, when Charlie died in 1959, Gordon continued with it until his own unexpected death, at the age of 52, in 1972.

'Charlie was my father-in-law,' Margaruite said. 'Gordon and I had two sons, Peter and Christopher. Gordon ran the business with the help of Arthur Dixon, Pop's half-brother. The business didn't feature domestic hard-wear and garden products like it does now. That came about after the cattle market and auction yard moved to Harlescott. Gordon was a wonderful man. Wonderful. After he'd gone I took over the business.'

Gordon would be proud to see Margaruite still in the shop forty-one years later – and so would Pop. At first, Margaruite found herself thrown in at the deep end, knowing next to nothing about running a business. 'But the boys came in with me as they finished college, Christopher and Peter. And the customers were wonderful. Particularly the old farmers – they knew where everything was. And then, of course, there was Freda.'

Freda Middle, I'm reliably informed, is an honorary Birch. She came straight from school in Bishop's Castle in 1960, and works in Birch's to this day.

'Peter, me and Freda, we have some wonderful memories,' said Margaruite. 'Like the time a pig escaped from the market and came rushing through the shop. It crossed Smithfield Road, leapt into the river, swam across it – which is how I know that pigs can swim – and tried to get away across the grazing fields of Frankwell. I'll never forget the drovers chasing it. There was no footbridge then, so they had to go round by the Welsh Bridge.'

While Margaruite was talking, a little man came into the shop asking for a glass of water. Peter fetched him one. They shared a few words about the weather. The man drained his glass. 'Do you feel better for that?' Peter said. The man nodded and left. 'He comes in sometimes for chocolates,' Margaruite said. 'I don't think he has a clue where he is. But then over the years we've seen some funny people. Only the other week a man came in asking for a chamber pot. He'd already tried Rackhams, with no success, his bladder was weak and his feet didn't work well in the night, so we sold him a bucket with a lid. It would hold more than a chamber pot, we said.'

Margaruite's a great mimic. When she tells a story, you can hear voices as she remembers them. Like the man who had a mouse visitor for breakfast every day, for whom he provided grapes and digestive biscuits. He was a very nice mouse, the man said, but now he was bringing his family with him and the man couldn't feed them all. They had to go. Could Birch's help?

Margaruite has a stack of mouse tales involving people of kind disposition towards the little creatures cosied up in their homes. Mr Kershaw of School Gardens, for example, couldn't bear to kill his mouse so wanted a trap to catch it humanely – which he did every day and removed it as far as the greenery at the end of his garden. Only every day there would be a new mouse. What could he do?

'Have you considered that it might be the same mouse?' suggested Freda. The next time Mr Kershaw came into Birch's, he was in a real temper. He'd taken Freda's advice and branded his next catch with a dash of paint. 'And you know what – I've caught that same mouse forty-five times!' he said.

Margaruite and Peter Birch

Then there's the old Welsh woman who rang up with a problem. 'Oh, Mr Birch, have you got a piece of wood, 36" x 4", for the bottom of my bedroom door?' 'Do you want a draught excluder?' asked Christopher. 'No,' said she. 'I'll tell you what it is. I was in bed and I felt a wriggling on my back. I turned over, and it was still there. I got out of bed, and a mouse shot out of my nightie. Well, I don't want to kill it. It has a right to life. That's why I want the wood. To stop it coming back.'

Driving out to attend to people's needs seemed to be part of Birch's service to its customers. 'There was an old couple by the name of Minshall,' Margaruite said. 'He was blind and she was dizzy, but they mostly got along all right.' One time, though, they phoned the shop in a bit of a state. Where's the lad, they wanted to know. 'We need him, see.' Why did they need him, Margaruite asked. They were locked out of their house, they said. They wanted him to break in. But he mustn't break the glass. And he didn't. 'The lad' undid a latch and squeezed in through a window. All part of the Birch's service.

'We miss the old farmers,' Margaruite said. 'After the market closed the wives still came in for a while to leave their baskets. But now that generation has gone. We miss the equine business too. When Pop started Birch's he used to make cart greases, and embrocation for the horses. You'd see him in the shop cleaning harnesses. We sold all sorts of riding equipment. Pop's red, white and blue halters were for full-sized horses, red striped ones for cobs and blue ones for ponies. Some are still hanging up in the back of the shop to this day, but the riding schools started selling cheaper gear from India and China and mostly we gave up.'

Back in those days, the area between Birch's, Mardol and Pride Hill buzzed with activity. Where the new flats are now, stood a maltings. Then there was the Queen's Hotel, its large car park packed on market days. Then up Roushill Bank was Mr Ryden, the saddler. Then there was the brush factory, then the corn people selling seed to the farmers. Then there were the two pubs, the Sun and the Horshoes on opposite corners. Margaruite said that actors from the theatre (now Granada Bingo) stayed at the Horseshoes. Their shows were wonderful.

'I remember the blind man who used to sit outside the row of cottages up Roushill,' she said, 'making wicker baskets. Back in those days, I remember Bythell's Passage coming out on Pride Hill next to Mac Fisheries. That got knocked down, like the Old Mint. I remember standing on Pride Hill, looking all the way down the Seventy Steps towards the river. Now the Darwin Shopping Centre has put an end to that.'

But there's one thing Margaruite reckoned hadn't changed. The River Severn. C.R. Birch & Son sits right in the middle of what was once flood-plain marshland. Flood defences guard the far side of the river on Frankwell Quay, but strangely there's nothing on the town side. 'When the river rises, everything has to go upstairs,' Margaruite said. 'It's a tried and tested routine. We hose the place down afterwards and wait for it to dry, then everything comes down again.'

When Gordon died, he left behind a file on flooding compiled by Pop, detailing the best procedure for avoiding damage. This highlights the continuity that is one of Birch's great strengths. When Margaruite and her boys took on the business, they found cupboards and files full of fastidious notes, including Pop's accounting system, which was easy to pick up.

What did Birch's have to offer that its modern out-of-town superstore competitors couldn't provide? For a moment Margaruite seemed stumped. 'Nothing really,' she said at first. Then, haltingly, 'Well, it's probably us. The service we give. People come to Birch's because we offer service. They come because of us.'

I've got to tell you something about Margaruite. A few years ago, on a research trip to Belize, I visited the indigenous Kekchi-Mayan people and spent one evening with their village elder. By candlelight, with the jungle croaking and whistling outside, I heard the story of how he'd founded the village. That man had the demeanour of royalty, and here it is again. Would it be stretching a point too far to say that this quiet, friendly, smiling lady is Shrewsbury royalty? I think not.

9th September: THE FLAX MILL MALTINGS

A year of getting behind closed doors in Shrewsbury has to include the town's famous Flax Mill Maltings. Such an important building, of international significance, couldn't possibly be left out. Yesterday was its Open Day, including a laser show in the Silo, so I went along. I'd always been fascinated by this extraordinary building, in recent years covered in scaffolding and in desperate need of repair, but had never been inside. Now was my chance.

The Flax Mill Maltings was built in 1796, after extensive tests on the structural properties of iron. It was designed by Charles Bage, one of the pioneers of structural engineering, at the behest of brothers Thomas and Benjamin Benyon and their partner, John Marshall of Leeds. Mills at that time were highly dangerous, built of brick and stone, with wooden floors. The dust from the spinning process, along with the volatility of lubricants for machinery and the use of candlelight to work by meant that it was easy for them to burn down. Charles Bage's Flax Mill, however, built of brick and iron, was completely fireproof. This was to be a new type of mill.

The Flax Mill benefited from good transport links by road, river and canal, and a ready market for the mill's products. Shrewsbury also was able to offer the new enterprise skilled workers. The building remained a mill for over a hundred years, then in 1897 was adapted by William Jones Maltsters and functioned as a maltings until the company's bankruptcy in 1934.

In World War II the building was used as a barracks. In 1948 it became a maltings again, for Ansells, which is how it remained until 1987 - which means that there may well be people in our town who remember working there.

Laser show inside Ditherington Maltings & Flax Mill

The value of the Flax Mill Maltings isn't just its history, however. Its value lies in its innovative design. The Main Mill, which now faces regeneration, is the oldest remaining iron-framed building in the world. This means that New York and every other city that has ever put up a skyscraper owes a debt of gratitude to the Ditherington Flax Mill Maltings, still standing here in Shrewsbury 217 years after it was first conceived.

Together with the Cross Mill and Warehouse, the complex has three of the ten oldest iron-framed buildings in the world, and the design of the Flax Mill by Charles Bage is of international significance for its use of structural engineering within building design.

Interestingly, John Marshall of Leeds is the entrepreneur who purchased the rights to the flax-spinning machine when it was first invented, bringing cutting-edge manufacturing technology to Shrewsbury as well. In addition, he became Mayor of Shrewsbury, as did Charles Bage. Both were important men in their day.

Last autumn, whilst in Toronto, I visited the Distillery District, a part of that very modern city's preserved past. Housed in a massive old distillery and accompanying outbuildings and warehouses are craft shops, high-end jewellers, boutiques, bars, restaurants and exhibition spaces. This is a quality destination full of interest and charm, away from Toronto's skyscrapers, reminiscent of the city's industrial past. People flock to it. They love it. If you're coming to Toronto, you've got to see it, they say.

And the same could go for the Flax Mill Maltings. People could flock to it as well, locals and tourists alike, making it not only a commercial destination, but also a significant destination on the national heritage tourist trail.

13th August: THE PHIL GILLAM DOUBLE INTERVIEW

Throughout the year, I've enjoyed Phil's column, and sometimes I bump into him on Twitter. I know he's interviewed some fascinating and, in many cases, famous people. Now here in the Boathouse pub was the man himself, tall, smiling, slightly self-deprecating, sitting over his notebook just as I was sitting over mine. This was the Phil Gillam/Pauline Fisk double interview, him 'doing' me for his column in the Chronicle. Me 'doing' him for my blog.

Phil is a journalist for the Midlands News Association, working as one of five editors running ten newspaper titles across the region (including the *Shrewsbury Chronicle*). But where had he first caught the writing bug?

Phil caught the bug early, he said, spending time with his brother making up comic magazines populated with superheroes.

He grew up in Castlefields, where he went to the Lancastrian School (designed by Charles Bage of Flax Mill Maltings fame). He left school and went straight into journalism.

'I belong to that lucky generation of young people for whom that was still possible,' Phil said. 'The Midland News Association put me through five months of intensive training. Afterwards I worked on the *Shrewsbury Chronicle*. It was the year of the Queen's Silver Jubilee. I certainly had my fill of buntings.'

From there Phil went to the *Sunday Independent* in Devon, then onto Yorkshire's *Hull Times*, in which city he and his wife Carol met. He returned to the Midlands to work on the *Staffordshire Newsletter*, then to Shropshire in 1988, spending sixteen years on the *Shropshire Star*, both in features and on the news desk. After that, Phil had a stint on the *Wolverhampton Express and Star* before taking up his present position, Editor of Market Drayton's and Newport's *Advertisers*.

Over the years, Phil has interviewed everybody from Neil Kinnock to Michael Heseltine, Joan Collins to Jimmy Tarbuck. What was Collins like, I wanted to know. Frosty, Phil replied. And Tarbuck? Naked but for his underpants, Phil said. He was doing his show, it was the interval, he was in his dressing-room and he was running with sweat.

Phil Gillam

On the subject of sweat, Phil once interviewed Labour leader, as he was then, Tony Blair, who'd just made a speech and sweat was pouring off him. He'd go on stage, take off his jacket and roll up his sleeves. That impressed. Back in those days, politicians didn't do that.

During the miners' strike Phil interviewed Neil Kinnock. He'd covered a meeting at which Kinnock had been speaking. When it finished, Kinnock swept through to the back of the hall and Phil and his photographer followed him. They ended up sharing a few whiskies. Phil got his interview.

Another time Phil found himself huddled in the back of a car with Roy Hattersley. It was the mid-eighties. Hattersley had given a good speech and as he left somebody asked Phil if he fancied coming along too and grabbing the chance of an interview – which he did.

What was the best thing about being a features writer, I wanted to know. Going into people's homes, Phil said. Seeing what their lives were like. It had also been great to do unusual things like flying in a jet fighter, or going to sea with the RNLI.

Recently, Phil has brought out his first novel, joining the growing trend of authors who've abandoned traditional publishing for doing it themselves. The book's called '*Shrewsbury Station Just After Six*'. Even in its title, Phil's love of Shrewsbury is plain to see. He once ran a column entitled '*Down Your Street*', which had him knocking on doors all over Shrewsbury, getting invited in to talk to people about their neighbourhood.

In his Chronicle column too, Phil is always banging the Shrewsbury drum. He wouldn't want our town turned into a museum piece, but he reckons no more old buildings, including The Stew on Frankwell Quay, should be demolished. 'Who in their right mind came up with the idea of knocking down the Raven Hotel?' he said. 'We can't allow a thing like that to ever happen again.'

Phil reckons that Shrewsbury has as many fine buildings as Chester, maybe even more, but that it doesn't sell itself enough. 'It's a gorgeous place,' he said. 'The other day I was crossing Kingsland Bridge, and I just stopped and stared. I couldn't move on. The view was breathtaking.'

25th September
HUGH OWEN & JOHN BRICKDALE BLAKEMORE

Meet Reverends Hugh Owen and John Blakemore, my new best friends. I met them in Candle Lane Books, which is where I also found Georgina Jackson & Charlotte Burne. Burne's *'Shropshire Folk-Lore'* has enlivened my writing life with all sorts of fascinating Shropshire characters, including Wild Edric and the highwayman Humphrey Kynaston. And thanks to Jackson's *'Shropshire Word-Book'*, I've been able to converse with Shroppiemon (another post, another day) on Twitter using Old Shropshire, which, believe me, is no mean feat.

The friends one makes through books are friends for life. Now Owen and Blakeway have joined that number, their *History of Shrewsbury*, in two hefty volumes, taking pride of place on my desk.

John Brickdale Blakeway was born in Shrewsbury in 1765 and educated at Shrewsbury School, Westminster School and Oriel College, Oxford. He was called to the bar in 1789, but entered the Church of England instead and in 1794 became vicar of St Mary's Church, Shrewsbury. In 1807 he was elected a fellow of the Society of Antiquaries of London. Nineteen years later, he died at the Council House, Shrewsbury, and was buried in St. Mary's Church, where a monument, executed by John Carline, was erected to his memory.

Hugh Owen was the son of a Shrewsbury physician, educated at St John's College, Cambridge, becoming vicar of St Julian's, Shrewsbury, in 1791. Like his friend, John Blakeway, he became a fellow of the Society of Antiquaries of London. He also became Mayor of Shrewsbury and, after the death of John Blakeway, vicar of St Mary's.

The *History of Shrewsbury* was published in 1825. There are modern facsimile copies of this book (one notable American version with snow-capped peaks on the cover, as if Shrewsbury was in the Alps). But to own the original is so exciting that I can scarcely contain myself.

From Roman times until the early Victorian period, Owen and Blakemore meticulously covered it all. Here Shrewsbury is in the days of Canute, in the reign of Edward the Confessor, in the life and times of

The History of Shrewsbury, by Owen & Blakemore, first edition

Edmund Ironside. Here's Shrewsbury as described in the Domesday Book. Here's the impact Henry II had on our town, and here's a facsimile copy of his son Richard the Lionheart's charter to the burgesses of Shrewsbury, dated three months after the Coeur de Lion's return to England from fighting in the Crusades (a brief return, as it turned out). It grants the town of Salopesbiri to be 'holden by the burgesses thereof' for forty marks of silver in annual rent.

This isn't the only charter in the book. One of Henry III's reveals the conditions under which freedom should be granted to slaves (referred to as 'natives'): *'If any native of any person shall remain in the said borough [ie. Shrewsbury], and hold himself in the said gild and hanse, and in lot and scot with the said burgesses for one year and one day without challenge [ie. without being claimed by his lord]: he may not be again demanded by his lord if he freely continue in the said borough.'*

And I thought slavery was something that happened elsewhere.

Did you know that Edward IV happened to be Christmassing in Shrewsbury when his father died, making him next in line to the throne?

Owen and Blakeway describe the presence of his brilliant court imparting upon Shrewsbury *'somewhat of the consequence of a second capital.'*

And did you know that Edward's IV second son, one of the doomed Princes in the Tower, was named Richard Shrewsbury because he was born here in our town?

There's more fascinating stuff like this – and I haven't even got to the Tudors yet, or the town's part in the English Civil War, or the Jacobean period when Shrewsbury's medieval street plan was added to with new-build Georgian houses.

Owen and Blakeway's book is a big one in every sense, setting Shrewsbury in a national setting, which is fascinating to discover. Be sure that over the next few months there will be more posts like this.

28th September: A BIRTHDAY PRESENT TO MYSELF

Over the year I've interviewed a lot of people, shining the light on Shrewsbury and what a fascinating place it is. But today, seeing as it's my birthday, and one with a significant number attached to it, I've decided to tell you a bit about myself.

I've lived in Shrewsbury for sixteen years, and before that in the south Shropshire village of Worthen for twenty-four, moving there from London, where I was born. A summer spent in a bit of a writer's retreat on a farm in Worcestershire was what brought me to the Marches region. I love living in Shropshire. I came here feeling as if I didn't belong anywhere, and have put down deep roots.

A year ago, my daughter Beulah lent me *'The Gift'* by Lewis Hyde. It explored the concept of giving in an historical context and looks at the value and purpose of gifts across differing world cultures. Time and again, I found the importance cropping up of giving back to the source that has nurtured one's gift.

I was thinking about this one night, walking up Castle Gates having spent the day in London. The air was fresh. It had been raining and the streets and pavements shone. The sky was clear, the road empty. Ahead of me I could see the great bulk of the library.

I was just thinking how much my surroundings had nurtured my writing life, and from nowhere seemingly the words 'my tonight from Shrewsbury' rose into my consciousness. What did they mean? I didn't know then – but it didn't take long to find out.

Over the years I've written eleven novels for children and young adults (a number based locally) the first of which won the Smarties Book Prize and the latest of which was set in the jungles of Belize, which I toured courtesy of an Arts Council grant. I started making up stories when I was three, telling them over the wall to the big children next door.

Pauline Fisk

I started writing stories as soon as I learned joined up writing. I made my big career decision at the age of nine. My first book was published when I was twenty-four.

A few months ago, the film company R & A Collaborations made a film to celebrate the e-publication of my novel, *'Telling the Sea'*. In close-up on the beach, lit by sea-light, the lines on my face are plain to see, and I feel affection for them. I feel as if I'd earned them. As much as the books I've written, or my family, they're part of my life. I'd never stretch or tuck them. I'm proud of my age. I'm still running round, bright-eyed at the world around me, ears pricked up at sixty-five.

PS. Here's the link to R & A's short film: http://vimeo.com/55155636

OCTOBER

4th October: ERIC LOVELAND HEATH

I'm having coffee with the musician E.L. Heath. He's shiny, sharp and button-bright, enjoys the bizarre and has an original take on things. His mind works super-fast, jumping from subject to subject, grasping connections out of thin air. He's very intense about ideas.

Eric (Loveland Heath, to give him his full name) is fascinated by words, and Welsh ones in particular. He was born in Athens, Georgia, but his mum hails from Swansea. His name came from his grandfather, passed down through the family. Eric was bullied for it at secondary school. 'But then I didn't much enjoy school anyway,' he says wryly.

Eric grew up in Snailbeach. The village school was Stiperstones, the secondary school Mary Webb. He lived in Snailbeach until sixteen and has a thing about the significance of the number six. He left the US aged six weeks, lived in London until he was six, lived in Snailbeach until he was sixteen, and returned to Snailbeach aged twenty-six to produce an album loosely based around Snailbeach life.

It always rains in Snailbeach, Eric says. I protest, but he insists. 'You'll get pockets of cloud. Even after the sun has broken through elsewhere, Snailbeach can be swathed in mist. There's an atmosphere about the place – weird and slightly sinister.'

Eric has been writing and producing albums for years. He started by messing around on the guitar, then 'did things' on his laptop, joined a band, played bass and started writing. His home is packed with instruments. Synthesisers, keyboards, guitars – 'You wouldn't believe the things you can pick up on Freecycle,' Eric says.

Plainly Eric is a man who pursues his interests in thorough-going fashion. He joined a Welsh-speaking band called Strap the Button and started learning Welsh through them, then developed it courtesy of the Open University, and later continued his studies in Welshpool and at Shrewsbury College of Arts & Technology.

Another of Eric's interests is the Ondes Martenot. He first heard it on Gerry Anderson's 'Captain Scarlet' and wanted to find ways to make the same sound. Years later he discovered that it came from an instrument devised by the cellist Maurice Martenot. 'Playing it became a bit of an obsession,' Eric says. 'It's always been the technical side of music that's fascinated me, the creation of sounds and the effect they have – and the Ondes Martenot makes things sound really weird.'

With Strap the Button, Eric made it onto Radio One. After that, however, he went off on his own, making his own music and 'messing around with machines'. He also hooked up with the band epic45. 'It's they who've been my biggest musical influence,' says Eric. 'Ben Holton and Rob Glover. I met them years ago through friends, put on a gig for them and in return they asked me to play at their festival. After that, they went off to Japan and I didn't see them for six months. Then Rob asked if I'd like to join the band. Since then I've been on three European tours with them, including Istanbul and Madrid.'

Epic45 have been making music now for more than a decade, inspired by their rural background, childhood summers in the countryside and their affinity with their surroundings. Amongst the radio shows they've played is the late John Peel's. Back in July 2011 they were *The Sunday Times'* album of the week. NME describes them as 'beguiling and beautiful'.

Eric's influences include the psychedelic music of Kevin Ayres and the classical electronics ('spacey noises', Eric calls them) of Joe Meek. The band is currently concentrating on releasing albums in their own names, but the hub of all their activities, as much as ever, is still epic45.

Eric calls it the 'mothership'. He has his own label, Plenty Wenlock Records, producing short runs of handmade releases, also available to download. His latest album, 'Ty' (lyrics in Welsh) will however be released on the epic45 label, Wayside & Woodland.

'It's knowing I have a CD coming out that inspires me to write,' Eric says. 'But it's ideas that excite me rather than the actual recording process – the drawing together of my interests, watching the ideas come alive.'

Eric is an avid collector of vinyl and books. As a reader he goes for the bizarre, citing the absurd tales of Ivor Cutler, the Mabinogion and the writing of Algernon Blackwood, the master of weird atmosphere.

Eric also loves the bizarre writing of Scottish satirist, radio producer and television director/writer, Armando Iannucci. 'All that stuff he wrote for radio before *In The Thick Of It* came along – it was brilliant,' Eric says.

Eric and I are sitting in the Shrewsbury Coffeehouse. He lives out of town but comes in frequently. A couple of years ago, the photographer Richard Foot and his sister, weaver Helen Foot, put together a series of network evenings, bringing together Shrewsbury artists, writers, filmmakers and craftspeople. Eric already knew Richard from before, but networking, he says, has made him less insular. Things are happening in Shrewsbury these days, and he's glad to be a part of them.

Eric Loveland Heath wearing a Helen Foot scarf

Eric's album is due out on October 28th. Pre-orders are already coming in. My order's going in after I've finished writing this post.

7th October
DOREEN WOODFORD, SIGNAL & THE DEAF COMMUNITY

The late Doreen Woodford was renowned worldwide for the work she did in the deaf community. Yesterday, in pursuit of her legacy, I visited the Woodford Foundation on College Hill.

The Woodford Foundation was set up in 2004 by four retired professionals, including Doreen Woodford, whose working lives had been spent with sensory-impaired children and their families, in particular overseas. For many years it worked in tandem with the Shropshire Deaf Association. Last week the two organisations merged, and are now known as Signal.

Interestingly, Doreen never wanted an organisation named after her. That was thrust upon her by the Foundation's other Trustees, in recognition of what her name stood for in the deaf community worldwide.

We're talking here about a woman whose exploits included sneaking into Afghanistan during the Taliban's rule, disguised beneath a burka, to bring support to deaf children in that country; flying fearlessly into the Congo; even taking on Somalia, coercing men with machine guns to allow her to pass through.

'There's a stigma to deafness,' said Matthew Gilbert, Signal's Chief Executive, 'especially in Africa, where superstition is rife and the deaf face serious social taboos. Often Africans regard the deaf as cursed. Even within the family, the deaf can find themselves excluded. And where the deaf community forms itself into groups, those groups are still often separate from the rest of society.'

Not that it's enormously different in the UK, Mat reckoned. 'Maybe people don't see deafness as a matter of being cursed, but our society isn't much better at helping the deaf to find their place.'

Helping the deaf to find that place is what Signal is all about. Its global mission is to integrate deaf people. It offers local-to-local assistance both in Africa and here in the UK. 'A massive amount of time is spent listening to people and talking through issues,' Mat said. 'It would be far quicker to go in saying *we know what you need,* but then we wouldn't be half so effective.'

In Tanzania, the Woodford Foundation has done a great job assisting deaf children in their out-of-school lives. They've worked with parents too, and their first vocational training centre for the deaf was opened in 2010, funded by the Tanzanian government.

In Malawi, the Woodford Foundation found a need in the north of the country that wasn't being addressed. For the last four years, along with the Central African Presbyterian church, they've been running awareness communication training up in that region, and encouraging families to put their deaf children into schools.

The Woodford Foundation, and now Signal, very much see their role as project management. They don't have staff on the ground, but work instead with overseas partners. 'It's important to build capacity locally,' Mat said, 'so that local people can undertake training themselves. We're the catalyst bringing together money and help, and formulating plans and programmes to be implemented by trained and trusted outreach workers.'

Currently Signal has been asked by Comic Relief to create a model to be replicated elsewhere. This speaks for the success their approach is achieving. In order to build that model they have starting pilot schemes in Malawi and Uganda. 'In Malawi,' Mat said, 'we're seeing increasing government involvement, but very little by way of funds. The Ministry is keen, but often lacks money or resources. The United Nation's Millennium Development goals call for the highest number of children to be in schools. But higher class numbers mean a reduction in the quality of teaching and inevitably the hearing impaired miss out.'

Many deaf people end up being completely dependent because thought hasn't gone into what will happen to them post-education. Making links with the vocational world is vital, as is the need to raise awareness that the deaf can be as productive as anybody else.

This is where James Cousins' work comes into its own. He's been busy liaising with hard-of-hearing groups here in the UK, social workers, councils and other gatekeepers, working towards creating a deaf and hard-of-hearing hub.

The Signal team: Rachel Baxter, James Cousins, Mathew Gilbert, Alex Hiam, Karen Goodman-Jones.

Currently James is working with clinical commissioning groups to find a place in Shrewsbury where focus groups can meet – somewhere hopefully that could offer access to a variety of users. 'Did you know,' he said, 'that 43% of people who go to their GP about hearing problems don't get referred on?' I didn't, and I was shocked.

The merger between Woodford and Shropshire Deaf was facilitated by Rachel Baxter. 'It was natural for all our resources to be pooled,' she said. 'Both organisations' objectives were virtually identical, dealing with the same issues, raising awareness and working against stigma and isolation, the only difference being that one worked for the deaf community in Africa, the other in the UK.'

The 'deaf community', Mat added, was actually a whole variety of communities. There were the sign language users ('the noisiest language in the world' somebody once said – and having witnessed a group of deaf teenagers exuberantly signing on a train, I know what they meant). There were those who lip-read – historically speaking Shropshire has always been a lip-reading county. There were those who used hearing aids, whose deafness most probably was the result of a hearing loss at some point in their lives. And there were those who struggled with the effects of tinnitus.

As I write this, I can hear a swishing noise in my ears. First time I realised this was happening, I was in a hammock in a Welsh wood beside the sea. It was the middle of the night. Half way through telling myself how much I was enjoying the silence, I realised a) it wasn't silence, and b) it wasn't the sea; the sound I heard came from inside me. Since then it's upped the ante. I tell you this not to garner sympathy but to make the point that deafness isn't 'out there' happening to 'someone else'. It can happen to us.

10th October
THE LAST REAL PRINCE OF WALES – ARGUABLY

The story of Henry III ain't exactly impressive. Given that kings were meant to get out there and make their presence felt on the battlefield, Henry was an arty-farty weakling, more interested in kneeling before Holy Relics than taking to arms. Sure enough, there were occasions when he did do battle, but by the end of his reign, huge chunks of the Plantagenet empire had slipped through his fingers.

Henry's son however, Edward I, known as 'Longshanks', was another cup of tea. He made his mark as a young man in the Crusades, then made it at home too, charging round Wales, planting castles with his left hand, defeating the guerilla tactics of Wales's two famous princes, Llywelyn and his brother, Dafydd, with his right.

Llywelyn the Great, also known as Llywelyn the Last, was according to many even today the last real Prince of Wales. The night before he died in battle, legend has him sleeping in a cave on the banks of the Wye.

It so happens that I've been into that cave. I came across it whilst doing research for my novel '*The Red Judge*'. It wasn't easy to find – a low cave in a cliff set back behind a stream with nothing to mark it as special or important. However, once I'd stooped inside I found its walls and ceiling covered with graffiti. Some was modern, written in felt-tip, some beautifully engraved, dating back centuries. 'Sleep well, sweet prince,' I read. 'We'll never forget you,' someone else wrote. 'You'll always be our prince,' wrote a third.

So why am I telling you this? It's because the story of those two doomed brother-princes of the Welsh has its last chapter here in Shrewsbury. Every day I walk past its final full stop. I'm talking about Pride Hill's High Town Cross.

This is where Dafydd was hung, drawn and quartered. He and his brother had risen in rebellion against Edward I's heavy-handed replacement of Welsh customs and laws with English ones, which they saw as an attempt to crush the Welsh spirit. No tempting offers of English earldoms could deter them. They and their Welsh compatriots achieved some notable victories, but in the cold depths of a Welsh winter Llywelyn was slaughtered in battle near Builth Wells, and in April 1283 Dafydd was captured.

Dafydd was brought to Shrewsbury for the 1283 Michaelmas Parliament, where he stood trial. Regarded by Edward I as a betrayer, one who'd enjoyed his hospitality then turned his back on him, this wasn't just a political trial; it was personal.

Edward's revenge was to have Dafydd slaughtered as a common criminal. At the top of Pride Hill, 720 years ago Dafydd was hung on a scaffold, his body slashed open with a butcher's blade and his intestines ripped out without the nicety of waiting for his death. What was left of his body was hacked into quarters, and sent to different cities as a reminder of the king's power. Finally Dafydd's head was sent to the Tower of London, where it was set on a spike next to his brother's.

Llywelyn's head was wreathed with ivy, in derision of his claims to the crown of the Welsh. It's reckoned to be buried beneath a pub on a Cardiff council estate, or so I've heard. I've no idea where Dafydd's head ended up.

13th October: SOME BLOOMING GOOD NEWS

A Shrewsbury rose

It's ten past one in the morning and I should be asleep, but I've just picked up on Twitter that Shrewsbury's won a Gold Award for Britain in Bloom, so I thought that any of you who read my post about Shrewsbury going mad on Bloom Judging Day might like to know the outcome. Goodnight.

14th October: AN OLD SHROPSHIRE OAK CALLED SHROPPIEMON

In 140 characters the Tweeter Shroppiemon is the living embodiment of Georgina Jackson's Shropshire Word-Book. His 'gallus chundering' (muttering, collected from Newport) 'wasna quite o' Georgina Jackson's standard,' he tweeted to me. But that didn't ever seem to stop him.

Shroppiemon's a tweeter with attitude. Here he is on Princess House in our town square: 'It shudna bin put up in the furst place. Owd nick himsen couldna built a more drodsome pigcote.'

If Georgina Jackson were alive, she'd be delighted to see him using its 140 characters to put Shropshire's fast-fading dialects on Twitter. But who is Shroppiemon? We've been 'following' each other for months, but all I can say with confidence is that Shroppiemon is to Shropshire what Batman is to Gotham City – and Twitter is the mask behind which he hides.

However, after terse negotiations (how could they be anything else at 140 characters a tweet?) I'm thrilled to introduce the Shroppiemon interview. 'Ow do, lass. Here goes nothing,' he emailed back the answers to my questions. And of course they're not 'nothing'. See for yourselves. Shroppiemon in his own words:

'I was born in Cross Houses hospital on my mother's 21st birthday. Er obviously didna want a boikin for a present and soon left. This meant that I got ter be that most Shropshire of Shropshireness – granny reared.

'I 'ave spent most o' me life in the town of Salop but Shroppieoomon says that 'er is still waitin' for me ter grow up. I went ter Wilfred Owen, then Holy Cross Cof E, an' then the Priory (the owd boys' school, not the modern 'un). I had such a gud time that I forgot ter leave with many qualifications. The more we got towd off at the Priory for sayin' inna, gonna, canna etc the more we said 'em.

'When we was childers we had a milkmon an' a breadmon, the Corona mon brought pop, Davenports brought beer and Mr Jones brought the veg on his horse-drawn dray – an' I miss 'em all. Havin' worked at the Abbey, the Castle, Clive House, Rowley's House and shops and cafés in the past, I feel that the town is getting' on jest fine without my meddlin' these days. But I still love ter help promote it, an' the rest o' Shropshire, whenever I con.

'I see myself as a barley child o'twitter. John Wood Warter wrote "An Old Shropshire Oak" about an anonymous tree watchin' over our sebunctious county an' I thought that through Twitter I could do summat similar. (So far I 'ave bin muchly wrong.)

'I love Shropshire and everythin' ter do with 'er, so I love findin' out things that I didna know, an' I love ter share it too. I have ter howd me sen back when I realise that I have crossed the very thin line betwixt interestin' others an' borin' em – Shroppieoomon thinks that I tend ter realise this too late for 'er likin'. I know a little about a lot, lass.

'I anna got a clue when I furst discovered Georgina Jackson and Charlotte Burne (of Shropshire Folk-Lore fame). They both jest snuck in ter me sub-conscious. They jest allus sim ter 'ave bin thar. I con still remember the kerbiffleypump feelin' when I walked out of Candle Lane Books clutchin' my copy of the Shropshire Wurd Book.

'Yer asked what was the best and wurst about Salop. Wurst = Princess House. Best = jest about everything else. Yer also asked what I'd do fer the town. I 'ood save The Stew, knock

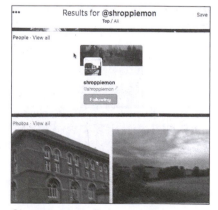

Shroppiemon's Twitter profile

down Princess House – or at least stop 'em filling the bottom in – open a university, restore the Shrewsbury Cut (canal), make all public transport and out-of-town parkin' free, and fund it by dearer parkin' in the loop. I would mek Sunday the day ter be sin in town, a sort of modern version of the monkey walk. Selfishly I 'ood reinstate the Loggerheads back on the Shrewsbury Town shirts.

'I love anything an 'eveything ter do with Shropshire, not jest Shrewsbury. I collect books, pictures, signs, postcards, owd tat memorabilia, bottles, clocks etc.

'I never realised until ternite how important women are ter Shropshire folklore – G. Jackson, C. Burne, Lady Milnes-Gaskell, M. Webb, E. Pargeter, yer gud sen, H. Stretton, Shroppieoomon, thrum the Caradoc & Severn Valley Mrs Hayward, Jean Hughes. Less famous but equally important, Annie E Smout, Sheila Hamer and Valerie Kilford.

'The oomon I left until last is Val Littlehales. She is an artist, storyteller, teacher, farmer and poet. She writes and recites in Shropshire dialect (sadly I have misplaced my copy of her live cassette).

'Yer want a clue ter who I am. It 'oodna help as I inna well known, but I will buy yer a drink one day lass, Shroppieoomon ull join us too. Thank 'ee very much for yo'em interest. Regards Shroppiemon.'

18th October: SIR HENRY SIDNEY'S HEART

I came across this story about the father of Sir Philip Sidney whilst investigating the history of the Council House. Here's how the 'Account of the Ancient and Present State of Shrewsbury' describes the great Privy Counselor, Knight of the Garter and Lord President of the Marches Council heading off to St Chad's Church on 1st May 1581, his 'knights following hym in brave order and after them bayliffes and aldermen in scarlet gownes, with the companies of all occupations in the sayde towne, in theire best liveries, and before every warden of every company, two stuardes with whit roddes in their hands'.

And here's Sir Henry departing 'from Shrewsberie by water', taking 'his Barge under the Castell Hyll by hys place (the Council House)' to a fourteen gun salute and 'lamentable orations' from Shrewsbury schoolboys, 'being apparelyd in grene, and greene wyllows upon their heads'.

When Sir Henry died, he directed that his bowels be buried in Bewdley, his body in Ludlow and his heart in Shrewsbury. However, no record was made of where any of those parts – or, indeed, the rest of him – ended up.

Enter Mr Hodge, whose historical account of Ludlow Castle recalls a leaden urn dug up in the garden of Edward Coleman Esq of Leominster, Herefordshire, where it had 'lain unattended for long years till the researches of a gentleman of that neighbourhood introduced it into notice and presented the editor with a drawing of it'.

Round the urn was this inscription:

HER LITH THE HARTE OF SYR HENRYE SYDNY
L P ANNO DOMNI 1586.

The urn was five inches deep and four in diameter, having lost its lid. Some believe it was originally placed in one of Shrewsbury's town churches and that during a period of what the 'Account' calls 'confusions and great rebellion' it was saved by a friend of Sir Henry Sidney's, who decided to bury it in a garden. In Herefordshire.

Where it is today, nobody knows, nor what became of the heart, because the urn was empty when Edward Coleman dug it up.

This tale is for any of you who say your heart's in Shrewsbury. Make sure you keep it there – or else you never know where it might end up.

22nd October

HOW SHREWSBURY ESCAPED THE WRATH OF A GIANT
(No, I'm not talking about the tallest MP in the House of Commons, Shrewsbury's Daniel Kawczynski)

This story was read by Thomas Wright to the British Archaeological Association in 1860, and also recorded by Charlotte Burne in her *Shropshire Folk-Lore*, mentioning several versions, including the giant being the Devil:

Once there was a wicked old giant in Wales, who had a spite against the Mayor and folk of Shrewsbury and decided to dam up the Severn and flood the town.

Off he set with a massive spadeful of earth, tramping mile after mile. Somehow he missed Shrewsbury and ended up in Wellington, puffing and blowing under his heavy load.

Along came a cobbler carrying a sack of old boots, on his way home from Shrewsbury where his business was based. 'How far is Shrewsbury?' the giant called. 'Why do you ask?' the cobbler replied. 'I want to fill up the Severn with this lump of earth,' said the giant. 'I've a grudge against the Mayor and townsfolk and mean to drown the place and get rid of it once and for all.'

Oh my, thought the cobbler. This'll never do. I can't afford to lose my customers. 'Eh!' he said, 'You'll never get to Shrewsbury, not today, nor tomorrow. Look at me. I'm just come from there and the journey has worn out all these boots.'

The cobbler showed the giant his sack. The giant groaned. 'If that's the case, I'll have to drop my load and go back home,' he said.

And that's what he did, scraping his boots on his spade and returning to Wales. Nobody heard of him again but, where he put down his load, there's the Wrekin, and the mud off his boots created Little Ercall.

And Shrewsbury's still standing to this very day.

23rd October: SHREWSBURY ABBEY CELBRATES BENJAMIN BRITTEN

The man next to me says his daughter is one of the elephants. The orchestra is tuning up. On the screen behind the stage images of flooded Shrewsbury are projected. God climbs into the pulpit in the person of Gareth Jenkins, my dentist. Cymbals crash, clouds fill the screen. God's angry with mankind and only one man is worth saving. You know the story. The show has begun.

Standing in the aisles awaiting their cues are rows of animals. Mrs Noye is onstage, winding up her old man. The sky darkens. Rain begins to fall. Water is rising. Behind Noye, an Ark begins to bob. 'Wife, come in!' sings Noye. 'I will not!' she replies.

Noye and their kids have to drag her in whilst the choir sings *Kyrie, eleison, Lord, have mercy,* accompanied by trumpets, cymbals and drums. I sit back, feeling a bit like one of those storm-chasers in the American mid-west. Here comes the rain – stair-rod rain, not polite English patter but rainforest stuff. First it's on the screen, then it's on the columns of the Abbey then it's up amongst its arches and down amongst the audience, stair-rods dancing over our heads.

Everybody in the Abbey is caught up in this. It might be Andy McKeown's light-show imitation rain, but I for one am feeling cold and wet, and to make matters worse, here are the storm dancers followed by the spirit of the storm kitted out in electric blue, presiding over waves billowing with rage.

Noye's Fludde in Shrewsbury Abbey

Wow. All around the Abbey, lightning flashes and thunder roars. The storm dancers rush about, surging like tides. Then out of the chaos comes that old hymn about those in peril on the sea. My hair stands up on end. It feels as if it's not just someone else's peril I'm singing about – it's mine.

The waters are high now. Shoals of darting fish (well, three first-year High School fish actually) leave trails of air-bubbles behind. The sky's still dark, but there's a shift in the music, something suggesting a hint of blue. Something on the screen hints at it too – enough blue for Noye to send out a ballet-dancing raven to look for land.

One moment the raven is on stage, on tiptoes, beating black wings. Then it's gone, leaving a huge bird image on the screen. Then that, too, is gone – and there's no land to be found.

Will this flood ever subside? 'Forty days and nights,' sings Noye. You can almost touch his despair. Next time round, he sends a dove.

Then (sigh of relief) we're into the olive branch scene.

Troubled waters are troubling no more. New life is found on earth. New life in the Ark too. Mrs Noye is at the helm, holding it steady as the waters subside. Transformed by the trauma of flood, she and Noye have made their peace.

Up pops God. 'Noye, come out of the shippie,' he calls in Gareth Jenkins' rolling Welsh tones. The door opens. It's time to leave.

A joyful procession stumbles out of the Ark. Twitchy little mice skip past my pew, prowling tigers and plodding elephants, the screen behind them alive with swirling lights.

'Noye! Noye!' God calls again. Then before we can think *'Oh no, here we go,'* God's promised that never again will such a cataclysm destroy the earth. The screen fills with rainbow colours. We start to sing rounds, supported by the orchestra, and I'm in a muddle because I don't know whom to follow. There's a sun on the screen, and a funny wobbly shaped moon. Stars like fireflies appear, and the screen turns the deepest sky blue.

Finally, to a fanfare of trumpets, Noye and Mrs Noye leave the Ark. 'The hand that made us is divine,' sing cast and audience as one. The last 'Amen' rings out.

Suddenly it's like the Cinderella story when the carriage became a pumpkin as midnight chimed. Animals turn back into children. They surge up the aisles and pile onto the stage. They're giggling and a few of them are shoving. It's hard to believe they all fitted in that Ark.

Thunder breaks out, only this time it's not orchestra or special effects, but parents and grandparents, proud music lovers all, stamping on the floor. Then God gets down from his pulpit, struggling with his robe, and the lights come on.

The applause peters out. Coats appear. It's amazing how quickly normal life is resumed. Everybody's switching their mobiles back on and clutching their kids. I'm swept along in the general press. A moment ago it was our town's children heading out into the world, leaving behind the Ark, now it's me, leaving the Abbey and blinking in the shiny darkness of a Shrewsbury night. What have I just been to? You have to have guessed. It was Benjamin Britten's *Noye's Fludde*.

29ᵗʰ October: HAS SHREWSBURY EVER LOOKED MORE BEAUTIFUL?

After storms with hundred mph winds, Shrewsbury awakens to clear blue skies. A perfect day for celebrating the town's beauty in autumn.

Once my jobs for the day are done, I head with Biffo on his lead, down Butcher Row, through St Alkmund's churchyard, down Fish Street, across the top of the Cop, up Belmont Bank, round Old St Chad's and onto the Quarry.

In the clear sunlight, the Quarry is even more beautiful with its shades of green and gold than in its summer colours. I cross Porthill Bridge by the Boathouse pub and climb Beck's Field to savour my favourite view of spires and domes. Then it's down to the river and Kingsland Bridge, and a

Shrewsbury roofscape from Beck's Field

saunter up sunlit Swan Hill, heading home via a network of the town's old passageways.

I wish I could distill the essence of today. I can't remember any occasion when Shrewsbury has looked more beautiful.

31ˢᵗ October: FROM THE URAL MOUNTAINS TO SHREWSBURY

Svetlana grew up in the mountainous region north-west of Kazakhstan, which forms the natural boundary between Europe and Asia. Her step-father wanted her to become an accountant with a good business degree. He didn't like her spending every spare minute painting and drawing.

When Svetlana went to Moscow to enroll in an Art College, she told her parents it was to study accountancy. Without the correct paperwork, however, she ended up training as an inspector of textile machinery.

These were the days before perestroika. Svetlana was discovered in the factory by a group of Agitation Artists looking for recruits. With them she learned the art of producing government propaganda. The money was good and the work kept coming in. A string of government-promoted festivals required slogans, posters and other works of art. 'Darling, you in the West only know about May Day,' said Svetlana. 'But there was also Soviet Military Day, International Women's Day, World War Victory Day and Victory of the Revolution Day.'

Svetlana Elantseva

For many Russians, Svetlana said, the years before perestroika were now seen as the good old days. There was an order to things. Society was stable. Now, however, all that stability had blown away.

Perestroika, meaning 'restructuring' was meant to be about reform within the Soviet Communist Party. However, it led to the collapse of the Soviet Union and end of the Cold War. This may have seemed good to the West, but it was frightening for ordinary Russians. When the old political certainties went, so did the certainties of ordinary life. People lost their jobs, Svetlana said. Their money counted for nothing. Factories closed. Art studios closed. People were offered shares that meant nothing to them as a form of redundancy package, and found themselves prey to shysters who'd buy them up for a shadow of what eventually would be their real value.

Having lost her job, Svetlana studied accountancy, achieved her diploma and ended up with a good job, providing her with a nice flat, driver, cook and cleaner. 'I was one of the lucky ones,' she said.

Very different however was Svetlana's introduction to life in the UK. 'I married an Englishman,' she said. 'I didn't understand what I was in for when he told me about the Shropshire home he shared with his father. My seventeen-year-old son from my first marriage, Nikita, moved to

England ahead of me and told me I wouldn't like it. But I'd always been a bit of an Anglophile. I wouldn't listen. Besides, I was in love.'

Svetlana arrived in Plox Green in her Moscow everyday fashionwear, including killer high heels, to find herself surrounded by fields full of sheep. Her new father-in-law was a lovely old man, but needed a lot of looking after. This was not what she had expected. The marriage didn't last.

'We were both to blame,' Svetlana said. 'Not just my husband, but me too. Neither of us recognised the cultural gulf between us. However, God must have been looking after me because at last I got my art education. I took BTEC in Shrewsbury, then did Art Foundation. Then I went to Stafford University and studied for a BA in Entrepreneurship in Culture & Heritage Industries, which taught me a great deal about business and marketing in Art industries.'

Back in Russia, Svetlana's paintings had reflected her Russian heritage. Here in England, she started exploring different landscapes and an entirely new culture. In addition, she pulled together a group of international artists who are currently exhibiting in Ironbridge, following on from Shrewsbury and Moscow.

'I've made some good friends here in England,' Svetlana said. 'There are teachers at SCAT, and other friends too, who helped me through some very difficult years.'

Currently Svetlana lives with her son Nikita, who works for a Shrewsbury electrical company who have put him through his training as an electrician.

'Shropshire is a beautiful place,' she said, 'but it's not easy to make money here. Moscow's the place for money, but Shrewsbury is the place for art. Better to have a quiet life though – do what you wish and have enough – than to sacrifice your life and have no time or energy to spend all your money.'

Svetlana has worked as a volunteer for the Museum Service, conducting audio interviews with Russians in the county, and other Eastern Bloc ex-pats who have stories to tell. One woman told Svetlana, 'I never felt like a foreigner in Latvia, which is where I lived, or in my home country, Russia. And I do feel like a foreigner here, but even as a foreigner in Britain, I still feel more at home.'

This year Svetlana has organised ten exhibitions, both for herself and for the group Art International Gallery. Their 'Art Without Borders' exhibition is heading for Moscow in the New Year, and from 14th January until 3rd February will be housed in the National Gallery 'Varshavka'.

Svetlana has been painting too. I visited her studio in the light, airy conservatory at the back of Nikita's house. Fiancé, Paul, described Svetlana's painting life as a frenzy of activity. 'It's a case of *out of the way, artist coming through,'* he said. 'Lights, colour, action – that's what it's like.'

Plainly Svetlana is a perfectionist. In conversation she's continually heading for the dictionary. 'How you say, darling..?' 'Have I got that right..?' 'I don't know the word for...' But Svetlana doesn't need to worry. Her English is very good.

There's something tough about Svetlana. You can tell that she's been through a lot and come out the other side. Yet she's gregarious and warm – a charming, outgoing person whom you can't help but warm towards. Svetlana's made her home in England, but she'll always have a Russian heart.

NOVEMBER

5th November: CAKE

Ms X and I went on a cake-finding mission this morning. In case you haven't met her before, Ms X is my secret shopper, aged three-and-a-half. At the top of Roushill we discovered Empire Cupcakery, ordered drinks and cakes and sat down.

Ms X's choice was a monster-faced cake with red stringy hair. I went for rainbow cake in sugary stripes. When Ms X had stuffed down her choice (this didn't take long) she wanted a fair chunk of mine.

Before we left, lured by all the pretty choices, I made the mistake of buying cakes for later as well. Even midway through the afternoon, however, Ms X was so full that she couldn't eat. Don't tell her mother. I don't think she'd approve.

Empire Cupcakery's rainbow slice

8th November: SHREWSBURY ANTIQUES CENTRE

Round the back of Princess House lies a treasure house of collectables, but all that hints at it are a pair of glass doors through which can be seen stairs leading downwards. At the bottom of those stairs – under Princess House if my geography is right – lies a vast underground cavern with antiques, vintage clothes and bric-a-brac – a cornucopia of collectables, stretching in every direction with always something new to find.

I've been mooching about in the Shrewsbury Antiques Centre for the past thirty years. Originally set up by John Lanford, assisted by Matt

Smith (who, after John died, took up the reins) it may be underground, and therefore out of sight, but its magnetic power has drawn me back – and back. I've bought everything down there, from fine Coalport cups to costume jewellery, Victorian household items to old toys, vintage clothing to furniture.

Rumours abound that the place is haunted. I was talking about this the other day to the Antiques Centre's John Allen. Some people reckon this huge underground space once included holding cells for the police but, whatever stories it may have to tell, John has seen no ghosts.

These days, he says, a wind of change is blowing through the

Antiques Centre, with some older stallholders stepping down – a number moving on to open their own shops – and new stallholders trying their hand. The key to becoming a successful collector, reckons John, is to always buy quality. And the key to selling successfully is to find things that people don't have, but would like to. 'If it's quirky and priced well, it will sell,' John said.

John knows what he's talking about. As well as being a collector of fine art he's a stallholder who has come to selling for 'a bit of fun' after a life in business. It takes a while to get the

John Allen in the Shrewsbury Antiques Centre

hang of running a stall, he said. A while to find out what sells, and at what price. You need to understand your market too. And you have to expect people to haggle. The deferential 'Antiques Roadshow' attitude to pricing is over. 'It's all "Bargain Hunt" nowadays,' said John. 'People will haggle over pennies.'

Currently Shrewsbury Antiques Centre sees about 500 customers a day – not bad for an outlet without a shop front. I wondered what difference eBay had made to customer figures. John reckoned its effect was minimal. 'Ebay provides customers with an instant price list,' he said. 'But it can't compete in terms of seeing items and actually handling them. For customer service, a real antiques market is hard to beat.'

If there's something you want, the Shrewsbury Antiques Centre will put it into their 'wanted' book. People's choices were often inexplicable, John said. There was the young collector of vinyl who couldn't explain why he wanted a record by the West Midlands Police Choir, and a student looking for a party costume who'd no idea what SS stood for.

There have been some amusing moments, too. One night, when Matt had switched off the lights, a shriek arose from the bowels of the building and it became apparent that he'd been about to lock in no less than Jools Holland.

'This is a good business to get into,' John said. 'With everything so low, interest rates and the current price of antiques, now's a good time for young people to start. We charge £28 a week per stall and £9.50 a week for a cabinet, which is nothing compared to the risk of taking on a shop. Just a shelf in a cabinet is a good first move.'

The Shrewsbury Antiques Centre is big enough to get lost in, yet intimate enough for help to be available should you need it. Faces haven't changed much over the years. There's still Matt behind the desk, and Damon and Donna, and now John and Sandra too. Raisa the dog has gone, sadly. Her paws have proved hard to fill, but Mavis has come in her place, and is doggedly giving it her all. She has a fan club and has received mail from as far away as the US. Currently she's expecting puppies on Armistice Day.

Next year, as part of their 30th anniversary, Shrewsbury Antiques Centre will be fund-raising for the Air Ambulance Service. This December they'll be open on Wednesday evenings for the first time for late-night shopping. If you've never taken a time traveller's trip through their doors, this could be your chance.

13th November: SHREWSBURY SCHOOL'S ANCIENT LIBRARY

Shrewsbury School is part of the backdrop against which our town is set. Take a walk along the river, and you'll pass Shrewsbury schoolboys rowing on the Severn. Walk through the Quarry and you can't miss the main school building standing high above the river, or fail to hear its bell ringing out the hour.

Last Sunday morning I visited the school's Ancient Library and met Michael Morrogh, its Ancient Librarian. Thanks to him, I became acquainted with 'Dr Taylor's MS', a Tudor town chronicle dated from the late 1570s drawing on local annals, broadsheets and pamphlets, full of murders, suicides, executions, prognostications, freaks of nature, fires, floods, earthquakes etc. Has the world changed? I don't think so.

I also browsed through a collection of memorabilia from the First and Second World Wars, including a pamphlet on the Re-conquest of America ('the Most Astounding Document Ever Discovered in The History of International Intrigue') and the Ruhleben Prisoner of War Camp Magazine, which contained some quite extraordinary drawings. I also saw the School's chained library.

Shrewsbury School's chained library

These were the books I'd come to see, the old guys – the really old ones; the ones that make my 19th century acquisitions from Candle Lane Books seem like Johnny-come-latelies. And one book in particular interested me.

I found it in the library's inner sanctum – a strong-room so strong that walking into it felt like entering an air-conditioned safe (but then I was entering an air-conditoned safe).

I'm talking about the Tyndale Bible.

In its day, the Tyndale Bible was dynamite. Certainly for William Tyndale, who ended up executed in horrendous fashion, its effects were explosive. And for the English, who now had the Bible in their everyday tongue, not just the Latin of the educated few, it was dynamite too. Not only did Tyndale dare to translate the New Testament into English, he did so from the original Hebrew and Greek rather than the Catholic Church's 'received' text.

Some say that English as we now know it was formed out of Tyndale's taking of the unpopular Middle-English 'vulgar' tongue, improving it with the help of Greek and Hebrew phraseology and sentence structures and forming out of it an early modern English that Shakespeare and others would draw upon. I'm no historian or linguist, so wouldn't know about that, but I do know that Tyndale was a reformer and a man of principle and faith.

In order to translate his Bible, Tyndale was forced to move abroad and become a fugitive. His life became a series of betrayals, escapes and flights from the authorities. When he died (in 1536, by strangulation, followed by burning at the stake) he prayed that the King of England's eyes would be opened.

And indeed they were. The Tyndale Bible played a massive part in the Reformation. It was part of a new attitude – a freedom from authority. Featuring prominently in the Geneva Bible that went out on the Mayflower with America's founding fathers, it also found its way into the King James Bible, which is still read today.

For a book with such a history, the Bible I saw in Shrewsbury School's Ancient Library was surprisingly small. I'd expected some massive tome, but it was almost small enough to pocket. I saw other books in the Ancient Library – John Donne's poems in first edition amongst them – but none impressed as much as this.

The only MS that came anywhere near it was the Shrewsbury Fragment.

For almost a year, I've been holding back from writing about the Fragment in the spirit of saving the best until last. I knew it was one of Shrewsbury's treasures, but I'd no idea where it was housed. Certainly I never thought I'd actually see it. And now I have.

I left the library, my head spinning, heading down an avenue of flame-coloured trees with old boy Charles Darwin's statue at one end of it, representing the Sciences, and Sir Philip Sidney's at the other, representing the Arts.

Thank you Michael Morrogh, Ancient Librarian, for allowing me to browse so freely. Thank you too, Andrew Dalton, Head of Philosophy and Theology, for being my fixer behind the scenes.

15th November: WHAT'S CRICKET IN INDIA GOT TO DO WITH SHREWSBURY TODAY?

My Tonight From Shrewsbury is slightly thin on the ground when it comes to sport, so why, if I'm writing about cricket, does it have to be in India, not Shrewsbury, I hear you ask.

The answer lies in a photograph I saw this morning of a crowd of outstretched hands all reaching for the cricketer, Sachin Tendulkar, who first played for India the year the Berlin Wall came down, and yesterday stepped out for his final 664th international appearance.

Sport doesn't do much for me, but heroism does, and so does the striving of the human spirit to leave its mark. Prior to Tendulkar's final match at the Wankhede Stadium, umpires and opponents (the West Indies) formed a guard of honour for the forty-year-old cricketer and his team-mates. 'After breaking nearly every record in international cricket, scoring more runs and more centuries than any other player, Tendulkar seemed the calmest person in the stadium,' wrote Guardian journalist, Dileep Premachandran.

Certainly, at the sight of Tendulkar, the 32,000 capacity stadium went wild. Banners waved, fans roared and feet were stamped. As the West Indies went in to bat, the stadium roof was ringed by fifty-one massive photographs, one for each of Tendulkar's Test centuries. Each time he caught the ball, roars broke out, whilst a giant electronic screen threw up messages from around the world.

Why am I telling you this? It's because the article made me cry. Even before hearing about Sachin Tendulkar's mother receiving a standing ovation on this first of her son's matches she'd ever attended, I had tears in my eyes.

Partly it was the unshowiness of Tendulkar that got to me, remaining extraordinarily calm whilst the rest of the stadium was in ferment. But, most of all, it was the sheer doggedness of the man that reduced me to tears.

I felt the same the other day when I read about the jockey A.P. McCoy and his 4,000th win. There are people out there who don't just win the short, sharp sprint. They hunker down for the marathon – and they don't shout about it either. They just get on with it.

I'm guessing that describes most of our lives. In fact, I'd like to think there's a bit of Sachin Tendulkar in all of us. A bit of A.P. McCoy too. Sporting achievements aren't just notched up somewhere else. Quietly and unheralded, we in Shrewsbury, as much as anywhere else in the world, notch up triumphs every day. Maybe no one sees them, and no crowds come to cheer, but a job well done can bring its own rewards.

15th November: RICHARD II AND THE REVENGE PARLIAMENT IN SHREWSBURY

A few nights ago I had a ticket to watch David Tennant, in live link from Stratford, performing Shakespeare's Richard II. For days in advance I researched him (Richard, not David), interested to find out whether he had any Shrewsbury connections. And did he, by gum.

In 1387, the young underage king, Richard II, paid a visit to Shrewsbury that in no small part led to his being deposed, and eventually to his tragic and thoroughly unpleasant death. Accompanied by his powerful and not-to-be-trusted uncle, the Duke of Gloucester, Richard was licking his wounds after a trouncing in parliament had stripped him of a number of his powers.

In Shrewsbury, Richard called together the chief justice of the day, Sir Robert Tresillian, and a group of other judges and eminent lawyers, and invited them to deliberate upon the validity of parliament's actions – and to put their deliberations in writing.

When parliament discovered what Richard had been up to, they punished Richard's legal experts in the 'Merciless Parliament' of 1388. Those with seats in parliament were impeached. Some were fined, others imprisoned and their advice overturned. The Lords Appellant who acted against the king included Henry Bolingbroke. Keep an eye on that name.

In 1389, the young Richard seized control of power, declaring himself to be old enough to govern without his uncle, who was subsequently murdered. Peace negotiations with France began. Westminster Hall was rebuilt. Treaties were made, truces sealed and opposition put down.

Now was the moment for Richard to have revenge on parliament. It was convened in Westminster in September 1397, and then prorogued and moved by the king – to Shrewsbury.

Yes, you heard me. Shrewsbury.

In history there is a name for the parliament that sat in Shrewsbury in 1398, and that is the Revenge Parliament. Every Shrewsbury child should know about it.

The king arrived in Shrewsbury determined to have his way, and to do so by overwhelming parliament, here in this remote corner of his kingdom, with a demonstration of regal splendour. On 25th January he entered the town with great pomp and circumstance. He then put on a sumptuous feast that dazzled parliament with the awesomeness of monarchy and indulged his taste for all things extravagant.

By the time it sat, Richard had parliament eating out of his hands. This obsequious parliament is how it's described by Owen and Blakeway in their *History of Shrewsbury* – and it's not hard to see why.

In full assembly, all the proceedings of the previous parliament were overturned. Lord Chief Justice Tressalin's legal advice to the king was agreed to be totally constitutional. All powers gained by the earlier parliament were returned to the king. Parliament even went so far as to grant subsidies on wood and leather to the king for life, and to provide a generous sum of money for the purpose of making compensation to anyone who had suffered for their attachment to the royal cause.

Richard had what he wanted – but it wasn't enough. He forced all lords, spiritual and temporal, to swear in parliament on the cross of Canterbury, (brought in for the occasion) that the statutes of this parliament would be kept for ever. The clergy had to swear too. So did the knights of the shires.

Then, as if that wasn't enough, Richard sent out a proclamation to the people of Shrewsbury, demanding to know if these new parliamentary measures had their assent. In an act of solidarity with their king, the good folk of Shrewsbury lifted their hands and cried aloud that they were well pleased. Highborn and low, common men and lords, at the Revenge Parliament in Shrewsbury all gave their assent.

Richard must have left Shrewsbury in a fine frame of mind. But his victory was short-lived. What the country really wanted wasn't kingly elegance and pageantry. It was wisdom in government and courage on the battlefield, and though Richard II had shown great promise in his youth (the way he stood up in person to Wat Tyler and the mob was nothing short of extraordinary) he was to finally fail on both counts. In fact, the final years of Richard's reign were a time of unbridled tyranny.

In 1398, Richard's cousin, Henry Bolingbroke, was exiled to France. In 1399, Bolingbroke's father died and Richard seized his lands. This was a big mistake. Enraged, Bolingbroke returned, gathering an army around him. It was the end for Richard.

By the time that Henry Bolingbroke seized the crown as Henry IV (that usurper is how Blakeway and Owen refer to him), the tide in Shrewsbury had turned too. Henry's arrival in the town that only two years before had so vocally supported Richard, was greeted by an outpouring of apparent joy, Shrewsbury's townsfolk describing themselves as Henry's 'loyal liegemen of the county of Salop' who, with 'their most entire will and heart' would attend on the new king to the utmost of their power, 'supporting and strengthening him and his adherents'.

So there you have it – the life and times of Richard II, as viewed from Shrewsbury. Richard's end came swiftly. Forced to abdicate, he's reputed to have been starved to death in Pontefract Castle while his cousin ruled in his place.

PS. I'm gutted. After all that research, I never did get to see David Tennant play Richard II. Typically I wrote the wrong day in my diary! However, by happy coincidence, I did get to hear David Natzler, Clerk Assistant to the House of Commons, giving a fascinating talk at Shrewsbury's Sixth Form College on the subject of our town's connection to parliament, including the Revenge Parliament.

PPS. I'm with David Tennant on Shakespeare. Apparently Julian Fellowes (who's just adapted Romeo and Juliet for the big screen) reckons you need a 'very expensive education' to understand him. But Tennant disagrees. 'I don't have an expensive education,' he's recorded as saying. 'I went to a comprehensive in Paisley, and I don't think Shakespeare's plays are remotely difficult.'

What do you think?

20th November: OFFICIAL WINTER STARTS HERE

This morning's dog walk is accompanied by dark clouds over the castle, rain and a weird reindeer wire-thing in front of the Darwin Shopping Centre. Tonight's dog walk is accompanied by crowds on Pride Hill, Father Christmas in the Square and the switching on of the town's Christmas lights.

Shrewsbury school children's lantern procession

On the High Street I find our Town Crier, Martin Wood, followed by a Boy Scout drum band and a lantern procession directed by Maggie Love in a hat with flashing lights. They pile into the Square and I pick up my dog before he gets trampled underfoot. The Mayor on the podium, is presiding over the countdown. '10-9-8-7-6-5-4-3-2-1,' we all yell – but nothing happens.

Apparently we're not loud enough. We try again. It works this time. Where's the year gone? The Christmas lights are on again.

Official winter starts here.

26th November: FILM NIGHTS AT THE HIVE

I first met Peter Pack at the Shrewsbury Film Society, which meets at the Hive on Belmont Bank. He's Assistant Head at Adam's Grammar School. His favourite author is Philip Roth. He's ex-Chair of the international board of Amnesty. He's also a film buff, and has been helping to run the Shrewsbury Film Society since he, wife Sally and friend Corinne started it back in 2011.

Initially, said Peter, they began with six films and tiny audiences, an ancient projector and a large white sheet. One of their main preoccupations was whether equipment might fall apart and hit someone on the head.

Figures remained small for the first year, but at the start of the second year in September 2012, seventy-five members turned up. 'The word must have got out,' said Peter. 'It wasn't down to us. It was down to word of mouth.'

Two grants from Shropshire Council provided a new screen and surround sound. The Co-Op Community Fund provided a projector and DVD player. This year the Film Society bought a hundred chairs with arms for the knock-down price of £400. 'So now films can be watched in comfort too,' Peter said.

Every year, Peter and the rest of the committee sift through a mass of films, aware that people wouldn't necessarily like the same as them. People want humour as well as drama. They want specialist films alongside broad interest ones. They want popular cinema, and art house too. 'What we're after is a balanced programme,' Peter said.

This season's first film – 'Welcome to the Sticks' – was suggested by a member. So too was 'Moonrise Kingdom' and Woody Allen's 'Crimes and Misdemeanours'. My personal favourite so far has been Wim Wender's 'Pina', about the life of the legendary, now deceased choreographer, Pina Bauer. 'Tokyo Story' has been one of Peter's most enjoyable showings – a gentle film on the subject of parents' disappointment with their children. 'I'd also like to show some Hitchcock,' he said, 'or do a Jack Nicholson series. Nicholson was a fantastic actor in his early days.'

Peter grew up in North London, close to Hampstead and a local cinema called the Everyman, which showed different films every day. Sometimes there would be a double or even triple bill and the films were on a loop. You could go in at whatever point you wanted and stay for as long as you liked.

In addition, Peter remembers BBC2's Saturday night World Cinema evenings. Nowadays he reckons you'd be hard pressed to find a foreign language film on non-subscription television, let alone on a Saturday night. Back then, however, Saturday night TV was his introduction to Bergman, Antonioni, Truffaut, Jean Luc Godard and all the other great names.

Peter's choice of films, he said, always leant towards the concept of director as authorial voice. Was that voice unique? Did it have something special to say that made the film stand out?

I asked Peter what were his all-time favourite films. 'Citizen Kane' came up straightaway, followed by the 'The Travelling Players', directed by Theo Angelopoulos who was killed in a motorbike accident last year. Then there was 'Stalker' by Andrei Tarkovsky. The book *Zona* by Geoff Dyer was all about that film, taking it apart shot by shot. 'I heard Dyer speaking at Hay,' Peter said. 'He said, 'Hands up who's seen the film?' – after all, Stalker's not that well known – 'but every hand went up.'

The Shrewsbury Film Society committee go down to the British Federation of Film Societies' annual meeting and come away with new

Peter Pack

directors and films. 'Like Father, Like Son' by Hirokazu Kore-Eda is one of those, and 'No' is another.

Peter would love to put on a day of films, laced together with discussion. He likes it when members make choices, and are prepared to say something at the showing about what the film means to them.

Over the years, Peter said, he and the rest of the committee had got to know the regulars. A small number were film buffs. Others were just there for a good night out.

'If you're a member with a season ticket, you're getting a night out for £2.25, exclusive of drinks,' Peter said. 'Where else in Shrewsbury can you do that? And, if you turn up on spec and buy on the door it's still only £5.'

Coming up this Saturday night, 8.00pm at the Shrewsbury Film Society, is 'The Gatekeepers', which according to Time Out is gripping, unnerving and worthy of a Bourne movie, the Guardian calls it 'a compelling overview of a modern security agency,' and Film4 calls it 'a fascinating film offering a startling look inside one of the most tightlipped intelligence agencies on the planet.'

I won't be there unfortunately, but I attend showings as often as I can. It's not just films I know about that I've enjoyed, but ones I've never heard of before, discovering new directors, new actors and stories that challenge, fascinate, entertain and sometimes touch me deeply. What more can I say? I commend the Shrewsbury Film Society to you.

DECEMBER

4th December: SHOPPING

The sausages are on. The sandwich boxes are open on the work surface under the crystal chandeliers. The rolls are being buttered. The porridge should be in the oven for the B & B guests, but it isn't yet. Mae appears and collects her box. She pulls on her blue duffle coat, dons her helmet, gets on her bike and sets off for school. Charlie's still in pyjamas, sneaking back to bed with a slice of toast for a bit more telly before he officially gets up. Bethan will appear later, but she doesn't have to be up as early as the other two, or as early as their mum, Sarah Hopper of Ferndell B & B.

Ferndell sits on the corner of Underdale Road, looking across the park towards the river. It's a fine old house with a light and airy kitchen and an Aga to give it that extra bit of 'heart'.

Sarah's preparing breakfast for this morning's guests. She hears their voices on the stairs and slides the kettle onto the hob. The porridge comes out of the oven. The bacon is cooked. The eggs are ready to go.

Into the kitchen come sisters Diane and Sandy, shortly followed by Diane's daughter, another Sarah, who's on crutches, but not even a broken leg is going to come between her and the shopping that the three of them are here to do.

Christmas is only a month away. Ferndell's guests live out in Wales where there's little access to good shops. They've left partners at home and taken time off work to come to Shrewsbury in Sandy's van, which by tonight they will have packed.

Breakfast arrives at the table, along with tea and coffee. The food looks good, but the chatter scarcely stops. Coming here to Shrewsbury is a real treat for these three women. It's not just about the shopping. It's their chance to meet up.

'We love it here at Ferndell,' says Diane. 'Can't praise it highly enough. We've been made to feel so welcome and at home.'

Ferndell Sarah beams. She's hovering in the background making toast and scrambling eggs, refilling tea and coffee pots. You hardly notice what she's doing, but it never stops.

Her guests, it seems, never stop either. 'Do you know,' announces Diane proudly, 'Yesterday we shopped for thirteen hours solid, and only went round five shops.'

Below the Darwin Centre is the Shopmobility outlet where yesterday Daughter Sarah abandoned her crutches for a scooter, which enabled her to shop all over the town centre. 'They were so helpful,' she said, 'and all the scooters had names. You pay a small fee and add what you feel like as a donation. You can even park your car down there. Shopping with a broken leg couldn't be made easier.'

Sarah Hopper with shoppers Sandy, Di and Sarah

Yesterday Sarah's guests hit the big stores. Today it's the turn of Shrewsbury's little independent shops and the town's passageways and fascinating little shuts. Then tonight the three of them will head off for the cinema and a meal.

'We're going to the Pizza Hut next to Sainsbury's,' Sandy says. 'We've heard good things about it. I'm vegan and not easy to feed, and we hear they're good at talking through vegan options.'

Sandy is vegan for ethical reasons. She has a great love of animals, as witnessed by her seven cats and six dogs, many of whom come from a rescue home in Cyprus. Diane manages the agency European Lifestyle, supporting individuals living in their own homes with mental health issues. Daughter Sarah works for the same agency. As a support care worker she goes into college with clients and gets involved in their interests and activities, including music and drama.

This year Daughter Sarah will be a fairy in the pantomime, so yesterday saw her buying fairy-lights. Next September she'll be going to college to study to become a primary school teacher.

Daughter Sarah's also a musician, singing, playing the guitar, writing her own material, loving the blues and jazz. Sometimes she performs with her dad, who's a comedian and entertainer. Next week the two of them are putting on a gig to raise funds for the typhoon-struck Philippines.

The plates empty and the coffee and tea cups are drained. Ferndell's guests depart, saying that they've been made to feel like family. It's quiet in the kitchen after they've gone.

A cake goes in the oven and breakfast is cleared up. Sarah's expecting the arrival of her next visitor soon, so I slip away. Thanks for breakfast. That was great. Thanks, too, Sarah, for all the encouragement you've given this blog. It's developed a large following over the year, and your enthusiastic tweets about it have played their part.

6th December: TWO ANCIENT SHREWSBURY CELEBRATION CAKES

The Shrewsbury Simnel started out as a raised cake with a crust of flour and water, coloured with saffron. Its interior was a rich plum cake mix with candied lemon peel. The whole thing would be tied in a cloth, boiled for several hours, brushed with egg and then baked. By the time it was ready to eat, its crust would be as hard as wood. Yum.

Hardly surprisingly, local yarns abound of unfortunate recipients of Shrewsbury Simnels using them as footstools, not knowing what else they might be. By the time the poet Herrick wrote about them, though, Shrewsbury Simnels had become the distinctive marzipan cake that we have today.

It was the custom, apparently, for young people in service to take them home as presents on Mothering Sunday. The Foods of England website says that they were baked for Christmas, Easter or New Year. Charlotte Burne, in her *Shropshire Folk-Lore*, says that the Shrewsbury Simnel was known as a springtime celebration cake.

The origin of this cake is said to date back to the 13th century. I've failed to find an original recipe, but here is what I have found, from Emily Elizabeth Steele Elliott's *Copsley Annals Preserved in Proverbs*:

'She who would a simnel make,
Flour and saffron first must shake,
Candy, spices, eggs must take,
Chop and pound till arms do ache :
Then must boil, and then must bake
For a crust too hard to break.
When at Mid-lent thou dost wake,
To thy mother bear thy cake :
She will prize it for thy sake.'

Simnels aren't the only cakes associated with Shrewsbury. Another was known simply as 'Shrewsbury Cake'. Later it developed into the Shrewsbury biscuit, courtesy of Mr Palin of Castle Street, but in its heyday it was a large shortbread, flavoured distinctively with rosewater.

Here's a recipe for Shrewsbury Cake, taken from *The Complete Cook* of 1658:

'Take two pound of floure dryed in the Oven and weighed after it is dryed, then put to it one pound of Butter that must be layd an hour or two in Rose-water, so done poure the Water from the Butter, and put the Butter to the flowre with the yolks and whites of five Eggs, two races of Ginger, and three quarters of a pound of Sugar, a little salt, grate your spice, and it well be the better, knead all these together till you may rowle the past, then roule it forth with the top of a bowle, then prick them with a pin made of wood, or if you have a comb that hath not been used, that will do them quickly, and is best to that purpose, so bake them upon Pye plates, but not too much in the Oven, for the heat of the Plates will dry them very much, after they come forth of the Oven, you may cut them without the bowles of what bignesse or what fashion you please.'

8th December: STREET PASTORS

Shrewsbury's Street Pastors go out into the town centre on Friday and Saturday nights, aiming to help people who might get themselves into trouble. They've been doing this for several years now and their distinctive caps and jackets have become as much a part of the night-time scene as the police and other community services. If trouble's brewing in a particular part of town, doormen or police often call in the street pastors, not because their role is to get involved in sorting out fights but because their presence is recognised as having a calming influence.

'Many times it's just our being there that calms things down,' said Street Pastor Steve Jones. 'That's what we're told anyway. And it might be hard to explain exactly why, but yes, I can see that that does happen.'

This morning I witnessed the official commissioning of Steve, along with Jane Lamb and Pauline Jones on the outskirts of Shrewsbury at Holy Trinity Church, Meole Brace.

Street Pastors' commissioning at Holy Trinity, Meole Brace

'We go out in teams of four,' Jane said. 'Starting at Central (the Baptist building on the corner of Claremont Street, formerly Claremont Baptist Church) we meet for prayer. Relying on God for help is an important part of being a street pastor. Then around 9.00pm we'll set off to do a recce of the town. This will include the Rowley's House area, where there are a number of clubs, then up past the Shrewsbury Hotel in the direction of the Salopian and the Premier Inn. Maybe we'll take in the Mardol too. Then we'll loop round the station and up Castle Gates, up Castle Street, down Pride Hill, along Fish Street, along High Street - almost all the way round town in fact, getting a feel for what sort of night it is.'

The town has its moods. Sometimes its nights are quiet, but sometimes there's a definite hint of something in the air. 'We might get a shout,' said Pauline. 'Something's kicking off and we'll head for it. We might do this as a foursome, or split into pairs. But whatever we're doing, we're never on our own.'

There are twenty-four street pastors in Shrewsbury, representing all the town's churches. Mostly they find themselves handing out water to dehydrated revellers, flip-flops for sore feet and blankets for partygoers who may be out on the street and getting cold.

Sometimes too much alcohol makes people disoriented or distressed. They'll be on their own, maybe separated from their friends, and the street pastors help to get them back to the rest of their group, or point them in the right direction home.

Tragically, over the years Shrewsbury has had a record of river deaths, as high as six or seven per annum, attributable to night-time revelling. That's the figure Steve quoted, anyway. But since the street pastors started up, he said that figure, astonishingly, has dropped to none.

'People ask us what street pastors are,' said Jane Lamb. 'They want to know why we're doing it especially when they find out we're not paid. And the answer is always the same. We want to show people love, our love and the love of God. And we do this in all sorts of ways. Even with flip-flops.'

Jane was a street pastor down in Plymouth, but Steve and Pauline have only been on the streets for a few months. Mostly what they do is well received. People could be throwing up one moment, apologising the next. Shropshire people, they said, were very sweet.

How hard, I wondered, was it keeping going through the long night? 'At some point,' Pauline said, 'we'll head back to Central where we're based for a break of coffee, tea and toast. It's warm in there, so it's easy not to want to go out again. But we do.'

10th December: R & A COLLABORATIONS

Around this time last year I was on the coast of west Wales for a film about my novel, *Telling the Sea*, which was made by the film-makers, R & A Collaborations. We were reminiscing about the shoot the other day, and about their interest in filming artists, craftspeople and writers.

R & A Collaborations are Shrewsbury-based photographer Richard Foot and digital media artist Arron Fowler. Their first collaboration was for the Power of Making exhibition at the Victoria and Albert Museum, producing short films about weaver Helen Foot and stained-glass artist Nathalie Hildegarde Liege.

Being featured in the Power of Making exhibition against so much competition was a fantastic start for a working collaboration. R & A have been filming and developing ever since. In the early days they created a buzz by producing a film in a day. Shooting, reviewing footage, recording interviews, putting it all together – the pace was frantic and it produced a certain kind of film, immediate, lively, very intimate.

R & A's first few films were made this way. 'We called it the 5-5-7 Project,' said Arron. 'Five makers, five films, seven days. A week of almost non-stop filming to produce a distinctive body of work. It was an experiment – a mad, mad project that stretched our practice to the limits.'

R & A's willingness to give their all in the name of film is something I can attest to. Last winter, over two days in wild west Wales, Richard and Arron staggered over cliff-tops lugging equipment whilst I sounded off about writing in general and *Telling the Sea* in particular, creating a film that clearly spoke for me as an author as well as for my work. 'I feel as if I know you,' wrote the Belizean writer and academic, Zee Edgell, after seeing the film. 'When you came down those stairs,' said Su Barber of Mmm & Co 'I knew you immediately in a strangely intimate way – and it was because of the film.'

'If we're going to make films, especially ones about craftspeople,' said Arron, 'then the films themselves need careful crafting. There are some horrendous examples of craft film out there. People think any publicity is better than none, but that's wrong.'

In the craft community, Richard and Arron have discovered an open, friendly and very talented group of people, driven not by ego but the work itself. Many don't realise what fascinating stories they have to tell. And by means of film, R & A are telling those tales.

Recently R & A Collaborations spent some time filming for Texprint in Paris. They were there with twenty-four graduates from top UK universities who'd been selected to attend the influential textile industry fair, Premier Vision.

'These students were at Premier Vision for exposure,' Arron said. 'Our job was to interview them and their sponsors, and make films about them. All 24 of them. We had ten days' notice. We were already booked to do two films with Confessions of a Design Geek for the London Design Festival. So we knew we were going to be under pressure.'

R & A hit Paris on the Wednesday and returned that night for filming in London. The first London film was ready by that same Friday, and the second by Saturday. Paris, however, was more complex and took longer.

'We never storyboard,' Richard said. 'Over-planning takes the fun out of the thing. There's a danger of losing spontaneity.'

In two years, R & A Collaborations have produced thirty-five films. This has been achieved with stop-motion photography rather than by shooting video, creating what's now recognisable as their distinctive style.

'We can create an effect that you wouldn't get on video,' explained Arron. 'Our films are literally constructed frame by frame.'

'The way we work,' Richard added, 'every second counts. All the time we're getting better at this. I knew almost nothing about editing before Arron and I joined forces. Now I know a lot.'

'And I've learned a lot about photography,' Arron said, 'and about people. My experience has been that they're almost exclusively

Arron Fowler and Richard Foot

lovely. They can be challenging, but rarely are they awful.'

Richard and Arron are currently preparing to go to Milan for the major Science of Stuff project 'Light Touch Matters'. The aim of this project is to bring together scientists and designers, and R & A's role is to film what happens when they do.

This is a typical R & A adventure. They're interested in ideas and in new things going on. Interested in people too, and seeing how they grow and develop. 'We came to Alexandra Abraham at a pivotal moment in her career,' said Arron, 'and there have been others too. Kate Gilliland, for example. What we're doing, we hope, is not only enriching people's working lives, but their personal lives too.

'It's easy for craftspeople to think they're not worth much and to sell themselves on the cheap. When they do that though they undervalue the whole craft community. It's important for that community to appreciate its worth. And appreciating one's worth is what R & A Collaborations is all about.'

13th December
FRIDAY 13th – JUST ONE OF THOSE DAYS

Today has been One of Those Days. For starters, it rained. Every time I stepped out of either my house or car, it rained, and every time I got back inside again, it stopped. I felt targeted. It was heavy rain. Shrewsbury doesn't look so good in heavy rain. I didn't feel so good either.

All morning I was in and out of the car, to the supermarket, to the council tip, into my basement to remove piles of junk, out to the car, to the tip again, finally back home along roads clogged with traffic, hoping the traffic wardens would recognise (which they don't always, I'm sorry to say) the difference between a parked car and one that was simply unloading.

Finally I had the contents of my car emptied into my house. How had I managed to come back with twice as much as I'd taken to the tip? My hall looked horrible, so did my kitchen. Staring at the sea of mess around me, two stark choices came into my head. Either I spent the rest of my dreary, irritating, unproductive day unpacking – or I went to the cinema.

I don't usually head off to the cinema in the middle of the day, but what had started out as 'One of Those Days' had turned into a 'F**k It Day'. You can guess which choice I made. Down Pride Hill I strode (in the rain), passing buskers and Big Issue girl without a hint of a smile, heading for the Old Market Hall cinema, which looks like a medieval building (it is) not a cinema, until you get close and see the posters behind the glass.

Is this the oldest cinema in the country? I don't know, and on that occasion I didn't care. In fact I didn't even care what I saw, which turned out to be 'Saving Mr Banks' with Emma Thompson as P.L. Travers, author of Mary Poppins – a film I'd wanted to see anyway.

Was the day turning my way? I thought it might be as I sank into my seat – but then the awful thought came to me that I had forgotten something in my diary, which I'd left at home. A date with somebody. An interview for My Tonight. Somebody was going to be knocking on my door, and I wouldn't be there. Not only that, but I'd left blackcurrant sorbet (which should have gone straight into the freezer) in my favourite shopping bag, and now it would be ruined, and probably everything else in it too.

The Ark shop on Castle Street

Dashing out of the house had been nothing short of eccentric. People were going to think (indeed, I was thinking) that something might be the matter with me.

I hardly took in the film, except to notice that Tom Hanks gave a good performance and to wish I had it in me to be as acerbic sometimes as Emma Thompson's P.L. Travers. Afterwards I dragged myself up Pride Hill in yet another shower of rain, fretting about what I'd find when I arrived home. When I did, astonishingly the sorbet had held its shape. And the diary was empty. My cinema trip had been ruined for nothing.

It was around this time I discovered that it was Friday the 13th. I like to think I'm not superstitious, and yet I thought of course. Certainly it raised the second smile of the day.

The first smile, however – and the bigger one by far – came when I hit Castle Street and found that a new charity shop in aid of the Shrewsbury Ark would soon be opening in a unit just past H & M. I was thrilled to see their sign up in the big, empty shop. The work the Ark does amongst the homeless and vulnerable of Shrewsbury is second to none.

16th December: CASTLE GATES LIBRARY

Castle Gates Library is housed in what has to be one of the finest buildings associated with public lending across the country. We're lucky to have such a beautiful library, and the extraordinary thing is that everybody's welcome in it, seven days a week – and it's for free.

I've been a member since moving to Shropshire in 1974. I was a newcomer to the county, wintering amongst the library's shelves,

Caroline Buckley outside Castle Gates Library

discovering authors whom I've loved ever since, Charlotte Burne, Georgina Jackson, A.G. Bradley and Brian Waters to name a few, and through their eyes being introduced to Shropshire.

However, it wasn't until the other day, when I met Castle Gates' Branch Manager, Caroline Buckley, that I learned about the way the library works. Its smooth running, she said, depended on a mass of mundane but nevertheless important things that mostly happened before the public were let in. The hour before the library opened was always busy. There were date-stamps to be updated, newspapers to put out, daily deliveries of requested books and returns to be received and recorded, and shelves to be tidied on a rolling rota basis.

A typical library day would see people being helped to find the books they wanted, and to use the computers. On Story Times days, up to thirty toddlers and parents would turn up. For the monthly babies' Rhythm Time, the children's library could become a bit of a buggy park.

Staff from Castle Gates Library would often go out to smaller libraries too, like the Lantern on Sundorne, to help with activities. They'd organise author events, school visits, book quests, poetry reading and writing competitions.

Caroline has been at Castle Gates Library for fifteen years, but can remember it back to when she was a child. Everything has changed, she said. There was no internet then, of course, but then there wasn't when she started working in the library fifteen years ago. No online referencing. No emailing. No computers. But there were stuffed birds in cases, and an art gallery upstairs.

In the 1980s a massive revamp took place of the Castle Gates building, separating library and museum services. Then, in more recent years, the decision was made to open the library seven days a week. The biggest challenge of recent years, however, according to Caroline, was absorbing government cutbacks, which in Castle Gate's case meant having to house the Reference Library, which was losing its building.

'Some library services have faced far bigger cutbacks than that,' said Caroline. 'It was sad for the town to lose a separate reference library, but it could have been so much worse.'

Much of library staff's time is taken up with the actual, physical activity of looking after books. There are new ones to buy from lists put together by suppliers, old ones to repair. Looking after stock is of vital importance. A book's binding will often be the first thing to go, according to Caroline. A careful repair, or a simple re-jacketing, can give a book months more life.

The Castle Gates Library aims to have a bit of everything. Crime novels are popular, as are thrillers, books made into films and Booker Prize wins. You got to know the regulars' tastes, Caroline said. You followed reviews and picked up trends. 'The best thing about my job,' she said, 'is that two days in the library are never the same – and I'm never short of a good book to read.'

17th December: MEET DENISA

Meet Denisa, Pride Hill's *Big Issue* girl. She hails from Romania, but now lives in Birmingham. She's been selling the *Big Issue* for two years. Her sister looks after her little son Narcis while she's at work. Denisa collects her *Big Issue*s from the Shrewsbury Ark, which saves her having to haul them all the way from Birmingham. Sometimes she's

Denisa – Shrewsbury's Big Issue seller

really cold, but she wears lots of layers to keep herself warm.

If, like me, you're a town-centre resident, Denisa is a part of your local neighbourhood. She always has a smile. I can't think of a time when I've gone by and she hasn't said hello. She never pushes her wares on me, but just seems naturally friendly.

I don't know how she manages it sometimes. She'd love to see her parents again, and for them to see their grandson. But they live in Romania and there's little chance that it will happen.

I hope Christmas gives Denisa a bit of a break, and that she has a good time with Narcis. He's just under two. Denisa showed me a photograph of him in a ziggy-zaggy, red-and-black tiger suit with a soft fluffy hood. A little fellow with a big smile, just like his mum's.

18th December: CANDLE LANE BOOKS

The name 'Candle Lane' harkens back to a certain Princess Victoria visiting Shrewsbury, when the candle-makers' street was renamed Princess Street in her honour. Candle Lane Books is the only reminder of those bygone days. Yesterday I met its proprietor, John Thornhill, with his son and business partner, Edward. Next year will be the shop's 40th anniversary, and they shared with me its history, their lives as hands-on farmers, their years as collectors and their love of books.

For Edward, the family's book business was always a factor in his life. At an early age he learned pricing and handling from his dad. Helping out in the shop was a regular occurrence. 'I always knew I'd be going into the family business,' Edward said. 'I also worked on our family's farm, and I still do. I also did some travelling, visiting almost forty countries.'

For John, his lifelong obsession with collecting books began aged eight with *The Book of the Farm*, bought by his mother to encourage his love of reading. She'd no idea what she'd started. 'It's a good job we're farmers too,' said Edward, 'otherwise we wouldn't have the space to keep all Dad's books.' 'We always say no collection too large, no parcel too small,' added John. 'Once we purchased 10,000 books in one day. The staff on the farm became good at handling books.'

In John's personal collection is the twelve volume classic, Eyton's *History of Shropshire*. Only three hundred copies of this book were ever printed, as well as three large paper copies – and at one time John owned all three of them (he now owns only one).

Another treasure is George Garrard's *History of British Livestock*. Edward said it was the only book of which he'd been unable to find another copy on the open market, which, given his contacts, makes it most likely the only still in existence. 'When my father acquired the book,' Edward said, 'an article and photograph went up in the *Farmers' Weekly*. A lady phoned in wanting to buy it for her husband. We named a ridiculous sum, saying even if the offering price was that, we wouldn't part with it. The lady offered more – but we still said no.'

Candle Lane Books started out as an offshoot of John's massive collection. 'I'd bought so many books,' he said, 'that I thought I'd better start a shop'. The shop in question was an old butcher's shop half the size of the current premises. John filled it with old books, and a book binder, Mr James, was employed to do repairs. For thirty-two years he worked for Candle Lane Books. Even in his eighties he was still coming in and picking up boxes of books.

'Thanks to him we saved many important books,' John said. 'The Parish Registers for example – by buying and binding them they were preserved. We have registers for most of Shropshire in the shop. They're of particular use to people looking up their family history.'

It didn't take long for the shop to be in need of expansion. The family bought the shop next door and went up three floors. Now even the furthest corner of Candle Lane Books is stuffed to the gunwales with good reads. 'We'll buy anything we think will sell,' Edward said. 'I tend to focus more on modern publications and my father on the older books. But Candle Lane Books has no specialism apart from local books.'

Over the years, some of my greatest book treasures have been bought Candle Lane Books, including a first edition Graham Greene, a signed Malcolm Saville and several books by one of my favourite authors, A.G. Bradley. Candle Lane Books always has something that I want – and more often than not that something is in the window, pleading to be taken away.

John, Edward and Maureen (who's worked in the shop for the last twenty-six years) have window-dressing down to a fine art. They know that showing the right thing will bring in the customers. Many of their regulars are simply looking for a good read, but others are on the lookout for certain books, and Candle Lane Books will put these on their 'Wants List' and look for them too.

'Once a book's on the list, it doesn't come off,' said Edward. 'Even years later, if it hasn't been found it'll still be there.'

Mostly nowadays John and Edward buy from private collections. 'We never buy from auctions for resale in the shop,' said Edward, 'but we sometimes do for ourselves. We keep an eye on the auction houses, and if something we want is going at the right price then we'll buy.'

How did they decide which books were for the shop, and which for their private library, I said. Edward and his father looked at each other. Plainly this wasn't a simple question to answer. If a book was rare, they finally said, or it had a certain something about it, a uniqueness of some sort, they would keep it. Once they bought seventy tea-chests of books from a known collector in Japan, mostly dated before the 1850s. Every single book was good enough to buy in its own right. They kept three hundred, but sold the rest in the shop. It didn't take long for the word to get round, then they had dealers beating a path to their door.

Another book, too, is worthy of mention. 'Shall I tell her about the...' said Edward. The word hung in the air. Again the two of them looked at each other. It was the Vaughan book they were talking about – a book that brings new meaning to the word unique. Starting with Adam and Eve, the writer of this book had traced his family's history from the beginning of humankind to his own times in the 19th century.

Every word of this massive tome has been written by hand. To begin with the hand was steady. By the end of the book, though, it was shaky and plainly old.

As soon as I heard about this book, I wanted to see it. For twenty-six years I'd lived out at Worthen in a farmhouse bought from some branch the Vaughan family, for whom it had been home for over a century. John and Edward agreed to bring in the book for me to see another day.

The conversation then moved on to John Thornhill as a publisher. Three books came out under the imprint 'John Thornhill, Candle Lane Books' – Georgina Jackson's *Shropshire Word-Book*, Garbett's *History of Wem* and *Shrewsbury Street Names*.

John would have published Charlotte Burne's *Shropshire Folk-Lore* too, he said, but his printer in Yorkshire went out of business and it never happened, which John regrets.

For all that he's a bibliophile, John's a farmer too. His love of books may have come from his mother, but from his father came the family farm. 'My farm is my life,' said John. 'This other thing, books, well it just developed. There was one time, you know, when I worked for three whole years on the farm without coming into town once.'

Edward and John Thornhill

John left school at thirteen. He broke up for the Christmas holidays, had his thirteenth birthday and never went back. Extraordinary changes in farming have happened in his lifetime. He farmed through the Depression and the Second World War, and now his son, Edward, runs the farm. 'We're hands-on farmers,' Edward said. 'Everything we have in town, this shop and other properties we own, come from the farm.'

The Thornhills have 260 acres and a herd of Pedigree Herefords. Theirs is an old family farm with a big old manor house and its own church. John remembers a time when all their staff lived on the farm, but things are different now. A few years ago when two of their workers – John Lewis and Michael Lewis (not related) – retired, between them they'd clocked up a massive one hundred and five years.

'They're a wonderful family to work for,' Maureen said later, when

John and Edward weren't around. I've got the best job in town. I suppose that one day I'll retire, but definitely not yet.'

I asked John what stood out most in his long life. I expected the answer to be a book, but I was wrong. 'It's the people who've worked for us,' John replied. 'They've been wonderful throughout the years. Without them, we couldn't have done what we've done. That's what stands out.'

PS. As promised, I did get to see the Vaughan Family History. It's folio-sized, several inches thick, with craftsman-like penmanship, beautifully bound in leather. Not only is Adam linked to the Vaughans, but the writer of the book links them to Brutus, and the same King Locrinus who featured in the legend of Sabrina, the spirit of the River Severn. What a treasure it must have been to its family in its heyday. I can't imagine what it's like to own such a thing, let alone to have written it.

20th December: THE HIGH SHERIFF OF SHROPSHIRE

A few afternoons ago, Shropshire's High Sheriff came round for tea. Very nice it was, too. From the moment she arrived we didn't stop talking.

Diana Flint was installed as High Sheriff of Shropshire on 5th April 2013 at Shrewsbury Castle. She grew up on a farm near Ellesmere and became the first girl to attend Ellesmere College, going on from there to university. During her London days, she worked for Thames and Hudson as a picture researcher. She also worked voluntarily as secretary of the Camberwell Society. After returning to Shropshire, she volunteered to work for The Art Fund, for whom she served as Shropshire's Chairman for ten years. She also became involved in supporting her local church at Dudleston Heath.

It's something of a leap, however, from supporting local causes to becoming High Sheriff. By what arcane process was Diana selected, I wondered, and were there any likenesses between those silver-starred men with their lantern jaws who kept law and order in the Wild West, and Diana's role in Shropshire today?

The likeness, it turned out, lay in the words 'law and order'. As High Sheriff Diana is the Queen's representative in Shropshire for the Judiciary. She's also official Returning Officer for parliamentary elections and has responsibility for proclaiming the accession of a new Sovereign. Hers is a position that goes back a thousand years, and even in these modern times it comes with a degree of ceremony.

Diana may not have turned up in full kit for afternoon tea, but there are occasions when she would. On ceremonial occasions she wears

a knee-length dark green velvet coat designed by herself, complete with antique buttons, a hat decorated with an ostrich feather, lace jabot around her neck, and cuffs finished with handmade Irish lace, passed down through her husband's family from his great- great-grandmother.

Male High Sheriffs, Diana said, carried swords as well. Should the occasion require, she could have one carried behind her on a cushion.

Once the High Sheriff would have been responsible for looking after royal properties, collecting taxes and presenting them to the Chancellor of

Diana Flint

the Exchequer. This would literally mean laying out the cash on the Chancellor's table [covered with a checkered cloth, from which the title 'of Exchequer' is supposed to derive] in the full knowledge that if it wasn't as much as expected, the High Sheriff would have to make up the shortfall.

Hardly surprisingly, the High Sheriff of a county was a powerful figure. So much so that Henry VIII felt the need to bring in a degree of moderation by creating a separate role of Lord Lieutenant. This was a lifetime position, 'life' extending to the age of seventy-five, whereas High Sheriffs were only appointed on a yearly basis.

'You'll know four years in advance that you're going to become High Sheriff,' Diana said. 'Your name is submitted to the County Consultative Panel. Nominations are discussed and the current High Sheriff will propose a name to the Privy Council. The nominee will be written to, ascertaining whether they are happy to be appointed, and then their name will be read out by the Queen's Remembrancer at an annual Nomination Ceremony in the Royal Courts of Justice in London. This has to happen three times, on three consecutive years before being submitted to the Queen for her approval. This means, in effect, that you have three years in advance to learn about the role.'

The actual appointment takes place in the Privy Council at what's known in rather Gormenghastly fashion as the Pricking Ceremony. The idea behind it is that not everybody called upon to become High Sheriff might see the office as an honour, but the pricking of their name on vellum with a bodkin makes it impossible for them to claim they'd never been nominated.

'Becoming High Sheriff once brought with it a great financial burden,' Diana explained. 'Even today the role comes at a cost. It's not paid for out of the public purse. High Sheriffs take the expenses of the year upon themselves.'

Next March, prior to the annual church service to recognise the work of legal services in the county, Diana will host a lunch for County Court Judges, senior members of the clergy and Chiefs of Police. In addition, she's hosted an event at Enginuity in Ironbridge, at which the speaker was one of the world's foremost scientists, the Astronomer Royal (also recent President of the Royal Society), Lord Rees of Ludlow.

Evenings like this allow Diana to stamp her personality upon the office of High Sheriff. So, too, does her charity work. During her year in office, Diana is supporting the county's museums and galleries as well as various charities. She has a particular interest in the work of volunteers, especially those in the justice system. A visit to the Midlands Air Ambulance shop, to encourage its volunteers on their first anniversary, or to see the work of the Probation Service in Telford, or Police Cadets in Shrewsbury are all special events.

The position of High Sheriff is the oldest secular office in the country outside of the monarchy, and it exists in its modern manifestation to work for the good of the community. Diana Flint sees her year as an opportunity to showcase some of what's best about Shropshire. You can only want to support an endeavour like that.

25th December: OPEN STUDIO – AIDAN HART

A couple of days ago I met icon painter, Aidan Hart, at his studio in the English Bridge Workshop, and we talked about his life and work. He grew up in New Zealand, he said, read English Literature at university, then taught in secondary school. In 1983, as a result of studies in Early Church history, he converted to Orthodoxy. After this, he began making carvings on religious themes, and studying the human body, which led into painting. He started examining icons, taking them apart in forensic fashion, trying analyse the component parts of beauty and why icons were so beautiful.

Aidan Hart

In addition, Aidan studied *Philokalia*, a collection of writings on prayer. The word meant 'love of the beautiful', and he came to realise that prayer was a form of beauty too – a work of art as much as any icon.

But what was an icon, I wanted to know. Was it just a religious painting, which was how I guessed most people thought of it? The way he was talking, Aidan seemed to be suggesting something else.

An icon, Aidan explained, was a painting of a holy person put together in such a way that one could be lead through the image to the actual person depicted. A window between heaven and earth, he called it, one that abstracted the human form to express the spiritual.

Making an icon, Aidan said, involved discerning timeless principles and expressing them in one's own indigenous way. His icons, for example, drew on Celtic and Romanesque traditions as well as Byzantine.

Currently Aidan is one of only three or four full-time icon artists in the UK today. He has two years' worth of commissions ahead of him; a second studio out at Pontesbury, where his student, Martin Earle, helps with carving commissions, and another assistant working in Telford making cabinets to house icons.

All of this is a far cry from the hermit's life that for many years Aidan experienced out on the side of the Stiperstones. Rural myth has it that he was visited there by Prince Charles. I put this to Aidan, and he said no myth. In fact, Aidan now teaches the Diploma in Icon Painting at the Prince's School of Traditional Arts.

Aidan's years as a rasophore monk [one who hasn't yet taken his final vows], was one of the busiest periods in his life. Icon commissions were coming in. His daily church services took about four hours. He had twenty acres of land to manage – which he did by planting 5,000 trees – and then there were visitors.

Aidan is now married, with a family. He may have left the hermitage (leaving behind another hermit in his place) but he still sees his ministry as an iconographer and he definitely hasn't left behind that inner calling. 'Strange as it may seem,' he said, 'as a hermit I had little time to paint.'

Nowadays, as well as taking on commissions for church icons, carvings, frescos and mosaics, Aidan also gives talks and lectures. 'What a finished icon presents you with is a transfigured world,' Aidan said. 'An icon isn't naturalistic, but it is realistic. In the way that Moses saw the burning bush alight but not consumed, and the disciples saw Christ's garments shining with light at his transfiguration, so an icon depicts the world aflame with the presence of God.'

'Icons are an affirmation of the incarnation,' Aidan said. 'What they're showing is that God became man in Christ. That's what the Christmas story is all about.'

Even the actual, physical making of an icon, Aidan said, is a bringing together of heaven and earth. The pigment of the paint speaks for the mineral world; the egg that binds the paint for the animal world; the wood upon which the icon is painted for the kingdom of the vegetable. And the icon painter's is a priestly role, binding the elements together, discerning the word of God in each created thing.

Aidan is currently working on a huge mosaic commission for a church in Houston, Texas, also a stone Mother and Child for Lincoln Cathedral, two icons of British saints for Hexham Abbey and an Annunciation for Caius College, Cambridge. In the pipeline is a fresco for a Benedictine Catholic monastery and a Prince Charles commission to sculpt the members of his immediate family.

Though connected to The Prince's School of Traditional Arts, based in Shoreditch, Aidan's Diploma in Icon Painting is taught here in Shrewsbury, at the Trinity Centre at Meole Brace Church. Its students are drawn from around the country and beyond, three making the huge commitment of commuting from Ireland, Germany and Sweden.

Aidan may have left the hermitage, but he's still a busy man. I got up to leave, aware that he had an icon to finish before flying out to America next day. Was there anything I'd left out, I asked – anything Aidan still wanted to say. He considered this. 'Life with God is beautiful,' he said. 'It makes you beautiful. I'm trying to bring seeds of Paradise into the world, so that people can nurture them and make them into little trees.'

28th December: A WHISTLE-STOP TOUR

There are all sorts of things I'd hoped to write about this year, but I'm running out of time. There's Hmmm Squad, hosted by the indefatigable Pip Bayley, providing Shrewsbury's answer to the TED talks, tackling every subject from Death to Halloween and back again. Then there's Network Rail who've spent the last few months wrapping up Shrewsbury's railway bridge in plastic as if it was Christo and the bridge its work of art.

Goodbye to Jane Dyas shop in Shrewsbury's Square

I've been meaning to find out what they're up to, hopefully get a glimpse behind the scenes –but it hasn't happened, much to my regret.

I've also tried unsuccessfully to get behind closed doors at Shrewsbury's railway station. Emailing, phoning, even turning up in person has got me nowhere. I've found out that it's listed (Grade II), that it was built in 1848, and that its imitation Tudor style, complete with carvings, came courtesy of architect Thomas Mainwaring Penson who was attempting to match the

Castle Gates Library. But the life of the modern station housed by that fine building remains a mystery.

Another Grade II building on my list is the old Granada Cinema, currently housing Gala Bingo. Built in 1934, its lavish interiors were designed by Russian émigré, Theodore Komisarjevsky. Its stage once hosted Eddie Calvert, Rosemary Squires, Joe Brown and the Bruvvers, Dick Emery and Sid James. More recently (1963 and 1964) the Beatles and Rolling Stones performed on it.

I'd have written more about the river if the year had contained a few more weeks. I apologise for all the regattas I haven't written about, and other river events. In fact I apologise for the lack of sport in general, but I did try (and failed) to contact Shrewsbury's Boxing Club. I offer you that in my defence.

Some time over the year I would have written about Hall's Auction House if it hadn't moved out of town, meaning that my days of mooching round its general sales are over for good. The Wakeman School has gone too, and so has Jane Dyas's shop, having graced the Square for over a hundred years, supplying generations of Shrewsbury ladies with clothes, shoes and underwear.

There are churches I haven't written about, including St Mary's with its windows full of jewel-like stained glass. Then there are people. Shrewsbury is full of residents and business people, shop owners, stallholders, school kids, street artists, traffic wardens, newspaper sellers, buskers, publicans, retirees and restaurateurs. And they all have stories to tell.

But the good news is, there are still a couple of days to go. Not long enough to fit all that lot in – but *My Tonight From Shrewsbury* isn't over yet.

29th December: THE SHREWSBURY FRAGMENT

The Shrewsbury Fragment. Have you ever even heard of it? You should have, if you live in Shrewsbury. According to the University of Maine, it stands at the point where liturgy left the church and drama hit the streets, which, extraordinarily, places Shrewsbury at a pivotal point in the history of Western drama.

Wow. Not only is our amazing little town the setting for one of Parliament's most infamous moments, the birthplace of Charles Darwin and the site of what *the Guardian* has recently called 'possibly Shakespeare's greatest plays' *(Henry IV Parts One & Two)*, all of which I've written about on other occasions, but it's also in at the birth of modern drama.

I saw the famous Fragment in the flesh a few weeks ago in Shrewsbury School's Ancient Library. However it was Bill Morris, ex-Meole Brace Labour councillor, who first told me about it. That was years ago, but he and I talked about it again the other night. According to Bill, it's all that remains of an extant cycle of mystery plays whose content is reckoned to predate those of the great cycles at Chester, Wakefield and York.

The seed of all these plays can be found in church liturgy, and in particular, according to Bill, the great three-day ecclesiastical liturgy which took place every year in Lent, summing up of all the major Bible events. By the 10th century, this summing-up was becoming increasingly complex. Parts of it were re-lived and the crowds, flocking to the churches to witness these dramatic enactments, eventually became so vast that proceedings had to be moved out of the main body of the church into its immediate precincts.

Shrewsbury Abbey is thought to be one of the early places in our town where this happened. As the crowds grew, so did awareness of commercial opportunities. Trades became involved in sponsoring parts of the enacted Canon. By the 1500s, these segments of Canon had outgrown even the immediate environs of the church, and taken to the streets.

A fragment of the Shrewsbury Fragment

Shrewsbury's trade guilds started competing to produce episodes. By the end of the 16th century, some of these had distinct elements of high drama, others were more slapstick. According to Bill, time was when ropes were hung across our Square, enabling angels to fly between earth and heaven.

All of this, of course, was also taking place across Europe, as part of the democratisation of religion. What started out as liturgy, by means of drama became commonplace. Once in a language [Latin] that few could read, the Bible had become more widely accessible. It had escaped the restraining bounds of the church and become the people's story, performed by their guilds on their streets.

In Britain this happened widely too, in Scotland and across the waters in Ireland. But the material recorded in the Shrewsbury Fragment suggests that one of the first places where the liturgy left the church was right here in our town.

So, how did Shrewsbury School's Ancient Library come to house this tiny (well, 43 pages, the first thirty-six of which contain Latin anthems set to music) fragment of an illustrious past? I've failed to answer that question, but I have come across a Dr Calvert who, realising the value of what he'd lighted upon, made a transcript of the Fragment which eventually reached the Reverend Professor Walter William Skeat, philologist, compiler of the Concise Dictionary of Middle English from AD 1150 to 1580; expert on Chaucer and editor of Piers Plowman; Fellow of Christ's College, Cambridge; also Elrington and Bosworth Professor of Anglo-Saxon at Cambridge.

On January 4th, 1890, Reverend Professor Skeat called public attention to the Shrewsbury Fragment in a letter to the Royal Academy. Then, a week later, in the Academy's journal, he published its text. Fifteen years later, Professor John Matthews Manly, American professor of philology and English Literature at Chicago University, turned up at Shrewsbury School during the summer holidays, keen to publish his own transcription of the Fragment, wanting to examine the manuscript in the flesh.

Unable to find anybody to give him permission, Manly was forced to leave. At the beginning of the following term, however, he wrote to the Headmaster still seeking permission – but received no reply.

Nowadays it's reckoned that the Shrewsbury Fragment is an actor's copy, containing only certain parts and cues. Even so, the scholar's view is that enough text remains for the Fragment to be regarded as that vital missing link between liturgy and vernacular religious drama as developed and represented by the great mystery cycles of York, Chester and Wakefield. This makes it a very big deal indeed.

Of the three plays represented in the Fragment, the first relates to Christmas, the second to the events leading up to Easter (this one's fairly free adaptation of the Vulgate places it at a very early date) and the third takes the story of Christ's appearance to Jesus's post-Resurrection appearance on the Emmaus road. This is a version of what was known more widely across Europe as the 'Peregrini'. From what I gather, it's the only existing extract from that play remaining in the UK today.

I'm no historian, as I've said before, but I've done the best I can, digging around in the archives of the University of Maine and the Wilfred Laurier University in Ontario, Canada, to find out not only about the Fragment but about the professors who did so much work on it. If anyone in Shrewsbury is looking for a project, perhaps translating the Fragment into modern English, and building around it a credible modern mystery play might be worth considering. Here are a few words from the third play, in very loose translation from the Latin and Middle English:

> *Christ is risen.*
> *We have witnessed it this morning.*
> *He is our hope, our help,*
> *our best health since ever we were born.*
> *If we will seek him for to see, our lessons*
> *from him will not be forlorn.*
> *We will follow him unto Galilee.*
> *Here we shall find him now before.*

30th December
MEET SHREWSBURY'S OWN GARETH JENKINS

...aka God. 'I've been plagued by that,' Gareth says. We're in the Lion Hotel having a drink, and Gareth is looking back upon his role in the recent production of Noye's Fludde. 'You go into a restaurant and ask if there's a table, and the answer comes back Yes, for God. All my priest and minister friends warned me about the danger of becoming God with a hat,' says Gareth, 'but I had to do it, didn't I? I thought I'd be behind a pillar booming forth, but oh no, Maggie Love had me up in the pulpit in a gold wallpaper frock. Now I'll never live it down.'

Whether it's dressed up as God or popping up on the telly in *Come Dine With Me*, Gareth Jenkins is a continual 'watch this space'. The one thing you don't expect from him is a quiet life. When the phone goes, his wife Elizabeth hands it to him, saying, 'It'll be for you.'

Gareth couldn't do anything without Elizabeth's tolerance, he readily admits. Everybody knows he married someone quite amazing. Along with their four wonderful children, she's top of Gareth's list of things that define

Gareth Jenkins
Dentist Extraordinaire

him – along with the word 'Dentist'.

Gareth Jenkins is my dentist. Thanks to him I still have my teeth – and I'm no longer terrified of dentists. Perhaps he hypnotised me; I can't quite remember. Or perhaps he cast a spell on me.

At five years old in his home town, Llanidloes, Gareth mastered his first magic trick. During his primary school years he developed his skills. At the age of ten he put on an hour-long show at the church Christmas party. 'My parents had two other sons who were quiet, reasonable sort of children,' Gareth says, sitting back in his chair, glasses stuck on top of his head, beaming at the memory. 'Then there was this middle brother, me, who liked nothing better than performing. I was a bit of a star turn over the next few years. I'd do church events and then the Liberal Party got hold of me and, to prove I had no political bias, I performed for the Tories.'

Gareth became a regular feature in the *County Times*. One day his Headmaster called him into his office. If he carried on this way, he said, Gareth would get nowhere in life. The Head didn't want to see his photo in the County Times again.

'My next show was at a Young Offenders' institution.' Gareth says. 'But I had to insist on anonymity. I got my own back on that Head, though. I won a £100 of book tokens in an essay competition and spent the whole lot on magic books. Because the competition was entered via the school, the Head had to sign for them.'

That was Llanidloes County School. Gareth was Head Boy. 'The way they worked things there,' he said, 'if you were a girl you studied French and History and if you were a boy you were channelled into Physics and Maths. I wanted to study Biology too, and then Music on top of that, and for some reason that threw them. Finally I was allowed to take my chosen subjects, but when it came to the exams the teacher had taught the wrong syllabus. We opened our exam paper and didn't have a clue what it was about. But the Headmaster swung it somehow. He wrote an impressive letter to the exam board and that did the trick.'

Gareth won a lot of essay competitions. One gave him an all-expenses-paid trip to the Eisteddfod, where he discovered choral music, especially that of Eastern Europe. He's since visited Eastern Europe on a regular basis – Bulgaria, in particular, where he's made many friends. He likes the complex rhythms of their music and has got to know Bulgarian conductors and composers.

'They're very hospitable,' Gareth says. 'I was invited to a lot of festivals representing Great Britain. Flights, cars, dinners etc – it would all be paid for. When communism went, though, so did all of that.'

For the last few years, Gareth and his wife have been sponsoring a Bulgarian boy and looking after him at weekends, so that he can study at Shrewsbury School, where he has a scholarship. He's a remarkable pianist, Gareth says. One of the best the school has ever had. He has a great career ahead of him. His name is Galin Ganchev.

In addition Gareth composes, coming up with works that he describes as quirky and done for his own interest, largely as an academic pursuit. 'I'll have a shot at anything,' he says. That could well be the motto for Gareth's life.

Everywhere the conversation takes us, a new interest pops up. Take Gareth's fascination for garden architecture, which he designs and builds. His garden, he says, is littered with pergolas, pagodas, potting sheds and other exotic structures.

Then, of course, there's the dental practice that Gareth has built up from scratch. 'I was always good with my hands,' he says. 'All that practising of magic probably did that for me. When I was growing up, everybody said that Llanidloes needed a good dentist, so from an early age my path seemed set.'

'But you don't practise in Llanidloes,' I point out. 'The plan after college was to do a couple of years in Shrewsbury,' Gareth replies, 'then move home to Wales. But I stayed.'

My early memories of Gareth are of him dazzling my children with coins appearing magically from behind their ears. One time I remember him hypnotising a friend of mine who'd refuse to let a dentist anywhere near her teeth.

'I used to lecture on medical and dental hypnosis,' Gareth says. 'It's effective at eliminating phobias, and that includes fear of dentists.'

As well as being an NHS dentist, Gareth is also a Draper. In fact he's this year's Master Draper, with the flashy fur-edged cloak to prove it. It was the Drapers, he tells me, who first provided housing for the poor in Shrewsbury. From the old almshouses at St Mary's (now long since gone) to their current almshouse project out at Holy Cross, they've had a long-standing interest in providing housing in Shrewsbury for those with little means.

Gareth describes the Drapers as genuine, public spirited, three-dimensional people who want to carry on the Guild tradition that first brought Shrewsbury to eminence and made it what it is. Their current project is a massive £2.7 million scheme which, as well as providing housing, will also provide facilities to benefit the neighbouring community.

Gareth is also a Governor of Priory School. He runs the annual Gregynog Young Musician Competition with a £3,000 prize, for under eighteens. He's a member of the Shropshire Magic Circle, performing throughout the year in gigs as far-flung as Norway and Welsh Patagonia. In addition, he organises an annual November concert in aid of the Huntington's Disease Association, to which he persuades eminent musicians to come to Shrewsbury and perform.

I could go on, but won't (this is turning into a very long post). However, there's one final story that I simply have to share with you. Until recently, Gareth looked after an elderly relative who was once a piano teacher at the High School. When she died, he found a bureau in her house with a locked compartment. Inside it he found a hand-written letter to his relative from King George VI, thanking her for what she'd done for her country.

So far Gareth hasn't been able to find out what exactly it was that this relative, Doris, actually did. But as the letter came at the end of the Second World War, it doesn't take too much imagination to figure out what it might have been.

In addition, in this locked compartment Gareth found evidence (despite Doris's protests to the contrary) of a great love in her life. The man in question had been an eminent author, and locked away in the bureau Gareth found his life's work – manuscripts, lecture notes, books and private correspondence. All on the subject of sex.

We haven't had much sex yet in *My Tonight From Shrewsbury*, but it's never too late. The love of Doris's life was an eminent sexologist who travelled the world lecturing on the subject. That's how Doris met him. As an asthmatic, she attended his clinic. They fell in love. She was in her early twenties, he forty years older than her.

These were the war years. Doris lived in Shropshire near to an air base. To keep out of danger's way, or so she said, she moved to the relative security of mid-Wales. According to a Shrewsbury friend, 'We don't know what Doris did during those years'. Maybe she'd simply moved closer to the new man in her life. Or maybe she'd spent those years spying for king and country.

'Doris was a direct descendant of William the Conqueror,' says Gareth. 'She'd worked it all out. Her mother came from Yorkshire, and was a stunning artist. Her family name was Grosvenor, but she painted under the name 'Minnie Duck'. When Doris died, I found sixty of her mother's water-colours in tight roles. The colours were vivid and the technique beautiful.

'Doris's grandfather was the first man to produce crown plate glass. Twenty thousand people went to his funeral. There were only fifteen for Doris. Doris Grosvenor-Davies was her full name, but we always knew her as the daughter of Mother Duck.'

31st December: THE LAST POST. GULP

This arrived in my email box in the early hours this morning:

FINAL BLUES
(apologies ter that Auden mon)

Stop all the clocks, cut off the telephone,
Prevent the dog from barking with a juicy bone,
Everything else seems drowned in fog
Because Fiskyoomon's ending her blog

Let aeroplanes circle moaning overhead
Scribbling on the sky that her blog is Dead,
Put crepe bows round the clock on the market hall
As Darwin and Clive mourn with us all.

Fiskin North, and South, and East and West,
Full working week and no Sunday rest,
Pauline's "my tonight from Shrewsbury" became my song;
I hoped that it 'ould last forever: I was wrong.

Salopians are not wanted, she's spoke ter every'un
Pack up the moon and dismantle the sun;
Unplug yer computer,yer know that yer shud;
For nothing now can ever come to any good.

Thank you, Shroppiemon, legendary Shropshire Tweeter, who has kept me smiling all year long. Gulp. *My Tonight From Shrewsbury*'s final post. For it, I headed down to the Shrewsbury Coffeehouse, the scene of so many of my interviews. Here I drank more coffee than was good for me and talked to friends – which is why I'm at my desk now, writing this whilst everybody else is out round town having fun.

It's been a strange and very special day. After the Coffeehouse, I went to Castlefields to watch parents and children launching candlelit paper boats to float downriver to the weir. All those shining faces, those little Shrewsbury people growing up – what will the future bring for them? What will they remember of 2013?

I'll remember a year the likes of which I don't expect to ever have again. Twelve months ago I started this blog not knowing what the year would bring. And what a year it's been! Thank you everyone who's been interviewed for this blog, followed it, retweeted it, 'liked' it on Facebook and encouraged me to keep going. There have been moments when I've been exhausted – but Shrewsbury itself has driven me on. It's a place like no other. I feel privileged to live in it. It's given more to me than I could ever give back, no matter how many *My Tonight From Shrewsbury*s I might write.

I live in a glorious town, one that deserves being shouted about from the rooftops. And that's what I hope this blog will continue to do.

Pauline Fisk, Nathalie Hildegarde Liege, Linda Edwards, Carla Risden, Sarah Hopper

---

Also published by Merlin Unwin Books
www.merlinunwin.co.uk

A Shropshire Lad A.E. Housman

Nearest Earthly Place to Paradise Margaret Wilson & Geoff Taylor

It Happened in Shropshire Bob Burrows

Beneath Safer Skies: a child evacuee in Shropshire Anthea Toft

A Most Rare Vision: Shropshire from the Air Mark Sisson

The Temptation & Downfall of the Vicar of Stanton Lacy Peter Klein

A Farmer's Lot Roger Evans

A View from the Tractor Roger Evans

Over the Farmer's Gate Roger Evans (ebook edition only)

For Pauline Fisk's other books

including her gap year novel *In the Trees*, and the recent Kindle publication of her Smarties Prize winning novel, *Midnight Blue*, go to

www.paulinefisk.co.uk